THE MURDER CLUB

"Well, I do not like accidents," replied Mrs Mush. "there's no meaning in them: but," she added confidentially, "I dearly like a murder. Of course I do not wish for murders," she continued, in a tone of resigned virtue: "but when there is one, why, I like it. It is human nature."

(Julia Kavanagh, *Sybil's Second Love*, 1867)

THE MURDER CLUB

Guide to

LONDON

Devised and Edited by Brian Lane

HARRAP
London

ACKNOWLEDGEMENTS

Sincere thanks go primarily to Derek Johns, Publishing Director of Harrap, whose imaginative response to the proposal for these *Guides* provided their initial impetus, and whose continued encouragement and practical support have ensured their realisation. Thanks also to our editor, Roy Minton, whose knowledge and understanding has saved us from more than a few pitfalls; and to Tim Pearce, who helped turn our ideas into books.

On the Murder Club side there are people too numerous to mention whose contributions to our Archive of illustrations and texts have made the compilation of these books possible. In particular, credit must be given to Steve Wheatley, whose work on the overall concept of the *Murder Club Guides* was of immense value, as were his written contributions to Volume One. And to John Bevis whose creative application to the layout and overall appearance has helped make the concept a tangible reality.

For the kindness and generosity we have been shown in scores of libraries and museums, large and small, all over Britain, and for all those people who knew about things and were willing to share, we hope these books may represent our thanks.

First published in Great Britain 1988
by HARRAP Ltd
19-23 Ludgate Hill London EC4M 7PD

© Brian Lane 1988

ISBN 0–245–54680–4

Designed by Brian Lane and John Bevis

Typeset in Times by
Falcon Graphic Art Ltd
Wallington, Surrey

Printed by Biddles Limited
Guildford and Kings Lynn

THE MURDER CLUB
GUIDE TO LONDON

CONTENTS

GENERAL INTRODUCTION: On Apologias 8

KEY TO MAPS 11

MURDER IN LONDON 13

THE MURDER CLUB 14

NORTH LONDON
"Reject all the values of society..."
Kenneth Halliwell (1967) 16
The Meanest Murderer of them All
Frederick Henry Seddon (1911) 19
The Hen-Pecked Killer
Dr Hawley Harvey Crippen (1910) 24
"This all counts for nothing"
Dennis Andrew Nilsen (1983) 29

NORTH-WEST LONDON
Cut off their tails...
Mary Eleanor Pearcey (1890) 36
In and Out The Eagle
Robert Wood (1907) 38
A Tale of Two Passions
San Dwe (called Sandy Wee) (1928) 42
The Fellow in a Long Black Cloak
Thomas Henry Hocker (1845) 46
I Find Murdered By Rogues
Robert Green, Henry Berry, and Lawrence Hill (1678) 48
"Thou tyrant, tyrant, Jealousy"
Styllou Christofi (1954) 52
"The Woman Who Hangs This Morning"
Ruth Ellis (1955) 56
The Case of the Anaemic Housemaid
George Baron Pateman (1911) 59

SOUTH-EAST LONDON
"I never liked him very much..."
Frederick and Maria Manning (1849) 62
The Poison Pen
Dr Thomas Neill Cream (1891) 66
A London-Wide Distribution
James Greenacre (1837) 72
The Full 'Rigor' of the Law
Colin Lattimore, Ronald Leighton, and Ahmet Salih (1972) 76
Hanged by a Fingerprint
Alfred and Albert Stratton (1905) 82

The Button and Badge Murder
David Greenwood (1918) 85
Another Victim of the Blitz
Harry Dobkin (1941) 90
Pity the Poor Convict
William Colman (1809) 93
Starved of Affection
Louis and Patrick Staunton (1877) 95

SOUTH-WEST LONDON
One law for the rich...
Philip, Earl of Pembroke (1678) 102
The Abhorrent Alternative
John Bellingham (1812) 104
The Most Intimate Relations of Men and Women
Adelaide Bartlett (1886) 107
The Charing Cross Trunk Murder
John Robinson (1927) 111
A Murder from the 'Yiddisher' District
Stinie Morrison (1911) 113
The Real Ronald True
Ronald True (1922) 118
"A Daniel Come to Judgement!"
Daniel Good (1842) 121
"A slice of cake, young Percy?"
Dr George Henry Lamson (1881) 124
The Man in the Green Van
George Brain (1938) 126

EAST LONDON
The Ratcliffe Highway Murders
John Williams (1811) 130
"Come to see a man die have you, you curs?"
Henry Wainwright (1874) 136
Catch Me When You Can
Jack the Ripper (1888) 140
Murder on a Railway Train
Franz Müller (1864) 145
"An evil, cynical, and depraved man"
Ronald William Barton (1985) 147

EAST-CENTRAL LONDON
The Patriot Game
Michael Barrett (1867) 152
The Hangman Hanged
John Price (1718) 154
"My wife, or my life!"
Robert Blakesley (1841) 156
Murder in the Old Bailey
William Johnson and Jane Housden (1690) 157
Crime and Punishment
Elizabeth Brownrigg (1767) 159

WEST LONDON
Petit Treason
Catherine Hayes, John Billings, and John Wood (1726) 164

The Treacherous Valet
    François Benjamin Courvoisier (1840).. 166
The Butcher in Charlotte Street
    Louis Voisin (1917) 170
The Naughty Pantry-Boy
    Henry Julius Jacoby (1922) 172
"Pen, Pencil, and Poison"
    Thomas Griffiths Wainewright (1829-1837).. 174
The Man Who Shot a Ghost
    Francis Smith (1804)... 177
The Problems of 'Reggie No-Dick'
    John Reginald Halliday Christie (1943-1953) 178
Manhunt
    Harry Roberts, John Witney, and John Duddy (1966)........................ 184

WEST-CENTRAL LONDON
  A Matter of Honour
    Major George Strangeways (1658).. 188
  The Fine Art of Murder
    Theodore Gardelle (1761) 191
  The Oriental Underneath
    Marie-Marguerite Fahmy (1923) 195
  The Face of Crime
    Edwin Bush (1961)... 198

APPENDICES

One   **Some Brief Notes on the History of Newgate and the Old Bailey**.............. 200
Two   **The Coward's Weapon: 1**.. 206
Three   **The Prison Hulks at Woolwich** 208
Four   **Benefit of Clergy** 211
Five   **The Punishment of 'Peine Forte et Dure'** 212

SELECT BIBLIOGRAPHY 214

INDEX 217

General Introduction

On Apologias

Madame Life's a piece in bloom
Death goes dogging everywhere;
She's the tenant of the room,
He's the ruffian on the stair.
(W.E. Henley, 1849-1903)

A disturbing by-product of the new fashionable 'humanism' and its inseparable partner 'attitude-baring' is that the individual is under constant pressure to apologize for his passions. And nothing needs an apologia quite as much as a fascination with the darker sides of humankind.

There can be few notions more difficult to promote than that an interest in, say, the ritual of Magic does not of itself lead to nocturnal harvesting of the parish graveyard; or that a diet of gangster movies results in St Valentine's Day madness. An interest in crime is viewed as decidedly sinister; but a fascination with the crime of Murder – be it as academic or aficionado – renders a person particularly vulnerable, particularly in need of an apologia.

And so, for all those members, and prospective members, and closet members of The Murder Club; for all those readers of these, its regional *Guides*, here are some excellent precedents for our common need to justify.

One of the earliest examples can be found in the first issue of what was to become a popular illustrated weekly paper for a number of years around the turn of the century. Though its name was *Famous Crimes Past and Present*, like so many similar magazines of the period "crime" meant "murder". Editor Harold Furniss wrote, "Down the vista of crime which stretches from the first transgression of our Father Adam to the last little boy punished for stealing a pennyworth of sweets, there stand at intervals landmarks – milestones, as it were – on the road of iniquity. These are the doings of great criminals, of men whose cunning, wickedness or brutality have thrown out their lives into relief against the sordid background of everyday transgressors. It is of these that we propose to write, and we do so with a two-fold purpose; firstly that those who are interested in criminology, and desirous of furthering the science by which the moral welfare of the country is preserved may have before them a reliable record of typical criminals; and secondly, that as the natural bent of man tends towards crime, we may provide him with reading matter, interesting and dramatic, which will afford him food for thought."[1]

That there was a lighter side to the "interest in criminology" even earlier is evidenced by David Jardine's *Criminal Trials* being published, in 1835, by The Society for the Diffusion of Useful Knowledge as part of its series 'The Library of Entertaining Knowledge'. Just why such material should be considered 'Entertaining' is spelt out by another chronicler of the Courts, Horace Wyndham: "Of course, the real truth is (as De Quincey, who was something of a connoisseur on such matters, has asserted) crime in itself is intrinsically interesting. We may protest to the contrary, but there is no getting over the fact that the traffic of the dock does make an appeal. An extended one, too. Still, there is abundant reason for this. After all, 'crime books' are concerned with human happenings, with real life, with the stir and fret and thrill of everyday occurrences. Again, crime is essentially dramatic, and touches the whole emotional gamut. Thus, there is tragedy; there is comedy; there is melodrama; and there is occasionally sheer farce. Even romance, too, at times. Anyway, plot and passion and swift moving incident from the rise to the fall of the curtain. Hence, not nearly so astonishing that such volumes are popular as that they are not still more popular."[2]

Other writers have sought to give equal stress to the 'Useful' and to the 'Entertaining' sides of the crime story. Few people have done more consistently to popularize the twilight world of the criminal than the much respected writer, broadcaster, and former barrister, Edgar Lustgarten: "The main aim of one approach is to probe psychology – and thereby to illuminate and instruct. The main aim of the other is to tell a story – and thereby to divert and entertain."[3] But whichever of these two caps Mr Lustgarten chooses to wear, he is clear on the moral foundation of his apologia, "Certainly the arrangement adopted in the construction of the book does not signify any departure by the author from the received opinion that murder is the wickedest and gravest of all crimes."[4]

A different approach is taken by Colin Wilson, whose prolific path has taken him through such dangerous territory as Black Magic, Extra-Terrestrialism, ESP, Assassination, and Murder. One of his contentions is that the study of murder is a necessity – indeed, an obligation – if one is to understand the counter-balance, which is man's great creative potential. We have to be very grateful to Wilson for much of our contemporary understanding of 'criminality', though it is an approach which has has led to accusations of pomposity – not much dispelled by his published feelings about some fellow-authors: "It will be observed that my references to certain other writers on murder – particularly Edmund Pearson, William Roughead and William Bolitho – are hardly complimentary. I dislike the 'murder for pleasure' approach. I consider this book, like the *Encyclopaedia of Murder*, as a tentative contribution to a subject that does not yet exist as a definite entity, a science that has not yet taken shape."[5] Wilson's co-author on the *Encyclopaedia of Murder* was Patricia Pitman, who took a rather less pedantic view of the task in hand, concluding that the fascination with murderers is that they are so utterly different from us, and that that fascination is perfectly natural. Further, she brings a refreshing down-to-earthness to it all by adding that, aside from psychological justifications, the *Encyclopaedia* can provide "...plots for novels, questions for quizzes, and innocent entertainment for eerie winter evenings."[6]

But what of the "murder for pleasure" approach so despised by Wilson?

The late Edmund Pearson, tireless recorder of the classic American murders and controversial authority on the Lizzie Borden case

does, it is true, seem to take a wholesome relish in the retelling of a great murder story; England's own 'Brides in the Bath' killer, George Joseph Smith, he laments as a man "who only went to ruin because, like so many great artists, he could not resist one more farewell performance" [see *Murder Club Guide No.2*].[7] In the essay 'What Makes a Good Murder?', Pearson treats 'collectors' of murders with the respect that he feels due to a discerning cognoscente, noting that "...failure to recognise the elementary principle of an attractive murder is characteristic of many who should be better informed".[8]

Back on this side of the Atlantic, Pearson would recognize a soul-mate in Nigel Morland, who steers a course happily between detective fiction and criminology; he too is adamant about quality in a murder – "the critical eyes of aficionados recognise two distinct divisions of murder in the United States. There are the common-or-garden majority, whose ultimate destiny is the pages of popular magazines with lurid covers. The second, numerically minute, division is concerned with murders acceptable to the discerning taste, and here time has made certain classics".[9]

Edward Spencer Shew was one of the pioneers, with Wilson and Pitman, of the encyclopaedic approach to the recording of murder, and in the frank introduction to his indispensible *Second Companion to Murder*, Shew comes dangerously close to appearing to enjoy his subject: "Here the emphasis falls upon naked violence, raw and uncompromising, like the mallet strokes which destroyed Francis Mawson Rattenbury [see *Murder Club Guide No.6*], or the blows of the iron-stone brick with which Irene Munro was battered to death upon the sands of the Crumbles [see *Murder Club Guide No.2*]. Here murder wears its most savage face;[10] a face that Ivan Butler recognises: "it is in the strange vagaries of human behaviour that the persisting interest lies...the bizarre, the mysterious, the tragic, the gruesome, the just plain vicious".[11]

Two novel and distinguished vindications are advanced by Gordon Honeycombe in his introductory pages to *The Murders of the Black Museum* – "But the Black Museum made me realise what a policemen must endure in the course of of his duty; what sights he sees, what dangers he faces, what depraved and evil people he has to deal with so that others may live secure".[12] And later, "Murder is a very rare event in England. Its exceptional nature is in fact part of its fascination."

A counterpoint to this approach is provided by journalistic investigators, such as Paul Foot and Ludovic Kennedy. Their immediate motivation is the righting of a particular injustice, but they also have a wider purpose. As Kennedy writes in his introduction to 'Wicked Beyond Belief': "...once we start selecting those whom we think worthy or unworthy of Justice, we shall all in the end be diminished; for even if Justice is sometimes rough in practice, it is not for Cooper and McMahon alone that this book has been assembled; but for all those who, if Justice is allowed to go by default, may come to suffer in their time."[13] Kennedy's intention is to expose those attitudes and processes of the police, the courts, lawyers and judges which create an institutional tendency towards injustice.

A more academic, but no less absorbing, motive for the study of Murder derives from the fact that murder cases have tended to be so much better documented than the less notorious fields of human endeavour. The wealth of detailed information which can be gleaned from Court testimony and newspaper reports provides an eloquent picture of the everyday behaviour, social conditions, and moral attitudes of times past. We would, undoubtedly, be far more ignorant of conditions in London's East End in the 1880s if it were not for Jack the Ripper; the description of repressive middle-class life presented by the cases of Dr Crippen and Major Armstrong [see *Murder Club Guide No.4*] is, surely, as vivid as any novelist could invent; an examination of the predicament of Florence Maybrick [see *Murder Club Guide No.3*] or Edith Thompson provides a telling case study of the moral taboos of their time.

To be generous to the field, an example should be given of the "There but for the Grace of God..." argument. Take Tony Wilmot's introduction to *Murder and Mayhem*, "Why do we like reading crime stories, especially murder? For murder, that most heinous of crimes, both horrifies and fascinates at one and the same time...Could it be that deep down, we suspect that we are capable of committing murder, or other serious crimes, if we knew we could get away with it? That, perhaps, the only thing that holds us back is the fear of being caught and paying the price?"[14]

Probably not. But the one certainty is that there are as many reasons for a fascination with the "ruffian on the stair" as there are people to be fascinated by him.

References

1 *Famous Crimes Past and Present*, Ed. Harold Furniss. Vol.1. No.1, 1903.
2 *Famous Trials Retold*, Horace Wyndham. Hutchinson, London, 1925.
3 *Illustrated Story of Crime*, Edgar Lustgarten. Weidenfeld and Nicolson, London, 1976.
4 *Ibid.*
5 *A Casebook of Murder*, Colin Wilson. Leslie Frewin, London, 1969.
6 *Encyclopaedia of Murder*, Colin Wilson and Patricia Pitman. Arthur Barker, London, 1961.
7 *Masterpieces of Murder*, Edmund Pearson. Hutchinson, London, 1969.
8 *Ibid.*
9 *Background to Murder*, Nigel Morland. Werner Laurie, London, 1955.
10 *Second Companion to Murder*, E. Spencer Shew. Cassell, London, 1961.
11 *Murderers' London*, Ivan Butler. Hale, London, 1973.
12 *Murders of the Black Museum 1870-1970*, Gordon Honeycombe. Hutchinson, London, 1982.
13 *The Luton Murder Case*, Ed. Ludovic Kennedy. Granada Publishing, London, 1980.
14 *Murder and Mayhem*, Ed. Tony Wilmot. Harmsworth Publications, London, 1983.

Maps

The complexity of London's traffic system – particularly around the crowded central area of the city – makes it impractical to provide a detailed road map. Instead, individual cases are accompanied by a map of the immediate area, marked with Underground or British Rail stations, as well as locational information relevant to the crime.

To give an overview of the areas covered, each region is prefaced with a map of its postal districts, with murder sites roughly plotted on to it.

KEY TO MAPS

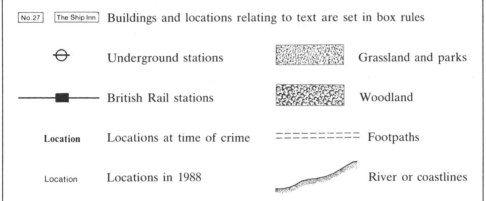

No.27 | The Ship Inn | Buildings and locations relating to text are set in box rules

⊖   Underground stations   Grassland and parks

━━■━━ British Rail stations   Woodland

Location   Locations at time of crime   ========== Footpaths

Location   Locations in 1988   River or coastlines

Location Photographs

In keeping with the status of this series of books as Guides, maps have been supplemented, where possible and appropriate, with photographs of buildings and locations relevant to the crime under discussion; in many cases, however, the precise spot on a landscape has been buried either by time or by the ubiquitous developer. Further research may unearth more precise information, and the compilers would be most grateful to receive it.

Public houses come quite naturally to the foreground in many of these cases, and provide a genuine excuse for refreshment in the amateur 'murder hunt'; but it should be remembered that those many private houses whose history has been blackened by dark deeds are not public monuments, and their present occupants' privacy should be respected.

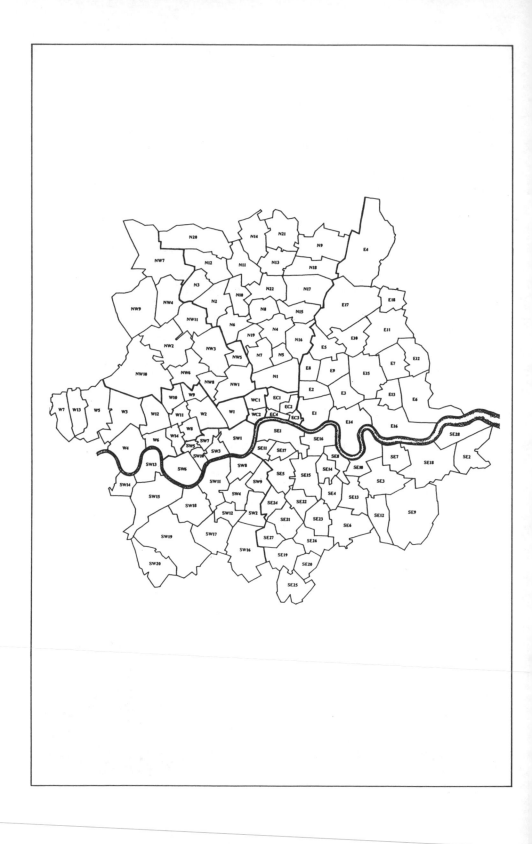

Murder in London

London: a nation, not a city.

(Benjamin Disraeli)

In compiling any series of books the essence of which is based on regional divisions, a pattern of identifying characteristics inevitably emerges which encapsulates the vital element of a particular area. This has been found essentially true during the research for the *Murder Club Guides*.

Thus the eight regions into which mainland Britain has been divided emerge with their own broad 'types' of murder, and this grouping depends on many factors – it is clear, for example, that a prosperous pastoral community will, through its crimes, reflect a vastly different image from the picture that derives from the desolation of inner-city slums.

London, however, appropriate to its status as one of the world's largest and most cosmopolitan agglomerations, reveals no such overall characteristic but, rather, appears as a microcosm of the nation as a whole. All the dirt and grime, the violence and squalor of its once sprawling docklands with that mysterious temporality which accompanies the vast traffic of any busy port. In its inner suburbs, like Hampstead, can be found the midddle-class 'gentility' which closets its blacker passions behind lace curtains, so strongly reminiscent of England's south-eastern counties. There is the glittering West-End with its theatres and hotels, its pubs and clubs; its thoroughfares trodden by the feet of representatives of every nation on earth. It will come as no surprise, then, that on our murder trail we encounter the occasional Arab, Canadian, Belgian, Swiss. . .

And so it is with great deference to this capital of ours that we have made this selection to stand witness to its darker Spirit. The following pages tell many of those stories to which superlatives must necessarily attach; there are a handful of firsts and lasts – the first railway murder (Franz Müller) for example, the first Identikit success (Edwin Bush), the last man to be publicly hanged (Michael Barrett). There are some 'big-

gests', like Dennis Nilsen's incredible sixteen victims; and the capital can boast more than its share of Britain's most gruesome and bloody killings.

DOOR OF NEWGATE.

If this metropolis is host to Scotland Yard, the world's best known police station, and to the Old Bailey the world's most celebrated criminal court, it has also been the home of some of history's most notorious assassins; lurkers in the dark like Jack the Ripper; cruel, calculating killers like the Staunton brothers. Those like Crippen who murdered for love, those like Wainewright who murdered for money; those like Thomas Neill Cream who killed for pleasure, and Major Strangeways whose excuse was 'honour'. There is John Reginald Christie who slew for perverted sex, and Ronald Barton for no reason but bestial depravity.

But this book is not merely a catalogue of carnage, for it has been rightly said that through the concentrated passion of murder we may uncover the many hidden layers of the social 'condition'; have spread before us. exposed, the whole range of humankind's emotions and aspirations.

Read on, then; London has a tale or two to tell.

Brian Lane

The Murder Club
January 1988

13

THE MURDER CLUB

Background

In the October of 1985, when Steve Wheatley and I first began to mould our mutual interest in Crime and Criminology into some more tangible form, it was as an occasional fireside activity. The first manifestation was the manuscript for a book of Execution Broadsheets. From there, as winter deepened, and the fireside became host to more frequent discussion, the ambitious concept for a new kind of periodical devoted to the Crime of Murder began to creep from our meditations. And the more of the blood-red wine that was sipped, and the more nimbly the shadows from the flickering flames darted about the room, the more of a good idea it seemed. It even stood up to the cold, thin reality of winter daylight.

It was, we decided, to be called *The Murder Club Bulletin* – though heaven knows why, the 'Club' wasn't due to emerge from the moving shadows until the next season's firelight. Indeed, at the time the first rough plans were put on to paper the 'Club' fitted round the editorial desk with more than enough room to spare.

It must have been around the mid-winter of 1986 that somebody said something like: "We've got the *Murder Bulletin,* what about the *Club*?"

I should say, though, that in the intervening months we had gradually begun to put together what will become a complete regional documentation of British Murders since the beginning of the seventeenth century; it's a big job. People in various parts of the country heard about it, and started to send us things – notes about famous local murders, regional press cuttings, pictures. We discovered people like Mr Mackintosh who had traced the last resting place of Bella Wright, the victim of the Green Bicycle Mystery in 1919, and had set up a fund to give Bella a modest memorial. We were becoming a Club!

Discussion began to revolve more and more around what we, as committed enthusiasts, would want out of a Murder Club if we were 'them'. The list on page 191 reveal some of those decisions which have already been adopted; other paths await discovery.

So, in the middle months of 1987 we had a prototype *Bulletin,* we had the partially clad skeleton of *The Murder Club,* and we had something else – we had a series of books demanding to be written; a series of Guides to the darker sides of Britain's landscape. Then came our first meeting with Harrap – long-established publishers of true-crime works – and their Publishing Director, Derek Johns. Derek it was who responded enthusiastically to the proposal for a series of eight *Murder Club Regional Guides;* Derek it was who enthusiastically adopted the suggestion to launch *The Murder Club* on the same date as the first four books – on the 30th of June, this year. And by the next season of flickering fires, Criminology will no longer be the exclusive preserve of the scientists, the lawyers, and the journalists. Our Members will already have become arm-chair detectives.

Brian Lane

London
April 1988

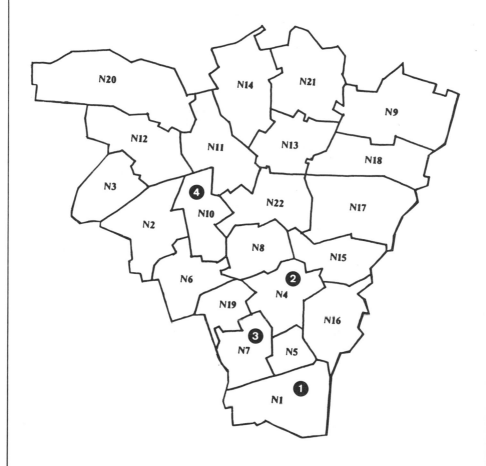

North London

1. Kenneth HALLIWELL 16
2. Frederick Henry SEDDON 19
3. Dr Hawley Harvey CRIPPEN 24
4. Dennis Andrew NILSEN 29

"Reject all the values of society..."

The Murder of JOE ORTON
by KENNETH HALLIWELL
on the 9th of August 1967
at 25 Noel Road, N1

It was in 1951 that the unlikely affair began between two drama students which set a ball rolling that would lead, within a decade and a half, to brutal murder and suicide.

The affair was unlikely only because of the disimilarity of the partners. At the age of seventeen, Joe Orton was a virtual rural innocent, the product of very basic formal teaching, and having never travelled outside his native Leicester. By comparison, Kenneth Halliwell was the urbane sophisticate; twenty-five years old, with the benefit of a classical education; in addition he had his own flat and a car – certainly high among the symbols of a young man with prospects. The couple met at the Royal Academy of Dramatic Art, where they studied acting; each must have recognised the comfort and support of a fellow homosexual in a world less tolerant than today.

Within a very short time they had set up home together. Home was one small room in which they were to live...and to die.

It was in this curious hermetic world that the brilliance of young Joe was given its early foundation; Kenneth adapted to the role of teacher and guide as well as of lover, steering Orton through a rapid literary education. They read together, they wrote together; and with the flowering of confidence Joe Orton began rapidly to overtake his companion. He began to develop a purposeful determination, and with it the brand of flamboyant sexuality which has caused him so often to be compared with another young giant of a former age – with Oscar Fingall O'Flahertie Wills Wilde. Like Wilde, too, he had achieved a remarkable and individual style of play-writing, and a firm position in the ephemeral artistic society of 1960s 'swinging' London.

1963 was Joe Orton's year – the year the BBC broadcast his *Ruffian on the Stair*, that *Entertaining Mr Sloane* was to open on the West End stage, with *Loot* soon to follow. Joe was being wooed by the media; he was in demand at social gatherings. He was leaving poor Kenneth behind. He had – to use the phrase of his biographer John Lahr – "edited Halliwell out".

Kenneth would never recover from the real and the imagined rejections, and his inability to adopt a 'supporting role' to Joe's by now extravagant life-style and promiscuous sexuality signalled disaster for them both.

On August 9th, 1967, Kenneth Halliwell smashed in his lover's head with a hammer. The life and times of Joe Orton had come to an untimely end, followed quickly by that of the tragic Ken – victim of a self-administered overdose of Nembutals.

After his suicide, Halliwell's enigmatic 'last words' were found by police in a scribbled note – it read "if you read his diary all will be explained." Orton's diary covering the

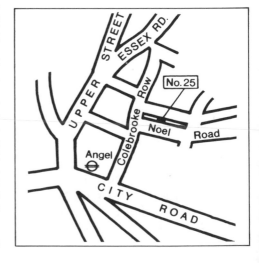

25 Noel Road, Islington

met a maniac. "See over there," he said. "Two men. They shag. And over there," he said, pointing to a clump of trees that were perhaps three feet away from a well-lighted pavement. "Please let me shag you," he said, "I'll be quick." "But we're in the light!" I said. "We can be seen." "Naw," he said, "nobody notice." Up against a tree. I dropped my trousers and he fucked me. He was quick. Afterwards he tossed me off. As we were walking away he said, "I shag a boy last week. I pay him £2. You don't want money, do you?" "No," I said, "I've plenty of money."

(13 July 1967)

There is acknowledgement, too, of the rapid degeneration of Ken Halliwell's reason; the black moods of hatred and self-doubt:

Suddenly I realised Kenneth was looking tight-lipped and white-faced. We were in the middle of talks of suicide and "you'll have to face up to the world one day". And "I'm disgusted by all this immorality". He began to rail savagely at Tom and Clive, and after a particularly sharp outburst, alarmed me by saying "Homosexuals dis-

period from December 1966 until his death, was published in 1987*, and even if Kenneth Halliwell's sad clue is not so dramatically apparent, it does reveal points at which Orton – wittingly or no – seemed to be deliberately goading his partner with the blatant sexual promiscuity that so hurt and frightened Halliwell; exploits that were written in colourful and wildly explicit prose into the pages of the 'diary' and then deliberately left where his companion could hardly fail to see them:

We went into the lavatory. Only one man was there. I stood next to him...He was a Greek-Cypriot. He wasn't very young. About thirty-five. Very stupid looking. "Come to the park," he said, in an ice-cream seller's accent, "I'll shag you." I thought it was a stupid idea. And when we got to the park it seemed as though I had

Kenneth Hailliwell's collage design for the poster for Orton's Loot

---

* *The Orton Diaries*, edited by John Lahr. Publ: Methuen, London, 1987.

gust me!" I didn't attempt to fathom this one out. He said he wasn't going to come away to Morocco. He was going to kill himself. "I've led a dreadful, unhappy life. I'm pathetic. I can't go on suffering like this". After talking until about eight he suddenly shouted out and hammered on the wall, "They treated me like shit! I won't be treated like this."

What is perhaps most remarkable, when viewed in retrospect, is that despite the painstaking observation and meticulous record-keeping that his diaries and other writing exhibit Orton was quite incapable of reading the warning signs of imminent danger; a naivety that would have kept him in blissful unconcern until he felt the first frenzied blow of the hammer. . .

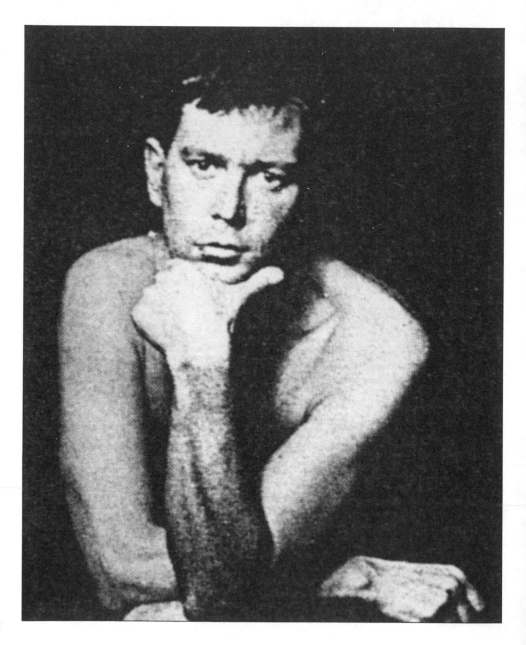

The Meanest Murderer of them All

The Murder of Miss ELIZA MARY BARROW
by FREDERICK HENRY SEDDON
on the 14th of September 1911
at 63 Tollington Park, N4

Frederick Henry Seddon has the well-deserved reputation of being perhaps the meanest murderer in the annals of crime. His activities have gained lustre over the years to the point where his name has become almost synonymous with cold, calculated greed, though his crime, in itself, was no more vicious or horrifying than many others. Edward Marshall Hall, trial counsel for his defence described him as the ablest man he had ever defended on a capital charge, and he was undoubtedly cunning. Yet he was, at the same time, remarkably vain and totally insensitive, qualities which he unwisely made no attempt to disguise at his trial.

Seddon was 40 years old, married, with five children and an aged father who lived with him. For twenty-one years he worked for the London & Manchester Industrial Insurance Co., reaching the position of Superintendent of Collectors and Canvassers in North London. The making and keeping of money had become the greatest obsession in his life, to the point where at one time he swelled his earnings by running a second-hand clothes business from his house using his wife's name. He also speculated in the buying and selling of property. One such house, 63 Tollington Park, Holloway, was substantial enough to tempt him to move in himself. There was room enough for his whole family and for an office on the ground floor, for which he charged his employers five shillings per week, while still leaving space to let the whole second floor at 12 shillings a week. His choice of tenant was Miss Eliza Barrow, a 49-year-old spinster in comfortable circumstances, but who was sour, argumentative, sluttish, deaf, partial to alcohol, and Seddon's perfect match in meanness.

Miss Barrow had been living in the house

of her cousin, Mr Vonderahe, just around the corner at 31 Evershot Road, before the inevitable arguments that she seemed to provoke forced her to rent the second floor of Mr Seddon's house, unfurnished, in July, 1910. She brought with her two family friends, Mr Hook and his wife and their ten-year-old nephew, Ernest Grant, who she had more or less adopted.

Since Seddon shared many of Eliza Barrow's preoccupations, it was not long before he had begun to wheedle his way into her confidence. Within a fortnight a row between Miss Barrow and Mrs Hook led to the Hooks being asked to look for alternative lodgings. Typical of Seddon was his pinning a notice to quit to their door, signed 'F. Seddon. Landlord and Owner'. Soon Seddon was advising Miss Barrow on financial matters, and after just two months in the house she had transferred £1600 of India Stock into Seddon's name in return for a small annuity and a remission of rent. This was all the more singular in that it was a most casual arrangement for a man who was a professional in the business of annuities.

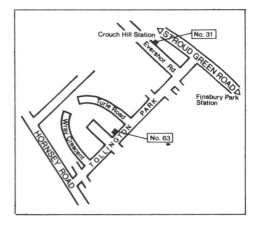

In the January of 1911 the leases of two properties in Camden were likewise transferred to Seddon; Miss Barrow's annuity rose to £3 a week. Later that year Miss Barrow became alarmed by Lloyd George's budget and the Birkbeck financial crash. On Seddon's advice she withdrew £200 in coin from her Savings Bank and placed it into Seddon's safe hands. It would subsequently be revealed that the old maid's remaining assets, a tidy sum in coin, notes and jewellery had also been lodged with Seddon. He now had his hands on the entire £4000 that constituted Eliza Barrow's worldly goods. It was around about this time that Mrs Seddon was observed changing thirty £5 notes in local shops, using the name 'Mrs Scott, of 10 [sometimes 18] Evershot Street'.

Miss Eliza Mary Barrow

In early August, 1911, the Seddons went on a short holiday to Southend, taking Miss Barrow and young Ernie Grant with them. Following their return, on August 26th, Seddon sent his daughter Maggie to a chemist's shop in Crouch Hill to purchase a threepenny packet of flypapers, which was prominently labelled 'Poison' and contained a considerable quantity of arsenic. On September 1st, Miss Barrow was taken ill.

As Miss Barrow's doctor was away, Seddon's own physician, Dr Sworn, was sent for and diagnosed epidemic diarrhoea. Miss Barrow was a heavy woman who suffered with asthma, and the risk of heart failure being evident, she was advised to keep to her bed. With sickness compounding her natural lack of basic hygiene, it took just a few days for her room to develop a most disgusting atmosphere, and was buzzing with flies. The Seddons claimed that they placed saucers of water containing the poisonous flypapers on the mantelpiece and this was the reason for their purchase, though Dr Sworn on his visits failed to notice this detail. Miss Barrow's most unpleasant solution to the problem was to abandon the room and move in with her young ward, Ernie Grant, sharing his bed.

At midnight on 13 September, Eliza Barrow was heard to cry out "I'm dying!" Mrs Seddon went up to attend to her, but when Seddon returned from an evening at a music hall, his main concern was to moan to his sister-in-law about a man who had, heaven knows how, swindled him out of a sixpence. While Mrs Seddon continued to minister to Miss Barrow, her husband settled down to a smoke and a read of the newspaper, without so much as visiting his stricken lodger on her sick-bed. At 6.30am, Miss Barrow died.

Seddon did not bother to call the doctor, though the next morning he obtained a death certificate from Dr Sworn, who deemed it unnecessary to make any examination of the body. Seddon then set about winding up Miss Barrow's affairs, not surprisingly in his own best interest. That evening, it was the turn of Mrs Seddon and her sister-in-law to visit the music hall. Seddon arranged the funeral of Eliza Barrow for two days after her death, at Islington Borough Cemetery, pocketing a commission of 12s 6d from the undertaker for his trouble. Only the Seddons and Ernie Grant attended, although Seddon claimed to have informed her cousins, the Vonderahes, by post, producing a carbon copy of the missive at his subsequent trial. The original, if it was ever sent, never reached its destination.

Seddon did contact the Vonderahes some time later, presenting them with his precise account of Miss Barrow's affairs. He produced a will, signed three days before her death, appointing him sole executor and guardian to Ernie Grant and Ernie's sister, who was away at school. This was accompanied by the documents detailing the transfer of stocks and property to himself. Finally there was an account explaining that only £10 in cash and valuables had been found in Miss Barrow's room and that Seddon was actually out of pocket to the tune of £1 1s 10½d after deducting the funeral expenses and the cost of Ernie's upkeep!

The Vonderahes, whose affection for Miss Barrow had always been firmly based on hopes of future advancement, were outraged, and it didn't take them long to visit the police and convey their suspicions about their cousin's sudden death. For some time the police cautiously investigated the various financial transactions between Seddon and Miss Barrow; after two months, they were sufficiently sure of their ground to order an exhumation. The autopsy was carried out by Bernard Spilsbury, the young pathologist who had so recently made his reputation in the Crippen case. Although the symptoms of epidemic diarrhoea and arsenic poisoning are very similar, the unnatural preservation of the body suggested foul play. This was confirmed when Dr William Willcox, the senior Home Office analyst, found traces of arsenic in the tissues and organs. On 4 December, Frederick Henry Seddon was arrested. His immediate response was to exclaim, in a shocked tone, "Absurd – what a terrible charge, wilful murder! It's the first of our family that has ever been charged with such a crime." In mid-January, the name of Margaret Ann Seddon, his wife, was added to the indictment.

The trial, which opened at the Old Bailey on the 4th of March, 1912, lasted ten days, a record for a murder trial at that time, and brought together some of the finest advocates of the day, under the stern eye of Mr Justice Bucknill. The counsel for the prosecution, as is traditional in poisoning cases, was the Attorney-General, Sir Rufus Isaacs. Edward Marshall Hall represented Seddon and Mr Gervais Rentoul represented Mrs Seddon.

The first portion of the trial was taken up with medical evidence. The defence claimed that the ingestion of arsenic into Miss Barrow's body had been chronic, rather than acute; that is, the poison had been taken in

small quantities over a protracted period, presumably by means of some relatively harmless medicinal preparation. Seddon was later to propose the additional theory that Miss Barrow might have drunk the flypaper water in her room by accident! Willcox and Spilsbury, however, remained firmly united in their initial assessment of acute arsenical poisoning.

63 Tollington Park in 1987

Now the scene was set for the main drama of the trial: the appearance of Frederick Seddon in the witness box. It has been said by many who attended the trial that Seddon's performance, more than any of the evidence, sealed his fate and condemned him to the gallows. The true odiousness of his personality was evident for all to see. His bearing was arrogant and vain. His hypocrisy and calculated poverty of spirit shone out at every opportunity. At one point, asked whether it was true that he had been seen by one of his agents counting Miss Barrow's money on the morning after her death, he vehemently denied the suggestion then, after a pause, added, "I would have had all day to count the money." Thus, in every way, he confirmed the impression of his character created by the financial evidence. Mrs Seddon, however, though not revealing a very flattering portrait of herself, was for the most part more effective, playing to perfection the meek, downtrodden wife who wouldn't dream of questioning, or even trying to understand, her husband's actions.

The outcome of the trial was uncertain to the end, but when the jury announced their verdict, it was evident that they had been greatly influenced by the conduct of the accused in the witness box. Frederick Seddon was found guilty. Mrs Seddon was acquitted. True to character, Seddon made a last gesture of arrogance. Giving a ritual masonic sign, he addressed himself to the judge: "I declare before the Great Architect of the Universe, I am not guilty." The Judge, a fellow-mason, seemed embarrassed and replied, with barely suppressed anger, "You and I know we both belong to one brotherhood ... But our brotherhood does not encourage crime." The final humiliation for Seddon was, however, the selling of his properties while he waited in the condemned

cell for his sentence to be carried out. Seeing the meagre price fetched by the fruits of all his acquisitiveness, he exclaimed in desperation, "That's finished it!"

Frederick Seddon was hanged in Pentonville Prison on the 18th of April, 1912.

Perhaps the major puzzle of the whole trial was the acquittal of Mrs Seddon. Throughout the proceedings, the prosecution contended that hers was the hand which had actually administered the poison; her husband does not seem to have had the opportunity. If Seddon was guilty, then Mrs Seddon must technically also have been. Her performance as the dominated, downtrodden wife (which had so affected the jury) did not long outlast the trial. Within three weeks of Seddon's execution, she had remarried and sold a lurid and fanciful confession to the Press for a considerable amount of money. A week later, she sold a retraction to a rival paper, also for a tidy sum.

The closing comment on the case must rest with the fact that Miss Barrow, whose burial in a common grave seemed such an outrageous example of Seddon's meanness, was allowed to rest for all time in that same meagre plot by her ever-loving relatives.

The Seddons in the dock at the Old Bailey

By Appointment to Henry Seddon, Suppliers of Poison

The first registration of the trade mark of William Mather's patent flypapers in 1877. The design was to become familiar with those attending Seddon's trial in 1911, being some of the strongest tangible evidence for his poisoning of Miss Barrow.

Ironically, it was fifty years previously that Mather had patented a new system in order to overcome the "danger to human life" inherent in the use of poisons to control household pests:

Apparatus for Catching and Destroying Flies, etc. Provisional Specification left by William Mather at the Office of the Commissioners of Patents, with his Petition, on 2nd April 1859.

I, William Mather, of the City of Manchester, in the County of Lancaster, Wholesale Druggist, do hereby declare the nature of the said Invention for *An Improved Apparatus for Catching and Destroying Flies and other Insects*, to be as follows:–

Instead of placing poisonous matter on plates, or other domestic vessels for the purpose of destroying flies and insects, the said system being dangerous to human life on account of the vessels being generally within the reach of children, I make shallow dishes or vessels of tin, zinc, or other suitable metal or material, with holes, perforations, or projections in the sides thereof to allow of string or other material to be easily attached to them, whereby the vessel can be hung to the ceiling of a room or other convenient position where it will be out of the way, and thus avoid danger. In the vessel I place any of the well-known poisonous or adhesive substance or substances generally used for such purposes.

The Hen-Pecked Killer

The murder of Mrs CORA CRIPPEN
(called BELLE ELMORE)
by Dr HAWLEY HARVEY CRIPPEN
on or about Monday the 31st of January 1910
at 39 Hilldrop Crescent, N7

The kitchen at 39 Hilldrop Crescent, Hollo-way was an unappetising sight. Piles of un-washed dishes made a squalid litter with bits of discarded female clothing, a box of spilled face powder and several empty gin bottles. At one end of the room a small and obviously depressed figure was furiously polishing several pairs of muddy boots. He was a dapper little man with a drooping moustache and gold-rimmed spectacles pro-tecting protuberant blue eyes which from time to time glanced anxiously at the kettle on the stove. When it eventually boiled he made morning tea with the precise gestures of a man of science, belying the role of the kitchen drudge.

Hawley Harvey Crippen – a trained doctor in America but not qualified to practise in his adopted London – was doing the morning chores before his wife would let him go to work. Each morning the lodgers' boots must be cleaned and their breakfasts cooked while his wife, Cora – or Belle Elmore as she preferred to be known to her theatrical friends and audiences – still lay dreaming of dresses and diamonds, compliments and champagne; and the time when her name would blaze in lights to dazzle the whole of England. In the meantime she vented her many frustrations on the meek little man to whom she had accorded, to her mind, the inestimable honour of marriage.

Crippen first met Cora Turner (whose real name was Kunigunde Mackamotzki) in New York and was dazzled by the vivacity of the attractive Polish-German girl. Cora, at nineteen, had already been the mistress of a wealthy stove manufacturer and she now looked to Crippen to keep her in the manner to which she felt entitled as a potential star of the operatic stage.

In 1900 Crippen's employers – Munyon's Remedies, a patent medicine company – sent him to England, and Cora prepared to take the London theatre by storm. Sadly, her ambition was wildly out of proportion to her talent and she never achieved more than occasional music hall or smoking concert en-gagements. But she did become something of a personality in off-stage theatrical circles and even attained the position of treasurer of the Music Hall Ladies' Guild, so enlarging her large circle of friends and admirers. When Crippen was called to Philadelphia for six months on business she made good use of the time to enjoy a tempestuous affair with an American performer and ex-prizefighter called Bruce Miller.

Crippen desperately tried to keep pace with his wife's imperious demands for all the trappings of luxury. He moved from venture to venture, all in vaguely medical fields, and even practised illegally for a time as a dentist and women's consultant; but their

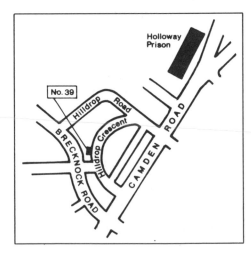

24

bank balance still would not stand the strain of Cora's extravagance and to make ends meet they were forced to take in lodgers to the large gloomy house they rented at Hilldrop Crescent. While Crippen was dispensing quack medicines to keep Cora in ermine, fox and jewels, she ruled him with a rod of iron, choosing all his clothes for him –right down to his underwear–humiliating him in front of the lodgers and her friends and treating him as a domestic skivvy.

She was unable to have children due to the ovariectomy that she had undergone shortly after her marriage, and so she was free to use her time as she pleased. She divided her energies between two personas: the charming and delightful Belle Elmore –beloved by her many friends–and the coarse and bullying Cora Crippen, cruel tormentor of her husband.

Then Cora discovered that her husband was having an affair with his secretary – Ethel le Neve. The love that had grown up between the 48-year-old Crippen and the younger Ethel was the only ray of happiness and pride in his otherwise miserable existence. Cora mocked and taunted him about the affair, cheapening it into something sordid and absurd and she used the situation to indulge her own extra-marital adventures more openly. That is, until she found out that Ethel was pregnant. This was too much for the childless Cora, who set out to spread slanderous stories about Ethel among all her friends and acquaintances. Finally, she threatened to desert Crippen and to take everything in their joint bank account with her – leaving him penniless.

When Ethel suffered a miscarriage, Cora decided to stay put, but by this time a resolve had formed itself in the mind of the otherwise mild and inoffensive Crippen – a resolve so desperate that it did not stop short at murder – and he quietly laid the groundwork for the plan that would rid him of the intolerable incubus of his wife. His first step was to visit a chemist in New Oxford Street where he bought five grains of hyoscine hydrobromide – an obscure but effective poison...

On the evening of January 31st 1910, Mr and Mrs Martinetti, retired mime artists and friends of the Crippens, dined at Hilldrop Crescent – Crippen insisted that they should

Hawley Harvey Crippen: Age 50, 5 feet 3 or 4, complexion fresh, hair light brown, inclined sandy, scanty, bald on top, rather long scanty moustache, somewhat straggly, eyes grey, bridge of nose rather flat, false teeth, medium build, throws his feet outwards when walking...somewhat slovenly appearance, wears his hat rather at back of head. Very plausible and quiet spoken, remarkably cool and collected demeanour.

(Metropolitan Police description of Crippen issued July 1910)

keep the engagement despite Mr. Martinetti's ill-health and the fact that Cora was not in her finest fettle either with a slight cold. When the Martinettis left at around 1.30am, she waved them goodbye from an upstairs window so as not to risk the chill of the cold night air. It was the last time that anyone, other than her husband, was ever to see Cora Crippen alive.

The day after the dinner party, Crippen called on the Martinettis to see if they had enjoyed the evening, and he promised to pass on Mrs Martinetti's love to Cora. The following day he was pawning some of Cora's jewellery, and Ethel le Neve spent the night at Hilldrop Crescent. Two days later, the Music Hall Ladies Guild received two letters

Mrs Cora Crippen, otherwise Belle Elmore: "A very charming lady, and very popular in the music hall world" (The Era, 1910)

signed 'Belle Elmore' – but not in Cora's hand-writing – resigning her membership of the Guild. The reason given was an urgent visit to America due to a family illness. Crippen made another sally to the pawnshop and, on February 20th, three weeks after Cora's supposed departure for the US, he coolly took Ethel, wearing one of Cora's brooches, to the Music Hall Ladies' annual ball. Neither the brooch nor the relationship escaped the scandalized eyes of the Ladies and their escorts and when on March 12th, Ethel openly moved into Hilldrop Crescent, the clicking of tongues became a clamour. Crippen started spreading the story that Cora had developed pneumonia in America and was dangerously ill. Finally, on March 24th, on his way to Dieppe for an Easter 'honeymoon' with Ethel, he sent a cable from Victoria station to the Martinettis saying baldly – "Belle died yesterday at six o'clock".

The clamour of gossip became a tumult and on his return to England, Crippen was bombarded with questions from Cora's friends demanding details of the death and funeral arrangements. Crippen calmly told them that Belle had died with relatives in Los Angeles – even going into details of who was by her bedside at the end; he assured them that it was too late to send flowers – Cora's ashes were already on their way.

He continued his normal quiet routine, returning each evening to Hilldrop Crescent and Ethel, who was now openly wearing Cora's furs and jewels. Then in May an old friend of Cora's returned from a business trip to California; a hurried visit to Los Angeles had revealed no trace of Cora or Belle, either alive or dead. His suspicions aroused, he took them straight to Scotland Yard.

Chief Inspector Walter Dew had been instructed to launch an enquiry into the disappearance and on July 8th he began by visiting Hilldrop Crescent; he was received by Ethel le Neve and a French maid. Later Crippen courteously showed the Inspector over the house, pointing out the trunks of clothing, furs and jewellery belonging to his wife. Then, with a shamefaced and dejected look, Crippen 'confessed' to the Inspector how he had fabricated the story of her death to cover up the scandal of the 'real story' – that she had run away with her lover (the American Bruce Miller) and the couple had disappeared together, he knew not where. Inspector Dew felt sorry for the pathetic little man and after making him promise to write a description of Cora for the US newspapers, he left Crippen with a warm handshake. His reaction was rather cooler when he returned to the house a few days later to find nothing but the signs of hurried flight.

Pictures and descriptions of the couple were circulated, and on July 13th the police began a systematic search of the house. It was not until the third day that Dew, armed with a poker, prised up some loose bricks in the cellar floor and discovered something wrapped up in a pyjama jacket and buried in lime. In the parcel was part of a human body – a headless, armless and legless torso.

Piece by piece the grisly remains were taken to the mortuary for analysis; side by side with the stoppered jars containing the body's organs were others displaying variously a pair of bloodstained combinations coated with lime, brown human hair in a curler, a tattered handkerchief, a cotton camisole and portions of a flannelette pyjama jacket which matched trousers found in Crippen's bedroom. A final jar contained a piece of skin from the abdomen which exhibited an old operation scar – the sort of scar that Cora Crippen bore as a reminder of the operation she had undergone when she was a young girl. Analysis of the organs revealed traces of hyoscine – the first time that this obscure poison had been used for the purpose of murder.

A warrant was issued for the arrest of both Crippen and le Neve and the story exploded into the headlines of every newspaper in the country...

Captain Henry Kendall of the S.S. *Montrose*, bound for Canada, fancied himself as an amateur detective and used his powers of observation to protect his passengers and crew against conmen and troublemakers. On this particular voyage he was keeping a weather eye on a curious couple who had boarded the ship at Antwerp; Mr and Master Robinson, who shared a double cabin, were not quite what they appeared to be. He watched them more closely and soon came to the positive conclusion that Master Robinson was a woman in disguise; Mr Robinson, he noted, carried a revolver under his jacket.

A police notice about Crippen and le Neve reached Captain Kendall and he studied the photographs minutely; despite the lack of spectacles and moustache, he felt a shock of excitement as he reached the certain conclusion that he had found the fugitives Crippen and le Neve in the Robinson couple. He took the dramatic step of sending a radio-telegraph to Scotland Yard, the first time

that the new wireless device had been used in the battle against crime. As soon as the news reached Inspector Dew, he boarded a fast ship and caught up with the S.S. *Montrose* before she docked at Montreal.

The international press were running a high fever about the story by this time, and a boat-load of journalists, disguised as shipwrecked sailors, had to be bribed from upstaging Dew, himself disguised as a harbour pilot, in getting aboard the *Montrose*.

Eventually Inspector Dew was welcomed on board by Captain Kendall and lost little time in recognising Mr Robinson as his quarry. Crippen, however, was at a disadvantage without his spectacles and did not at first recognise Dew in his pilot's uniform. The Inspector greeted him, "Good morning Dr Crippen" and was rewarded with a fleeting look of surprise, then fear and finally resignation as the cornered Crippen struggled to regain his composure.

Ethel le Neve, awaiting Crippen in their cabin, collapsed in a dead faint as Dew burst into the compartment. The couple were arrested, handcuffed and searched on board the *Montrose*. In Crippen's pocket Dew found two cards – both printed 'John Robinson' and bearing pencilled messages. The first read: "I cannot stand the horror I go through every night any longer and as I see nothing ahead and money has come to an end, I have made up my mind to jump overboard tonight. I know I have spoiled your life but I'll hope some day you can learn to forgive me. Last words of love. Yours H." The other card read: "Shall we wait till tonight about 10 or 11? If not, what time?"... Were these genuine suicide messages or were they part of a plan to foil the police when they searched the ship at Montreal? Crippen maintained at his trial that he had bribed someone to smuggle him ashore before the ship docked and that Ethel would have handed the two cards to the police saying that he had jumped overboard during the night. Such a plan might well have succeeded but for Dew's speed in reaching the *Montrose* when he did.

Crippen's trial at the Old Bailey became such a star attraction that over 4,000 applications were received for seats and half-day-only tickets were specially issued. The trial opened on the 18th of October and lasted for five days, the prisoner behaving throughout with courageous dignity – even when the jury pronounced the inevitable 'guilty' verdict and sentence was passed. Only when the Appeal Court upheld the verdict did Crippen give way to a moment's black despair; he penned his last love letter to Ethel: "...Death has no terror for me..." he wrote, "but Oh! wifie my love, my own, the bitterness of the thought that I must leave you alone without me in the world..."

On 23rd November, 1910, at Pentonville Prison, Hawley Harvey Crippen calmly met his death by the hangman's rope and was buried in an unmarked grave in the prison yard. In compliance with his last modest request, Ethel's photograph and letters were buried with him.

Ethel le Neve was acquitted of any complicity in the murder and to escape further publicity she emigrated to Canada soon after the trial. There she later married and had children and returned after many years to Britain where she died in old age and obscurity in 1965.

By all accounts, Hawley Harvey Crippen was a courteous, pleasant and unselfish man, in fact one witness at his trial described him as one of the nicest men she had ever met. Perhaps it is Cora Crippen who should have

Ethel Le Neve before her trial

gone down in history as the villain of the piece – in driving her husband beyond the bounds of what human dignity could stand and into a ghastly crime for which they both paid with their lives.

[*Based on* The Hen-Pecked Killer *by Susan Dunkley*]

The Ghost of Hilldrop Crescent

The Hilldrop Crescent of this story has undergone significant changes at the hands of developers since the Crippens' time, and the war-damaged site of number 39 (along with its immediate neighbours) was rebuilt as Margaret Bondfield House, a block of flats. But if Hilldrop Crescent has lost a house or two, then it would appear that it has gained a ghost: for some say that the shade of Hawley Harvey Crippen walks still, on the night of the 31st of January, replaying the night of Belle's death.

The first sighting of the ghost was recorded by Peter Underwood, President of The Ghost Club, in his *Haunted London*. On the night after Crippen's execution a man stood vigil on a piece of waste ground close to the house – a patch where the doctor was accustomed to walk – perhaps to clear his head...perhaps to plan...

It was just before midnight that the already chilly air developed an icier touch...and from the shadow of a high wall a form began to take shape...a shortish man with a drooping moustache...and gold-rimmed spectacles. As the figure moved out of sight it was seen to be carrying a parcel. When it returned some minutes later, it was empty-handed...and quickly evaporated into the night.

What was wrapped in the parcel is anybody's guess...But what would a man who has just killed and decapitated his wife be likely to dispose of at the dead of night?

"This all counts for nothing"

The Murder of KEN OCKENDEN, MALCOLM BARLOW, BILLY SUTHERLAND MARTYN DUFFY, JOHN HOWLETT, and STEPHEN SINCLAIR

by DENNIS ANDREW NILSEN

on various dates between December 1979 and January 1983 at 23 Cranley Gardens, N10 and 195 Melrose Avenue, NW2

Stumbling on a Mass Murderer

23 Cranley Gardens is a large, Edwardian, semi-detached house in the North London suburb of Muswell Hill. Most of the houses in Cranley Gardens are occupied by middle-class families, but in the early 1980s number 23 had been converted into six bedsit flats.

On Thursday, the 3rd of February, 1983, a number of the tenants were irritated to discover that their lavatories wouldn't flush properly. The local plumber was called, but when he arrived on the Saturday he realized that it was too serious a job for him to handle. Jim Alcock, the boyfriend of one of the tenants, Fiona Bridges, decided to telephone 'Dyno-Rod', the large plumbing company, while his girlfriend attempted to get in touch with the landlord.

It was not until 6.15pm on the Tuesday evening that Mike Cattran, a 'Dyno-Rod' engineer, arrived to investigate the problem. He managed to trace the blockage to a manhole at the side of the house without any difficulty, but when he removed the cover he was assailed by the most revolting stench. As he shone his torch into the murky depths he could just make out, twelve feet below him, a layer of white sludge, which was flecked with what looked appallingly like blood. Holding his breath and suppressing the desire to retch, he climbed down the rungs into the manhole. In the sludge he came upon what he was now certain were pieces of rotting white meat, some with hair still on the skin. After climbing back up he discussed his unpleasant discovery with the tenants. Had anybody been trying to flush pieces of chicken or pork down the toilet? They hadn't, but the man in the top flat did have

a dog. Perhaps he knew something about it? Mike Cattran turned to 'Des' Nilsen, a quiet man in his thirties who usually kept himself very much to himself. Had he been flushing meat down the lavatory? No, he replied, he was just as puzzled about the plumbing problem as everyone else. Mike Cattran was still suspicious. He hardly dared think it, but the meat just might be human remains. It didn't look like any meat he had ever seen before, and for some time he considered telephoning the police. Instead, he informed his supervisor of what he'd found and arranged to return to Cranley Gardens to take a further look in daylight.

Next morning Mike Cattran, accompanied by his supervisor, Gary Wheeler, prised open the manhole cover again, with considerable trepidation. To his surprise there was no nasty smell and when he looked down, the layer of white sludge had also disappeared. Had he been imagining things? He decided to climb down the manhole to have another good look. Feeling with his hand along the

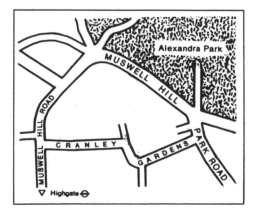

pipe which led into the manhole, he pulled out a chunk of flesh and four pieces of bone. The bones were horrifyingly reminiscent of human fingers. At that moment Fiona Bridges came out of the house. She and Jim had heard somebody scrabbling about outside during the night. Jim had gone out to investigate and nearly bumped into Des Nilsen coming back in. Nilsen had explained that he had just popped out for a pee, but both Jim and Fiona had been quite upset and had had some difficulty in getting back to sleep afterwards. Cattran and Wheeler decided it was time to call the police.

Detective Chief Inspector Peter Jay arrived at Cranley Gardens at eleven o'clock. A full search of the manhole was immediately begun and further pieces of flesh and bone were recovered from the drain. These were then taken in a plastic bag to Hornsey mortuary for identification, and from there to Charing Cross Hospital for detailed analysis by David Bowen, the Professor of Forensic Medicine at University College, London. Professor Bowen examined the remains at 3.30 in the afternoon and pronounced them human, the flesh coming from the neck region and the various bones from a male human hand.

By 4.30 DCI Jay was back at Cranley Gardens, accompanied by DI Stephen McCusker and DC Jeffrey Butler. They had to wait until 5.40pm for Des Nilsen to return from his work as a clerical officer in a Job Centre in Central London. Meeting Nilsen at the door, DCI Jay explained that he was a police officer and he had come about the drains. Nilsen expressed surprise that the police should be interested in something as mundane as drains, and the four men climbed the stairs. As they reached his flat and walked into the bedroom, Nilsen was informed that human remains had been found in the outside drain. "Good grief! How awful!" he replied. DCI Jay then said "Don't mess about, where's the rest of the body?" To his great surprise Nilsen replied, quite calmly, "In two plastic bags in the wardrobe next door, I'll show you." and led the detectives into the front room, offering DCI Jay the key to the wardrobe. The smell alone was enough to confirm Nilsen's statement without further investigation. Nilsen continued, unprompted, "It's a long story. It goes back

The official police photograph of Dennis Nilsen

a long time. I'll tell you everything. I want to get it all off my chest, not here but at the police station." Nilsen was cautioned and then arrested on a charge of murder.

While Nilsen was being taken by car to Hornsey Police Station, Detective Inspector McCusker turned and asked him, "Are we talking about one body or two?" Nilsen replied: "Fifteen or sixteen, since 1978. I'll tell you everything. It's a relief to be able to get it all off my mind."

In the charge room the questioning began: "Let's get this straight. Are you telling us that since 1978 you have killed sixteen people?" "Yes, three at Cranley Gardens and about thirteen at my previous address, 195 Melrose Avenue, Cricklewood."

The police were at first flabbergasted by Nilsen's apparent frankness, his cold, mat-ter-of-fact approach to the situation, and by the sheer scale of his claims. They also found themselves in the unlikely position of having found their murderer almost before the investigation had begun. Their task was – literally – to piece together whom he had kil-led, when and where the crimes had occurred and how such an orgy of killing could have gone so completely unnoticed for so long.

With Nilsen secure in a cell in Hornsey Police Station, Chief Inspector Jay returned to Cranley Gardens at nine o'clock that evening, accompanied by Professor Bowen and Detective Chief Superintendent Peter Chambers, the head of 'Y' Division, who had now been placed in charge of the inquiry. They took two large plastic bags from Nil-sen's wardrobe and returned to Hornsey mortuary to inspect the contents. Both of the bags contained a number of smaller, sealed carrier bags of the kind provided by supermarkets and department stores. The inventory of the first large bag listed the following: the left side of a man's chest; the right side of a man's chest with an arm attached; a torso minus legs, arms and head; a mess of internal organs, consisting of a heart, two lungs, a spleen, a liver, a gall bladder, kidneys and intestines. The second large plastic bag contained a torso with the arms attached, but the hands cut off; a skull with the flesh boiled away; a head with most of the flesh and hair attached, but the face removed.

On the morning of the following day, the 11th of February, at a quarter to eleven, the intensive questioning of Dennis Nilsen began, a process which was to take up a total of thirty hours over the next week. Throughout this ordeal Nilsen was always co-operative, straining his memory to recall the details of his murderous career. On the first morning he helpfully suggested that the police would find further remains under a drawer in the bathroom and in a tea chest in the front room at Cranley Gardens. In the tea chest, which was liberally garnished with mothballs and air freshener, they found another bundle of plastic bags under an old velvet curtain and some screwed-up pages of the *Guardian*. Inside was another torso, a skull, and an assortment of bones. In a plastic bag in the bathroom they discovered the complete lower half of a body.

The police next turned their attention to the other address that Nilsen had mentioned, 195 Melrose Avenue, Cricklewood. The house (which had been renovated since Nilsen's tenancy) was literally pulled apart. Nilsen had also confessed to burning as many as thirteen bodies in the garden. A team of policemen in green boiler suits and thirty police cadets working in shifts system-atically sifted every inch of ground over a period of thirteen days and nights. The trawl of Melrose Avenue brought in a pile of over a thousand charred bone fragments, including a piece of rib, part of a hip-bone, a jaw with the teeth intact and a six-inch length of thigh-bone. In addition, a cheque book, a silver medallion, a pen and several fragments of clothing were recovered, all the possessions of Nilsen's hapless victims.

Gradually, through the long hours of interro-gation, the police had begun to put together a picture of Dennis Nilsen's secret life of crime. His victims had all been unattached young men, many of them homosexual and most of them destitute. Few of them were missed when they disappeared, and this had undoubtedly been to Nilsen's advantage. Nevertheless, the extraordinary catalogue of crimes that Nilsen admitted to the police makes chilling reading.

The Case History of a Mass Murderer

23 November 1945
Dennis Nilsen was born, second of the three

children of Betty Whyte and Olav Nilsen, a Norwegian soldier. The couple had been married three years earlier, but from the beginning the marriage was unhappy, with Olav frequently absent from home and usually drunk. The situation resolved itself in divorce in 1949; Mrs Nilsen and her children living at 47 Academy Road, Fraserburgh, Aberdeenshire, the home of Mrs Nilsen's parents, Andrew and Lily Whyte. The grandparents were the driving force in the strict Presbyterian upbringing of the children.

31 October 1951
Nilsen's grandfather, Andrew Whyte, whom he idolized, died suddenly at sea at the age of sixty-one. Nilsen was much affected by seeing the dead body of his grandfather laid out in the parlour.

1954
Betty Nilsen was married to Adam Scott, a builder, and the family moved to 73 Mid Street in nearby Strichen. Dennis Nilsen developed into a solitary child and disliked his step-father.

August 1961
Nilsen enlisted in the Army Catering Corps at the age of fifteen to escape from home. He was trained at Aldershot for the next three years.

1964
Nilsen was posted to Osnabrück in Germany as a cook. It was at this time that he began to drink heavily and to discover his homosexuality. Over the next eight years he was relatively happy in the Army, being posted at various times to Berlin, Cyprus and Sharjah in the Persian Gulf.

October 1972
Nilsen decided to resign from the Army, partly because he was appalled by the way it was being used in Northern Ireland.

November 1972
Joined the Metropolitan Police, and was trained at Hendon before being posted to Willesden Police Station.

December 1973
He resigned from the police force, being unhappy both with the discipline and the restriction it put on his homosexual social life. He took a room at 9 Manstone Road, NW8, and began work as a security guard protecting various government buildings.

May 1974
After resigning his job as a security guard, Nilsen was accepted by the Manpower Services Commission as a clerical officer at the Denmark Street Job Centre, in Soho. He continued in this employment until his arrest in February 1983. A large part of his work was to interview the unemployed, the down-and-out, and the young rootless who hung about in Central London. At this time he was also regularly frequenting those public houses which atracted a homosexual clientele.

1974
Nilsen was evicted from his room in Manstone Road for entertaining male visitors late at night. He found new accommodation at 80 Teignmouth Road, Willesden.

1975
A young man called David Painter claimed that he had been attacked after rejecting Nilsen's sexual advances. Nilsen had met him at the Job Centre and invited him back to the flat. It was Nilsen who actually called the police after Painter had cut his arm in the struggle. Nilsen was interrogated for some time before being released.

November 1975
Nilsen met an unemployed man called David Gallichan at *The Champion* public house in Bayswater Road. Nilsen invited him back to his home; the pair of them decided to share a flat and moved to 195 Melrose Avenue.

May 1977
Gallichan left Nilsen, who felt humiliated and rejected by the sudden departure.

30 December 1978
Nilsen met a young Irishman at the *Cricklewood Arms*. After inviting him back to his flat to continue drinking, Nilsen strangled his guest with a tie during the night. The body was carefully undressed and washed before being stored under the floorboards, a procedure that became the pattern in Nilsen's subsequent crimes.

11 August 1979
Nilsen burnt the body of the Irishman in the garden. It had until then been stored in pieces in two plastic bags.

October 1979
Nilsen picked up a Chinese student, Andrew

Ho, in *The Salisbury* public house in St Martins Lane and took him back to his flat. Ho offered sex and agreed to be tied up. Nilsen attempted to strangle Andrew, but he broke free and ran off to inform the police. Nilsen claimed that Ho had been trying to "rip him off" and the matter was dropped.

3 December 1979
Nilsen met a 23-year-old Canadian student, Ken Ockenden, at the *Princess Louise* in High Holborn; Ockenden was in London on holiday after graduating. This victim was also strangled in Nilsen's flat and placed under the floorboards. Nilsen tore up Ockenden's money "because it would be stealing". Uniquely, Ockenden was missed, and his parents came to London, creating considerable publicity over his disappearance, but to no effect.

May 1980
Dennis Nilsen's next victim was a 16-year-old butcher called Martyn Duffey; he took his place beside Ken Ockenden under the floorboards.

July – September 1980
26-year-old Billy Sutherland, a Scot, went on a pub crawl with Nilsen and ended up with Duffey and Ockenden.

12 November 1980
Nilsen met Scottish barman Douglas Stewart at the *Red Lion* in Dean Street and took him back to Melrose Avenue. There he tried to strangle him, then threatened him with a carving knife, before deciding to let him go.

1980 – 1981
A succession of victims followed. A Filipino or Mexican was picked up at *The Salisbury*, followed by another Irishman, a building worker. There followed a half-starved down-and-out that Nilsen had picked up in a doorway on the corner of Oxford Street and Charing Cross Road. He was burnt whole in the garden almost immediately because Nilsen was so horrified by his emaciated condition. Of the next victim Nilsen could remember nothing, except that he had cut the body into three pieces and burnt it about a year later. The ninth victim was a young Scot picked up in the *Golden Lion* in Dean Street, followed by another 'Billy Sutherland' type. The next to fall prey was a 'skinhead' who was heavily tattooed, including a dotted line round his

neck, inscribed "Cut here". Ni while dissecting him.

May 1981
Nilsen had a major body-burning the garden at Melrose Avenue.

17 September 1981
Malcolm Barlow was sitting against a garden wall in Melrose Avenue, complaining that he couldn't use his legs when Nilsen found him; he phoned for an ambulance and accompanied Barlow to hospital. The next day, Barlow went back to Nilsen's flat to thank him, Nilsen cooked them both a meal, and strangled his guest when he fell asleep. Malcolm Barlow was the last of the Melrose Avenue victims.

October 1981
As a sitting tenant, Nilsen was offered £1000 to leave the flat in Melrose Avenue, so that it could be renovated. After a bonfire to remove the last vestiges of his murderous activities, Dennis Nilsen moved into the top flat at 23 Cranley Gardens, Muswell Hill.

25 November 1981
Nilsen met a homosexual student, named Paul Nobbs in the *Golden Lion* in Soho. Nobbs woke up next morning at Cranley Gardens with a worse than usual hangover; he went to University College Hospital for a check up and was told that someone had tried to strangle him. Nobbs did not pursue the matter.

March 1982
Nilsen met John Howlett, a young criminal known as 'John the Guardsman' in *The Salisbury*, and discovered they had drunk together before, back in December 1981. Nilsen invited him back to Cranley Gardens and tried to strangle him, but Howlett put up a struggle and Nilsen had to knock John's head against the bedrest before drowning him in the bath. Howlett was cut up quickly and portions of the body boiled in a pot, because an old friend was due to stay with Nilsen over the weekend.

May 1982
Picked up Carl Stotter, a homosexual revue artist known as 'Khara Le Fox' at the *Black Cap* in Camden High Street. Nilsen tried to strangle him and then drown him in the bath, but seems to have relented half-way through. Next morning, Stotter went for a walk in the woods with Nilsen, who hit him violently

over the head, pulled him back onto his feet and continued walking. The two agreed to meet again, but Stotter wisely avoided Nilsen from then on.

Late 1982
The next victim was Graham Allen, who was picked up in Shaftesbury Avenue. He was invited to the Cranley Gardens flat, and fell asleep while eating an omelette. Allen was dissected, some parts being put in a tea chest, some in a plastic bag, and others flushed down the lavatory.

26 January 1983
Stephen Sinclair, a 20-year-old 'punk' and drug addict, was picked up in Leicester Square and taken to Nilsen's home. Stephen's body was left, covered by a blanket, for several days and Nilsen was in the process of dismembering it at the time of his arrest.

9 February 1983
Nilsen arrested.

12 February 1983
Remanded in custody for seven days by the Highgate Magistrates Court. This became a regular weekly routine while police were investigating the case.

26 May 1983
Nilsen committed for trial at the Old Bailey on six counts of murder (Ken Ockenden, Malcolm Barlow, Billy Sutherland, Martyn Duffey, John Howlett, Stephen Sinclair) and two counts of attempted murder (Douglas Stewart and Paul Nobbs). The remains of Graham Allen were identified from dental records too late to be included in the first indictment. Likewise, Karl Stotter was traced too late for inclusion in the second, though his harrowing experience was used as evidence at the trial.

24 October 1983
The trial of Dennis Nilsen opened in Court No.1 at the Old Bailey, Mr Justice Croom Johnson presiding, with Mr Allan Green representing the Crown and Ivan Lawrence QC, MP, defending. That Nilsen had committed the crimes was never disputed. The main thrust of the defence case was a plea for manslaughter on the grounds of diminished responsibility.

4 November 1983
After a day and a half's retirement the jury found Nilsen guilty by a majority of ten to two on all six counts of murder and two of attempted murder. He was sentenced to life imprisonment.

Nilsen is at present serving his sentence, and it must be a matter of great doubt whether society will ever feel it safe to release him.

The Reflections of a Mass Murderer

Dennis Nilsen is an intelligent, articulate and self-analytical man. On the surface he was caring, compassionate and particularly socially aware, with strong left-wing political sympathies and a highly developed sense of morality which motivated his work in the Denmark Street Job Centre, and as a trade-union official. His personal life, however, became increasingly sad and unsatisfactory, leading him to seek solace in excessive quantities of alcohol and a succession of casual homosexual encounters, the unfortunate ingredients which brought about an appalling murderous obsession. Nilsen himself was fascinated by this apparent paradox in his personality and constantly explored his confused feelings through the written word.

I like to see people in happiness.
I like to do good.
I love democracy.
I detest any criminal acts.
I like kids.
I like all animals.
I love public and community service.
I hate to see hunger, unemployment, oppression, war, aggression, ignorance, illiteracy, etc.
I was a trades union officer.
I was a good soldier and N.C.O. I was a fair policeman.
I was an effective civil servant.
STOP. THIS ALL COUNTS FOR NOTHING when I can kill fifteen men (without any reason) and attempt to kill about nine others – in my home and under friendly circumstances.
Am I mad? I don't feel mad. Maybe I am mad.
(Poem written by Dennis Nilsen)

Never a man so sore afraid
To let his feelings shine;
Never a man so helpless
To stop and notice mine.
(Poem written by Nilsen in prison for David Martin, the bi-sexual police killer, for whom Nilsen developed a strong passion while on remand)

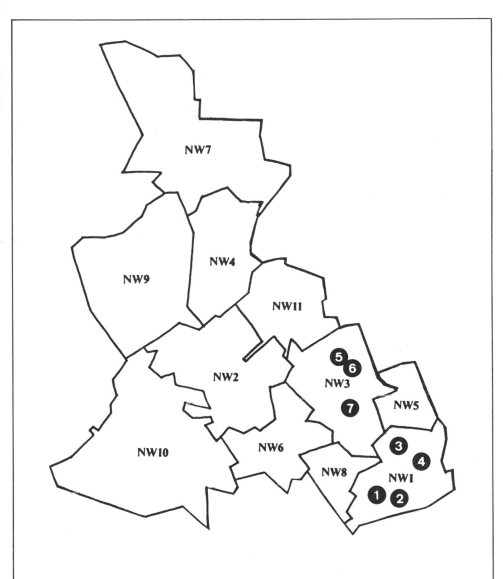

North-West London

1. Mary Eleanor PEARCEY 36
2. Robert WOOD.. 38
3. SAN DWE (called Sandy Wee) 42
4. Thomas Henry HOCKER 46
5. Robert GREEN, Henry BERRY, and Lawrence HILL 48
6. Styllou CHRISTOFI 52
7. Ruth ELLIS.. 56
8. George Baron PATEMAN... 59

Cut off their tails...

The Murder of PHOEBE HOGG and her Baby Daughter by MARY ELEANOR PEARCEY

on Friday the 24th of October 1890 at 2 Priory Street (now Ivor Street), NW1

Jealousy can be a powerful emotion and the murder of Mrs Phoebe Hogg and her eighteen-month-old daughter by Mrs Pearcey stands as a classic instance of that passion transformed into consuming fury.

Mary Eleanor Wheeler was not, in fact, married, but took the name Pearcey from a carpenter with whom she had lived for a period of time. In the two years before 1890 she resided at 2 Priory Street, Kentish Town, in a ground-floor flat which was paid for by a gentleman admirer. At the same time, she had developed a further intrigue with a local furniture remover named Frank Hogg. Hogg seems to have had an equally relaxed attitude to relationships, and contrived to get another girl, Phoebe Styles, pregnant and, constrained by family pressure, married her and set up house at 141 Prince of Wales Road, Kentish Town. This, though, did not bring the affair with Mrs Pearcey to an end. Indeed, when Mrs Hogg was poorly after the birth of her daughter, also Phoebe, Mrs Pearcey was introduced into the household to nurse Mrs Hogg and look after the baby. At the same time, Hogg was still visiting Mary Pearcey regularly at Priory Street.

On Friday, 24th of October, 1890, Mrs Pearcey sent a message to Mrs Hogg, inviting her and her baby daughter to tea. Mrs Hogg arrived at Priory Street, wheeling her child in a perambulator, at a quarter past four.

At seven o'clock on the same evening the body of a woman was discovered a mile away on a building site in Crossfield Street. Her throat had been cut, nearly severing the head from the body, her skull had been fractured and there was considerable bruising around the face. At first rumours circulated that Jack the Ripper was at work again.

At 8pm, a further mile away, in Hamilton Terrace, St John's Wood, an empty per-ambulator was found covered with blood; it was clear that the pram had been used to transport the body. On the following Sunday morning the body of a small child was discovered on waste ground in the Finchley Road. She had been suffocated.

Frank Hogg was not immediately concerned about the disappearance of his wife, thinking that she had gone to visit her sick father. On the Saturday, however, he became considerably worried by a description in the newspaper of the body found in Crossfield Road and sent his sister, Clara, round to see if his friend, Mrs Pearcey, had any idea where his wife might be. The two women then visited the mortuary to view the corpse. Clara immediately recognized the clothing but Mrs Pearcey tried to pull her away, saying "It's not her – it's not her, let's go! Let's get out of this." The police, most suspicious at this behaviour, took the women to Hampstead police station, picking up Frank Hogg on the way. When Hogg was searched and a latch key to Mrs Pearcey's lodgings was found in his pocket, he broke

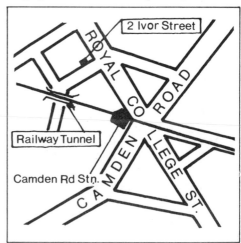

36

the busy streets of North London on her diabolical errand. It seems likely that she made a separate journey to dispose of the child; an extraordinary round trip of six miles!

The funeral of the two victims attracted large crowds, who hissed and cursed the hapless Frank Hogg. He attracted similar treatment at the coroner's inquest and the magistrate's hearing. The trial began on December 1st, 1890 at the Old Bailey, with Mr Justice Denman presiding, Mr Forrest Fulton for the prosecution and Mr Arthur Hutton representing Mrs Pearcey. It lasted for three days, and the result was never in doubt, the jury taking just fifty-two minutes to reach a verdict of guilty. A petition was submitted suggesting that Mrs Pearcey had been of unsound mind when the crime was committed, and there was evidence that she had suffered from epilepsy and had twice in the past tried to commit suicide; but

down and admitted his *affaire* with the lady, prompting the police to search the houses at Priory Street and Prince of Wales Road.

While Mrs Pearcey sat in her parlour, playing the piano and humming to herself, the officers discovered in the kitchen all the evidence that they needed. Blood spattered the walls and ceiling, two window panes had been broken, two carving knives were found to have blood on their handles, and a very ineffectual attempt had been made to clean blood from the rug with paraffin. Asked to explain the blood, Mrs Pearcey muttered "Killing mice, killing mice, killing mice." She was taken into custody and formally charged with the murder of Phoebe Hogg and her infant daughter.

Further police inquiries began to piece together the gruesome events of that tragic afternoon and evening. Neighbours had noticed that Mary Pearcey's curtains were drawn for most of the day, and they confirmed the presence of a perambulator in the hallway. Mrs Pearcey had "talked very funny and looked boozed". Later she was seen wheeling the pram, heavily laden, under the railway arch at the end of Priory Street. Passers-by had witnessed her progress along

Unchanged in almost a century, the cobbled road beneath the bridge at the end of Priory Street

such psychological subtleties were briskly rejected.

To the end, Mrs Pearcey sent impassioned but fruitless appeals to Frank Hogg to comfort her last hours in the death cell. His only positive action was to sell off the contents of her kitchen and the infamous perambulator to Madame Tussaud's Waxworks Museum for £200. Thirty thousand people attended the grand opening of the tableau in the Chamber of Horrors on the day of her execution.

Mary Pearcey was executed by the hangman, James Berry, in Newgate Prison on the 23rd of December, 1890. On the same day, by arrangement with her solicitor, Mr Freke Palmer, an enigmatic message was placed in the Madrid newspapers, "M.E.C.P. Last wish of M.E.P. Have not betrayed."

There is one final twist to this bloody tale. Almost a decade earlier, on November the 30th, 1880, Mary Pearcey's father, Thomas Wheeler, had swung from a noose at St Albans, convicted of the murder of a farm labourer.

Madame Tussaud & Sons' Catalogue.   51

THE HAMPSTEAD TRAGEDY.

MRS. PEARCEY.

A MODEL OF THE KITCHEN, containing the identical Furniture and Fixtures from No 2, Priory Street, where Mrs. Hogg and her Baby were murdered.

LIST OF FURNITURE, &c.,

TABLE, CHAIRS, OILCLOTH, COOKING UTENSILS, CROCKERY, FIREPLACE, GRATE, WINDOW AND FLOORING.

THE TABLE against which Mrs. Hogg was supposed to have been leaning when the blows were struck.

THE WINDOW supposed to have been smashed by Mrs. Hogg in her death struggles.

All the articles contained in the Kitchen have been removed from No. 2, Priory Street, and are placed in exact relative position as found by the Police when they entered the premises.

Mrs. PEARCEY'S SITTING ROOM, with her identical Furniture, Couch, Chairs, Table, Mirror, Carpet, Piano, Ornaments, Curtains, Blinds, &c.

The Piano is the one on which Mrs. Pearcey played whilst the Police were searching her house.

Mrs. PEARCEY'S BEDSTEAD and FURNITURE.

THE PERAMBULATOR in which the Bodies were carried.

CASTS OF THE HEADS OF Mrs. HOGG AND HER BABY, taken from Nature after death.

THE CLOTHES worn by Mrs. Hogg and Baby when murdered.

Mrs. PEARCEY'S RECEIPT in her own handwriting.

THE TOFFEE found in the Perambulator.

The Figures of Mr. and Mrs. Hogg and their Baby are placed in the Ground Floor Gallery.

In and Out *The Eagle*
The Murder of PHYLLIS DIMMOCK
on Wednesday the 11th of September 1907
at 29 St Paul's Road (now Agar Grove), NW1
and the Trial and Acquittal of ROBERT WOOD
for the Crime

The body in the case, that of 23-year-old Phyllis Dimmock, was found by Bertram Shaw, the man with whom she had shared the previous nine months of her life. Shaw was employed as a cook on the Midland Railways dining cars which plied the late night and early morning runs between London St Pancras and Sheffield; a job that had the double advantage of leaving Phyllis both the time and the space to pursue her own, more historic calling. In short, she made use of Shaw's nights away to hire out her natural, God-given attributes to such men as could afford her company.

On the morning of Thursday, September 12th, 1907, Bert Shaw arrived home off the 11 o'clock from Sheffield. Getting no reply to his enthusiastic knocks on the door of their first-floor flat, he obtained access via the duplicate key held against such emergencies by the landlady downstairs. The sight that confronted him in the parlour behind that front door was a shambles; cupboards and drawers had been ransacked and their contents scattered about the floor; there were the stale remains of a meal set for two, and some empty beer bottles on the table. The door to the bedroom was locked, obliging

Shaw to put his shoulder to it. The tableau that greeted his horrified eyes was worse by far than anything he might have imagined. The body lay naked on the bed; blood had seeped everywhere from a throat cut so far through that it was only the vertebrae that had prevented decapitation; pools of gore had flowed into sticky pools along the floor.

Subsequent examination by the police pathologist estimated the time of the attack as between three and six o'clock that morning, and from the position of the body, probably carried out while the victim slept. Small comfort for the heart-broken Shaw; for not only had he the shock of the discovery to contend with, but the inescapable evidence that his Phyllis had obviously returned to plying the trade which he fondly imagined she had rejected for love of him.

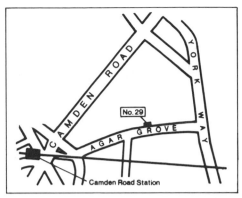

So you think that Bob's a killer?
Don't be silly he just couldn't.
You can say all night, 'twas Robert Wood,
And I'll say Robert Woodn't.

(contemporary doggerel)

Phyllis, the police soon found, was a popular member of the twilight world she inhabited while Bert was cooking mobile breakfasts, and it proved easy to piece together her movements while 'on call'. For example, she regularly used two local pubs as pick-up venues – the *Eagle*, and the *Rising Sun*; they tracked down one of her regular customers, a ship's cook named Robert Roberts. Part, at least, of Roberts's wages had been spent entertaining and being entertained by Phyllis (whose non-professional name, incidentally, was the more homely Emily Jane) on the three nights previous to the murder. In fact he freely admitted that he was prepared to rent the girl's affections for a fourth evening, but that she had protested a prior engagement for the Thursday. He also divulged what was to be vitally important information. On the Wednesday, the last evening that he spent with her, Phyllis had shown the young cook a part of a letter that she had received; he clearly remembered the words "Dear Phyllis, Will you meet me at the bar of the Eagle at Camden Town, 8.30 tonight, Wednesday. Bert." She then, inexplicably, showed him another communication, a picture postcard, on one side of which was the painting of a mother holding her child, and on the reverse the written message, "Phillis Darling, If it pleases you meet me 8.15pm at the [here was drawn a cartoon sketch of a rising sun with a winking face on it]. Yours to a cinder. Alice." She replaced the postcard in a drawer, dropped the letter into the fire grate, and set light to it. Both documents were, in Robert Roberts's opinion, in the same hand.

And the police did indeed find the charred remains of a note in the fireplace at St Paul's Road, the little that could still be read proving a credit to the memory of the ship's cook:

> ill...you...ar of the...e...Town...Wednes

[Dear Ph*ill*is, Will *you* meet me at the b*ar of the* Eagle at Camden *Town,* 8.30 tonight, *Wednes*day. Bert]

The second document, the postcard, turned up two days later when Bertram Shaw decided to pack up and move to a different room. At the request of the Commissioner of Police, the Press was invited to display the text on the card in the hope that a member of the public might recognize the hand responsible. Sensing that there might be more to be made out of the story, the *News of the World* offered £100 reward to anybody responding to its caption "Can You Recognise This Writing?"

Ruby Young recognized it; recognized it as the handwiting of her occasional boyfriend, a young artist with the extraordinary name of Robert William Thomas George Cavers Wood. Ruby liked to describe herself as a 'model' – which was to say, of the same profession as Phyllis Dimmock – and it was in this professional capacity that she had met Robert Wood. Wood, unlike many of the denizens of Ruby's world, was a talented engraver in a respected position with a glassmaker in Gray's Inn Road, earned a modest second income as a freelance cartoonist, and

lived with his father in St Pancras. Their worlds met on account of Wood's weakness for the company of inexpensive whores.

The *News of the World* offer must have reminded Ruby of the occasion, less than a week after the murder of Phyllis Dimmock, when Wood had extracted a promise from her to say, if anybody asked, that he always spent Mondays and Wednesdays with her. Now, before Ruby had a chance to claim her £100 bounty for Robert Wood the man in question presented himself at her door. On being taxed with the rising sun postcard mystery, Wood confessed "Ruby, I'm in trouble", and went on to tell the following story. He had, he said, been drinking in the bar of the *Rising Sun*, when he struck up a conversation with a young woman; they got to talking about picture postcards, and Wood impressed the lady by showing her the examples he had brought back from his holiday in Bruges. Phyllis (for it was she) had been particularly attracted by one of a woman hugging a child, and asked Wood if he would write something "nice" on it for her, and this resulted in the mock invitation embellished with the soon-to-be-famous rising sun cartoon. The signature "Alice" was supposed to be a device to allay any suspicion that Bert Shaw might entertain about the company Phyllis was keeping. At all events, the wretched card looked as though it would be big trouble

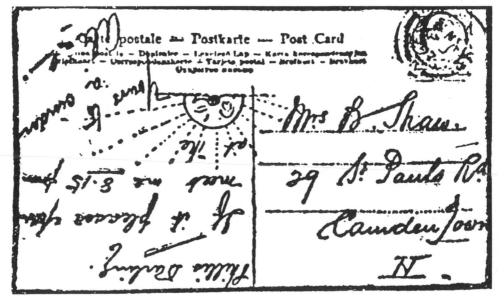

The Camden Town Murder, or *What shall we do for the rent?* Walter Sickert's tart painterly comment on the gruesome occurrence. Wood, a friend of Sickert, was said to have been the model for this picture, and Sickert was almost certainly instrumenal in raising money to pay for his defence.

for him. Unless. Ruby would have to tell the lie that Wood had spent the evening of 11 September with her – they rehearsed a complicated itinerary, but it must have seemed suspicious even to the uncomplicated mind of Ruby Young. In fact, it preyed on her mind so much that she passed the secret on to a 'gentleman friend', a journalist; he in turn shared the secret with Inspector Arthur Neil. Who promptly arrested Robert Wood for the murder of Phyllis Dimmock. At the police station Wood conveyed his explanation of the postcard's origin in the same words he had used to Ruby Young, ending with his alibi for the night of the crime – spent, as they had agreed, with Ruby. Robert Wood was not to know that she had already betrayed him.

At the two identity parades, the prisoner was positively picked out by a number of people, mostly the prostitutes of the *Rising Sun*, who associated him with Phyllis Dimmock.

Another sighting was provided by Robert McCowan; according to his own statement, McCowan had been walking along the St Paul's Road on the day of the murder, when hearing footsteps behind him he turned and saw a man leaving No.29. The time was ten minutes to five; the man he identified as Robert Wood. The coroner's inquest resulted in a verdict of wilful murder, and by the time Robert Wood stood his trial at the Old Bailey on December 12th, his conviction seemed a mere formality.

But that would be to reckon without the fickle, and often inexplicable, sympathies of the general public. For it was the very betrayal by Ruby Young – a prostitute, they saw, who had turned against her lover for money – that secured for Wood a small place in their hearts. A small place that, as the trial unfolded, and Robert Wood's defence was so ably handled by Mr (later Sir) Edward Marshall Hall KC, developed almost to mass

29 Agar Grove (formerly St Paul's Road)

hysteria in his support. As for Robert Wood, his attitude to his trial throughout was that of a somewhat distant and dispassionate observer, spending much of his time in sketching the proceedings from the dock. In the witness box he made a good impression, sticking to his original story, and clearly earning the support of Mr Justice Grantham, who summed up to the jury much in Wood's favour.

The jury retired at 7.45pm on the sixth day of the trial, and returned fifteen minutes later in order to free Robert Wood from the charge of murder. The court erupted in unrestrained cheers of pleasure and agreement, a jubilant swell that was soon taken up by the thousands waiting outside the court for just such a verdict. While Wood, his family and friends were escorted to a restaurant for a celebration dinner, the reviled Ruby Young was smuggled out of the side door of the building disguised as a cleaning woman.

Robert Wood had been a very lucky young man; and quite possibly a guilty one. But if the jury were right, who *did* kill Phyllis Dimmock?

A Tale of Two Passions
The Murder of SAID ALI
by SAN DWE (called Sandy Wee)
on Saturday the 25th of August 1928
in the Tapir House, London Zoological Gardens, Regents Park, NW1

The interest of this case is that it is a crime of intense passion - not as that word is usually applied to a crime, but the passions of two men from the East; their mutual passions for elephants and for money. Surprisingly, it takes place in the heart of London, at the Zoological Gardens in Regent's Park.

Said Ali was an Indian, a mahmout or elephant-driver by profession, and his intimate understanding of that animal's habits and temperament had developed throughout his early life in the jungles of his homeland. He first came to England in 1922, and found that his singular achievements were warmly welcomed by the Zoological Gardens in London. Over the next two or three years Said

Ali endeared himself not only to his employers – among whom his knowledge of elephants was legendary – but also to the many thousands of young visitors who came to look at, and ride upon, his charges. For the entertainment of these children Ali had taught the elephants a remarkably profitable trick – with their trunks these huge beasts would delicately pick up pennies thrown on to the pathway by visitors and deposit them, unfailingly, into their trainer's pocket – considerably boosting his weekly wage of two pounds and ten shillings.

The son of a warmer climate than England could offer, Said Ali's health could not easily sustain the damp, foggy, London winter, and

San Dwe

Said Ali

he liked to return to Calcutta during the colder months, coming back for the summer season at the Zoo.

In 1925 he returned to find himself faced with a potential rival. The newcomer was a Burmese elephant trainer named San Dwe, who had been sent over in charge of the sacred white elephant belonging to a religious sect in Burma. After a very popular stay in the London Zoo this valuable elephant was returned to its far-away home suffering, like Said Ali, from the English climate. San Dwe decided to stay on at the zoo as assistant to Said Ali.

The two keepers were, on the face of it, good, if not close, companions, and shared the modest accommodation above the Tapir House as well as the day-to-day pleasures and problems of caring for the elephants. And all might have remained in equilibrium

if the daily routine had not been changed. When he returned from his winter trip of 1928, Said Ali was given back the charge of the children's elephant ride, while San Dwe (by now he had been anglicized to 'Sandy Wee') was appointed to the back-room responsibilities of caring for the baby elephants in the zoo's sanatorium. But Sandy Wee's passions did not stop at elephants, they took in money as well – money that he hoped one day would take him home to a life of luxury – and he had looked to the tips that he got from a generous public to supplement his £2-a-week wage. Sandy Wee was passionately aggrieved.

While police-constables Buzzy and Evans were on their midnight patrol of the Outer Circle on August 25th, they heard the unmistakable sounds of a human voice in distress coming from the thick bushes that

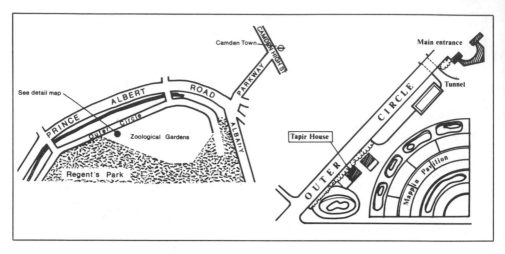

grew on the zoo side of the railing just beside the Tapir House. Prompt investigation revealed the pathetic sight of San Dwe clutching his ankle in pain and groaning on the grass. He was gibbering incoherently (or had perhaps lapsed into his native Burmese), but gave the officers to understand that he and Said Ali had been attacked in their quarters and that he, San Dwe, had had to jump out of the window to safety.

After alerting the Zoo's Superintendent, Dr Geoffrey Marr Vevers, and his assistant Mr Hicks, the policemen ran to the Tapir House, and the unfortunate Sandy Wee was removed to St Pancras Hospital where he was patched up and detained – for some reason best known to the medical authorities – in a mental ward.

Meanwhile the police party had discovered Said Ali lying on his bed cruelly battered about the head and body, the bloodstained murder weapons (in the shape of a heavy sledgehammer and a pickaxe) lying on the floor beside him.

When Detective Inspector Walter Hambrook arrived on the scene it was obvious to him that a ferocious struggle had taken place, amply supporting San Dwe's story of having been attacked by four men. On the face of it the intruders had used the sledgehammer to break down the entrance door before employing it to attack the occupants. Closer examination, however, showed bloodstains in the indentations where the door had been battered down, which could only mean – even to a less experienced eye than Inspector

Hambrook's – that the door had been attacked *after* Said Ali. Somebody was telling lies; and it could only be Sandy Wee.

The young man's story was that they had been standing by the open bedroom window, when Said Ali became involved in some abusive banter with a group of people outside on the Outer Circle road. Some time later San Dwe was awakened by a flashlight roving around the bedroom, and Said Ali shouting, "Who are you?", whereupon four men set on him. It was only by launching himself from the window and rolling to the place where the policemen had found him, said San Dwe, that he too was not as dead as his companion. The rest of the story lapses into virtual incoherence: "I saw two lights but I think three or four men. I cannot see the men. I only heard his voice. If they ask me if I like Said Ali I say no, I don't like him. I play my music and Said Ali do not like it. I want to see my friends to tell them what happen. I should be satisfied if I

The Tapir House seen from the Outer Circle, at the time of the murder

died with Said Ali. I know the people won't believe me. I know Said Ali was dead from the noise. I know everybody will say I killed him because they know I live with him. Me no kill Said Ali. Me no fight Said Ali..."

At his Old Bailey trial in November before Mr Justice Swift, San Dwe's jealousy was exposed as motive, and despite the best efforts of Sir Henry Curtis Bennett in his defence, the careless activity with the sledgehammer and door persuaded the jury to return a guilty verdict. Sentenced to death, San Dwe was later reprieved and committed to life imprisonment. Four years later the little elephant trainer was compassionately released and returned to his native land.

'The Indian Elephant, or Curtis Bennett' by George Whitelaw

THE LEGEND OF THE SACRED WHITE ELEPHANT

San Dwe and his charge 'Pa Wa'

It was with relish that the popular Press seized on the story of Said Ali's unfortunate death; not only for the saga's colourful 'oriental' protagonists, but for the romance of the Sacred White Elephant.

The rare white elephant in general was regarded as a holy animal in the religions of Burma and of Siam. They were revered as incarnations of the Buddha; they were not allowed to work, or to be ridden, and in an elaborate ceremony, at a time appointed by the Court astrologer, the King of Siam anointed the baby elephant, naming it "Most Magnificent White Elephant Lord", and feeding the beast pieces of fine red sugar cane with the name inscribed on it.

This particular Sacred White Elephant, that in charge of San Dwe, was called "Pa Wa" (meaning Mr White), and was caught and owned by Dr Saw Durmay Po Min, President of the National Karen Association of Burma. Dr Po Min describes the capture of the creature: "He was then only a baby of about twelve months old, and less than four feet high. No sooner had the stockade been erected than the white elephant and his retinue entered of their own accord. With the retinue of the white elephant was a big male elephant over nine feet high. He looked after all the others, especially protecting the little white one. It is said that sometimes he carried the white one on his tusks in the jungle."

A further intrigue not missed by the Press was that Pa Wa died on exactly the same day, in Calcutta, as its former keeper committed his horrible crime in London – giving credence to the legend that misfortune always follows when a white elephant leaves its own country.

45

The Fellow in a Long Black Cloak

The Murder of Mr JAMES DE LA RUE
by THOMAS HENRY HOCKER

on Friday the 21st of February 1845
outside Belsize House (now demolished), Belsize Lane, NW1

It was on a Friday evening, February 21st, in the year 1845, when a Mr Hilton, master baker of Haverstock Terrace, was distracted from the business of serving his customers by nearby cries of "Murder!"

Constable Jem Baldock was speedily summoned, and he in turn enlisted a fellow officer before setting off to investigate the disturbance. It turned out that the scene of the crime was Belsize Lane, in those days a grassy, tree-lined path that joined the Hampstead and Finchley Roads in North-West London. The crime itself was indeed Murder, and while his companion ran to seek further help, Constable Baldock was left with nothing but a man's corpse for company. Nothing but the corpse, that is, until the policeman became suddenly aware of the presence of another – "a chap who came on the scene like a happarition; a fellow in a long black cloak, who sprung up as if he had jumped from behind the trees there". The mysterious stranger knelt beside the body, took its pulse, and declared, "Yes, he's quite dead, Constable." Pressing a shilling into the puzzled officer's palm, he bade "good-night" and strode off.

When the corpse was removed to the *Yorkshire Grey* public-house, Hampstead, only a superficial examination was necessary by the surgeon, Mr R.R. Perry, to ascertain that death had resulted from the severe battering received by the victim's head. A search of the unfortunate man's clothing was rewarded by the discovery of the touching letter that follows:

My dearest James, – I find myself in a situation which makes it necessary for me to leave home shortly. I would rather die than doubt either your word or your honour; yet do not, oh! do not be ashamed to own me! If you cannot at the moment give me the title of wife, conceal from me the cruel fingers of scorn. Heaven has been my witness that I have loved you but too dearly. Let me be happy in the conviction that you will one day restore me to your arms for ever. Ease my suspense by meeting me tomorrow at the place where, alas! you have always made me happy; yet not so, if it will put one smile of hope and comfort in my countenance. You can render me forever light-hearted and happy, or forever heart-broken and conscience stricken. Oh, that a bended knee might procure me the former lot!

Ever yours. Caroline.

The inquest was convened for the following Monday; an inquest at which Mr Daniel de la Rue identified the murdered man as his brother James, a 33-year-old music professor who had resided off London's Euston Road.

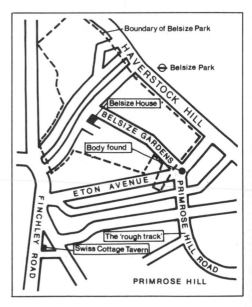

Subsequent inquiries by Messrs Shackell and Hayes of the London police force at the deceased's lodgings revealed a somewhat less honourable de la Rue than had been supposed – the rooms containing quantities of pornographic literature and pictures. It also provided the clue that led eventually to a police party raiding the Portland Town residence (11 Victoria Place) of the brothers Thomas and James Hocker, waking them from their beds and placing both young men under arrest for murder; a number of bloodstained articles of clothing were also removed, and later identified by the boy's father as belonging to Thomas.

Thomas Henry Hocker, "subtle and fixed of purpose in his general aspect, his features were remarkable, his eyes deeply embedded in his face, nose and mouth of unusually large dimensions. Narrow, retiring forehead, a long face, and flat cheeks. His head, remarkably thin towards the back part, surmounted by an ample crop of long brown hair, which looked as if it had never been disturbed by brush or comb. The conformation of the head would have formed a fine study for a phrenologist". So ran one description of the man now facing Mr Rawlinson, magistrate, at the Marylebone Police Court, charged with the murder of James de la Rue.

After conducting his own defence in a cheerful and confident mood, Hocker was sent to his trial at the Central Criminal Court. Arraigned before Mr Justice Coleridge and Mr Justice Coleman on April 11th, Hocker was prosecuted by Mr Bodkin and Mr Chambers, and was to be defended by Mr Clarkson and Mr Ballantine. In fact the prisoner dismissed these professional gentlemen and once more took on the burden of his own defence.

Rarely can there have been such a seemingly endless stream of damning circumstantial evidence presented against a man as there was that day against Thomas Hocker: Hilton the baker identified him as being around the scene of the murder at the time it was committed; Constable Baldock identified him as the mystery man whose behaviour had so puzzled him on the same night. William Latherthwaite similarly linked Hocker to the time and place of the slaying. Inspector Partridge produced the prisoner's bloodstained clothes, lacking one button which was found at the scene of the crime, and Hocker's

Belsize House

broken-hearted sweetheart told how she had seen him on the night in a bloody state and in possession of the watch and ring identified by Daniel de la Rue as having belonged to his dead brother. The letter from 'Caroline' luring the victim to Belsize Lane was shown to have been written by Hocker on paper of the same type a that found in his chamber.

Against the weight of this evidence, Thomas Hocker's spirited defence that it was another that had committed the dreadful deed fell upon deaf ears. It was, he claimed, the brother of a girl cruelly wronged by de la Rue, and whom he, Hocker, had introduced to the seducer. Hearing the cries of "Murder!" on the fateful evening, Hocker realized that the brother had had his revenge, and hurried himself to the place of assignation – to find a dead body in the charge of policeman Jem Baldock. For the sake of friendship and out of a sense of honour and personal responsibility, the prisoner could not reveal the name of the true culprit.

The jury took but a short time to return its verdict of "Guilty", and Monday April 28th 1845 found Thomas Henry Hocker dangling from the end of Calcraft's rope before a concourse of twelve thousand spectators.

The site of James de la Rue's murder as it looks today

I Find Murdered By Rogues*
The Assassination of Sir EDMUND BERRY GODFREY
by ROBERT GREEN, HENRY BERRY, and LAWRENCE HILL
on or about the 12th of October 1678
on Primrose Hill, NW3

Sir Edmund Berry Godfrey, the victim of this notorious crime, was born in Ashford, Kent in 1621. His family belonged to the comfortable Kentish gentry and Edmund Godfrey's early career as a merchant, supplying coal to the burghers of London, was notably successful. In October 1660 he was appointed Justice of the Peace for West-minster and Middlesex and quickly established a reputation as a fair-minded, charitable and particularly conscientious magistrate. During the Great Plague of 1665 Godfrey remained in the city to keep order after most of the nobility had fled in panic, an act of conspicuous courage for which he was knighted.

In the summer of 1678 an odious perjurer and scoundrel, Titus Oates, approached adherents of the Protestant cause with a list

* An anagram on the contemporary spelling of 'Sir Edmundburie Godfrey' given much superstitious significance at the time.

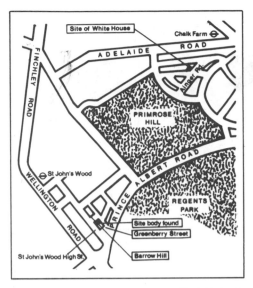

Sir Edmund Berry Godfrey

of fanciful allegations – the so-called 43 Articles – which claimed a conspiracy by Papists to assassinate the king and overthrow the Protestant religion in favour of his Roman Catholic brother, James, Duke of York. Concerned that the document might be suppressed by the Council of State, an independently minded magistrate was sought to affirm the allegations. It was the lot of Sir Edmund Berry Godfrey to be chosen for the task. On the 6th of October, he interviewed Oates and subsequently the infamous depositions were sworn. Now Sir Edmund, ever one of nature's gloomy men, began to offer dark hints that his life was in danger. Rumours of the plot had also

begun to spread, and to generate much wild speculation.

On Thursday the 12th of October Sir Edmund left his lodgings in Hartshorn Lane (now Northumberland St, W1.) at nine in the morning, and despite several unconfirmed sitings in various locations that day, Sir Edmund was never seen alive again. His disappearance, though, was taken as menacing proof of the feared Popish conspiracy, and a full-blown witch hunt against suspected Catholics was in the air.

The body of Sir Edmund Godfrey was found by a farrier and a baker, who were walking over Primrose Hill at 2.00pm on the follow-

TITUS OATES. D.D.   Cap. WILLIAM BEDLOE.   Mr Miles Prance.

The sense of outrage felt during the era of religious persecution in seventeenth century England found a popular propaganda outlet in several packs of playing cards recording incidents in the

ing Tuesday, the 17th of October. It lay in a ditch on the south-west side, a place known as Barrow Hill; the area in those days was open countryside – fields, hedges and bramble covered ditches. The body was transported to the White House, near to Chalk Farm, where it was officially examined by a local physician. An eye-witness described its condition.

His sword was thrust through him; but no blood was on his clothes or about him. His shoes were clean. His money was in his pocket, but nothing was about his neck, and a mark was round it about an inch broad, which showed how he was strangled. His breast was likewise all over marked with bruises, and his neck was broken. there were many drops of white waxlights on his breeches, which he never used himself; and since only persons of quality and priests use those lights, this made all people conclude in whose hands he must have been.

On the next day a jury was sworn and an inquest held. The evidence that Sir Edmund had taken his own life by falling on his sword was a transparent contrivance. The cause of death, it was agreed, was strangling, and further he had been murdered elsewhere by persons unknown and transported to Primrose Hill by horse or carriage. The persons unknown were assumed to be Papists.

so-called Popish Plot. In one of these packs, dating from around 1679, the suit of Spades relates the killing of Sir Edmund Berry Godfrey and the retribution on his assassins.

Sir Edmund's body lay in state at his lodgings in Hartshorn Lane for ten days, an object of curiosity and reverence to hundreds of visitors. His funeral took place amidst great pomp on October the 31st at St Martin-in-the-Fields and he was buried in its churchyard.

Rumours and accusations had by now become completely uncontrollable. Any person admitting to the Catholic faith was in very real danger of imprisonment, or worse. Eyes even turned towards the protected royal sanctuaries of Catholicism within the capital, to the establishments and retainers of the Duke of York and particularly the Catholic Queen of England, Catherine of Braganza, at Somerset House. The King,

though himself sceptical of the allegations of a plot, had felt it politic to offer a reward of £500 – a princely sum – for the apprehension of the murderers of his magistrate. With such a reward on offer, it did not take long for scoundrels to emerge, prepared even to implicate the servants of the Queen.

On October 30th, Captain William Bedloe wrote to the Secretary of State claiming knowledge of the murder of Sir Edmund at Somerset House and naming a number of Catholics as having some involvement. Then, on the 21st of December, a second perjurer, Miles Prance, a Catholic who was terrorised and cajoled into his treacherous role, came before Parliament with specific allegations that

Robert Green, cushion man of the Queen's chapel, Lawrence Hill, a servant to the treasurer of the chapel, and Henry Berry, a porter at Somerset House, had perpetrated the crime. The three men were arrested, Green being placed in the Gatehouse and the other two in Newgate.

Their trial took place on the 10th of February, 1679, at the Old Bailey. Lord Chief Justice Scroggs presided with the Recorder of London; the soon to be infamous Sir George Jeffreys also among the judges on the bench. The prosecution, presented by the Attorney-General, Sir William Jones, with the uninhibited assistance of the judiciary, was that... "he [Godfrey] was waylaid, and inveigled into the palace [Somerset House], under the pretence of keeping the peace between two servants who were fighting in the yard; that he was there strangled, his neck broke, and his own sword run through his body; that he was kept four days before they ventured to remove him; at length his

corpse was carried in a sedan-chair to Soho, and then on a horse to Primrose Hill." The evidence of Prance, Bedloe and Oates, which was at variance in almost every detail, was the main 'proof' of this fanciful tale. Green and Berry brought forward witnesses to vouch for their movements on the supposed night of the crime, but this was impatiently dismissed by the bullying Judge Scroggs. The three men were, with a sad inevitability, found guilty and sentenced to death.

Robert Green and Lawrence Hill were hanged from Tyburn Tree on 21st of February, 1679. Henry Berry, a Protestant, was allowed a further week of life in the hope that he might confess to his sins. All three died protesting their innocence, but to superstitious observers their guilt was confirmed by a strange coincidence; Barrow Hill, where the body of the unfortunate magistrate had been discovered, had a more ancient name – GREENBERRY HILL.

"Thou tyrant, tyrant, Jealousy"
The Murder of HELLA CHRISTOFI
by her Mother-in-Law STYLLOU PANTOPIOU CHRISTOFI
on Thursday the 29th of July, 1954
at 11 South Hill Park, NW3

Thous tyrant, tyrant Jealousy,
Thou tyrant of the mind!
(Dryden, *Song of Jealousy. Love Triumphant*)

Jealousy is an emotion of limitless strength – as overwhelming as love; as all-consuming as hatred; and more destructive than both.

This is the story of a woman whose intense and unreasoning jealousy caused her to kill not once, but twice; caused her to kill with unimaginable brutality; caused her to kill two members of her immediate family.

The tyrant is Styllou Pantopiou Christofi, and at the time that this episode of her life opens, she is living in a small village in Cyprus. She already looks old beyond her fifty-three years, wrinkled and dried out

by the heat of the sun and overwork. With little help from her reluctant husband, she spends most of her working life squeezing a

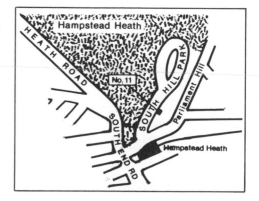

Mrs Styllou Pantopiou Christofi

have three healthy children, and live in South Hill Park, a stone's throw from Florence Nightingale's former home. The street, the house, the family, all fit easily into the civilized, very English life that is lived here on the edge of Hampstead Heath. To complete their contentment, Stavros holds a respected post as wine waiter at the internationally renowned Café de Paris in London's West End.

That life of contentment is about to end abruptly and explosively. The peace is about to be shattered by the arrival of Stavros's mother.

Were it not for the mean, intractable nastiness that characterized Styllou Christofi's personality, one could go some way to sympathizing with her position. An ignorant peasant woman set down in the sophistication of London, unable to speak a word of English – illiterate, even, in her native Greek – confronting a daughter-in-law and three young grandchildren for the first time, without the means to communicate directly. It would overwhelm anyone. And Stavros understood this; Hella understood it too; the whole family spared no effort to make the recently arrived member of their family as welcome as they were able.

But the old woman had been wrapped up in her own resentment for too long; the bitterness allowed to take too firm a grip. The mother began to cling to her son like an emotional limpet; began to develop a fanatical and jealous hatred of her daughter-in-law. She developed a hatred for the house; for Hella's stylish way of dressing, and her 'extravagance' in buying make-up; for the

small and indifferent existence from a small and indifferent olive grove. She had suffered enough of that relentless, debilitating poverty to have become a sour, envious old woman. And beyond this, Mrs Christofi carries in her heart a terrible guilt.

At the time this episode in her life opens she has already committed one horrible crime – in 1925, when two fellow-villagers had held open the mouth of the victim while Styllou Christofi rammed a blazing torch down her throat. The victim died; she was Styllou's mother-in-law. Incredibly, Styllou Christofi was acquitted at her trial.

Styllou Christofi's only son Stavros, has already left the claustrophobic, bitter atmosphere of the village; left the unproductive olive grove, and walked all the way to Nicosia where he worked as a waiter while he saved the money for his boat fare to England. By 1953, he has been in England for twelve years. During this time he has made a happy match with a 36-year-old German girl named Hella, a daughter of the Ruhr. The couple

Stavros and Hella Christofi

way Hella brought up her children. All this and more Styllou Christofi hated, and was not slow to say so – to shout it, in Greek, often. So oppressive did life become at South Hill Park, that Stavros twice arranged for his mother to live elsewhere; where Styllou rendered herself so objectionable that she was asked to leave on both occasions.

By now, by the July of 1954, even the good-natured Hella felt that she had endured enough. "Next week", she told her husband, "I am going home to Wuppertal for a holiday. I am taking the children, and when we get back your mother must be gone."
"But where can she go?"
"Back to Cyprus!"

It cannot have been easy for Stavros to break the news to his mother; harder still for her to accept it. To her it must have sounded like the announcement of the end of her world. She must surely have thought, this is all the fault of that girl; without her, I could be living here happily with my son.

When Stavros kissed his wife good-bye as

he left for work on the evening of July 29, he had no idea of the horror that was to greet his return.

The children in bed, alone at last with the woman who was destroying *her* family, Styllou Christofi struck. Struck from behind, smashing the cast iron ash-plate from the kitchen stove down onto Hella's skull. Struck again, winding a scarf around the unconscious woman's throat, twisting, pulling.

Dragging Hella's now lifeless corpse into the area behind the house Styllou Christofi, insane in her revenge, made mad with jealousy, soaked the body and a pile of newspaper in paraffin and lit a match. It is possible that she remembered another fire, twenty-nine years before.

At the time, John Young, a neighbour, happened to be looking in the direction of No.11, and saw the sudden blaze followed by the red glow of the fire. Thinking that the house might have caught light, he went to investigate. What he saw when he looked over the garden fence must have seemed

Left: the funeral of Hella Christofi leaving 11 South Hill Park in 1954; right: the same house in 1987

so incredible that Young's mind refused to register the obvious truth. Instead, to him, it looked as though someone was trying to burn a "wax dummy". "All I could see was from the thighs down, and the arms were raised and bent back at the elbow like some of the models you see in shop windows. There was a strong smell of wax." At that point it was about 11.45pm; Mrs Christofi reappeared to stoke up the fire, which seemed to reassure Mr Young, and he returned home.

Shortly before 1.00am a local restaurateur named Burstoff and his wife were returning home when they were forced to halt by a gesticulating figure in the road, shouting incoherently "Please come, fire burning, children sleeping." By the time they had got Mrs Christofi back to the house the fire was out, but the body was still there, like a charred shop-window dummy on the paving slabs of the area.

Wisely, Mr Burstoff decided to telephone for the police.

Three months later, Styllou Christofi stood in the dock at the Old Bailey listening, through a court interpreter, to the catalogue of evidence painstakingly collated by the police in support of their prosecution. The bloodstained kitchen, the petrol-soaked rags and papers, the fractured skull, the marks of strangulation around the neck. Most damning of all, the discovery of Hella's wedding ring, carefully wrapped in paper and hidden in the old woman's bedroom.

Styllou's defence was as pathetic as had been the rest of her life. As desperate an attempt to survive as had been her cultivation of the obstinate olive grove.

She had gone to bed before Hella, she claimed, leaving the girl to "do some washing" (it had been a never-ending source of puzzlement to Styllou that her daughter-in-law washed her body every day – clearly not a feature of her previous experience in the village). The next thing she was aware of was waking to the smell of smoke; she recollected going to the bedroom door, looking out and noticing that the street door was open; remembered going to Hella's room and not finding her there; rushing downstairs where the kitchen door was open revealing the body of her daughter-in-law lying on the ground in the yard, flames licking around her and

Police picking over the charred remains of Hella Christofi

blood staining her face. She had splashed water on the girl in an attempt to revive her, and when this failed to get a reaction had run in search of help – which was where she met the Burstoffs.

The trial did not last long. Had Styllou Christofi pleaded insane – as she almost certainly was – it might have been even shorter. In the event, in a final defiant gesture of dignity, she had claimed, "I am a poor woman, of no education, but I am not mad woman. Never. Never. Never."

And so Styllou Christofi, on the 13th of December 1954, gave herself up to be the first woman to be executed in England since Edith Thompson thirty years before. And she was nearly the last woman to hang, although Ruth Ellis (who also committed murder in South Hill Park a few months later) was to earn that distinction.

"The Woman Who Hangs This Morning"
The Murder of DAVID BLAKELY
by RUTH ELLIS

on Easter Sunday the 10th of April 1955
outside the *Magdala Tavern*, South Hill Park, NW3

A great deal has been written about the murder by Ruth Ellis of her boyfriend David Blakely, but it is as 'The Last Woman to be Hanged in Britain' that she has been most often remembered.

Ruth was the unremarkable, rather brassy manager of *The Little Club*, a London drinking house – and a not very salubrious place even by the standards such establishments set themselves. It was in 1953 that Ruth met Blakely – a good-looking, if somewhat degenerate, youth with a generous manner, a romantic occupation – he was a racing driver – and an above-average appetite for drink; they were instantly attracted, and for nearly a year (during which time Ruth found time to become pregnant and have an abortion) all seemed to be going as well as such a match might reasonably be expected to go. And then things began, perhaps inevitably, to sour. Blakely had started seeing other women, Ruth had started objecting; Blakely had begun to make his escape. He moved in with friends at 29 Tanza Road for a few days; Ruth tracked him down and smashed all the windows of his car.

Ruth in happier mood, showing no hint of the tragedy to come

Two days later Ruth intercepted David Blakely as he was coming out of the *Magdala Tavern* in South Hill Park, in Hampstead. On this Easter Sunday, April 1955, Ruth Ellis emptied the chamber of a Smith and Wesson handgun into the body of her former lover.

Ruth made no attempt to escape, and scant attempt to defend herself at her Old Bailey trial. The jury were in retirement for only fourteen minutes before finding her guilty. There was no appeal and, petitions having been rejected, Ruth Ellis became the last woman to hang in Britain, at 9am on Wednesday 13th July, 1955.

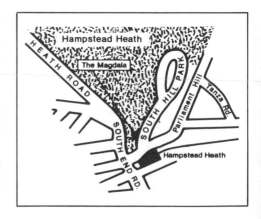

NO REPRIEVE

RUTH ELLIS TO HANG TOMORROW

Ruth Ellis has been refused a reprieve. The Home Secretary, Major Lloyd-George announced yesterday that there were "not sufficient grounds to recommend any interference with the due course of law."

This means that twenty-eight-year-old Mrs Ellis will be hanged tomorrow at Holloway Gaol for the murder of her former lover, racing driver David Blakely, 25.

She Had Seven Visitors

Blonde Mrs Ellis had just returned to the death cell from exercise in the prison yard, when a dispatch rider brought news of the Home Secretary's decision.

She was told immediately by the prison governor, Dr Charity Taylor, that there would be no reprieve.

Later, Mrs Ellis had seven visitors. They were her mother, Mrs Elizabeth Neilson; Mr George Rogers, MP for North Kensington; Mrs Jacqueline Dyer, a close friend; Mr J. Bickford, her solicitor; and three friends from the Kensington club where she met David Blakely.

Mrs Dyer, who helped to organise petitions to save Mrs Ellis, said afterwards: "It is difficult to see what we can do further, except perhaps to find some new evidence."

Quite Happy to Die

Mrs Dyer said she tried to interview Major Lloyd-George, but without success. While thousands of people were signing the petition for her reprieve, Mrs Ellis told friends: "I am very grateful to them. But I am quite happy to die."

Her friends said after their visit to her yesterday, that her attitude had not changed.

Mrs Ellis did not appeal against the death sentence, and the Home Secretary's decision has ended her last chance of life. So, at 9am. tomorrow, accompanied by two male prison officers and one wardress, she will go to the gallows.

(*Daily Mirror*, 12 July, 1955)

THE WOMAN WHO HANGS THIS MORNING

By CASSANDRA

It's a fine day for hay-making. A fine day for fishing. A fine day for lolling in the sunshine. And if you feel that way – and I mourn to say that millions of you do – it's a fine day for a hanging.

If you read this before nine o'clock this morning, the last dreadful and obscene preparations for hanging Ruth Ellis will be moving up to their fierce and sickening climax. The public hangman and his assistant will have been slipped into the prison at about four o'clock yesterday afternoon.

There, from what is grotesquely called "some vantage point" and unobserved by Ruth Ellis, they will have spied upon her when she was at exercise "to form an impression of the physique of the prisoner".

A bag of sand will have been filled to the same weight as the condemned woman and it will have been left hanging overnight to stretch the rope.

Our Guilt...

If you read this at nine o'clock then – short of a miracle – you and I and every man and woman in the land with a head to think, and a heart to feel will, in full responsibility, blot this woman out.

The hands that place the white hood over her head will not be our hands. But the guilt – and guilt there is in all this abominable business – will belong to us as much as to the wretched executioner paid and trained to do the job in accordance with the savage public will.

If you read this after nine o'clock, the murderess, Ruth Ellis, will have gone.

The one thing that brings stature and dignity to mankind and raises us above the beasts of the field will have been denied her – pity and the hope of ultimate redemption.

The medical officer will go to the pit under the trap door to see that life is extinct. Then, in the barbarous wickedness of this ceremony, rejected by nearly all civilised peoples, the body will be left to hang for one hour.

Dregs of Shame

If you read these words of mine at mid-day the grave will have been dug while there are no prisoners around and the Chaplain will have read the burial service after he and all of us have come so freshly from disobeying the Sixth Commandment which says thou shalt not kill.

The secrecy of it all shows that if compassion is not in us then at least we retain the dregs of shame. The medieval notice of execution will have been posted on the prison gates and the usual squalid handful of louts and rubbernecks who attend these legalised killings will have had their own private obscene delights.

Two Royal Commissions have protested against these horrible events. Every Home Secretary in recent years has testified to the agonies of his task, and the revulsion he has felt towards his duty. None has ever claimed that executions prevent murder.

Yet they go on and still Parliament has neither the resolve nor the commitment, nor the wit, nor the decency to put an end to these atrocious affairs.

When I write about capital punishment, as I have often done, I get some praise and usually more abuse. In this case I have been reviled as being "a sucker for a pretty face."

Well, I am a sucker for a pretty face. And I am a sucker for all human faces because I hope I am a sucker for all humanity, good or bad. But I prefer the face not to be lolling because of a judicially broken neck.

Yes it is a fine day.

Oscar Wilde, when he was in Reading Gaol, spoke of "that little tent of blue which prisoners call the sky."

The tent of blue should be dark and sad at the thing we have done this day.

(*Daily Mirror*, 13 July, 1955)

Mrs Violet Van der Elst, leader of the campaign against Ruth Ellis's execution, had taken up position outside the prison gates and refused to move. After a brief scuffle with the police Mrs Van der Elst insisted "I won't go until this shameful thing is over."

The Magdala Tavern, *1987*

The Case of the Anaemic Housemaid
The Murder of ALICE LINFOLD
by GEORGE BARON PATEMAN
on the 27th of April 1911
outside Ryhope House, Finchley

In the first decade of the 1900s forensic science as it is understood today – the application of medicine, physics, chemistry, and all the battery of new technological developments to the specific purpose of legal investigation – was in its infancy. The case that follows was a milestone in one branch of that blossoming science, the analysis of blood samples.

Alice Linfold was a 22-year-old housemaid in the employ of a large family household in North Finchley. On her regular day off, it was Alice's custom and pleasure to visit her parents. The senior Linfolds had for some years found it expedient to take in lodgers, the better to stretch family finances, and it

was during one of Alice's visits that she was introduced to the son of Mr Pateman, the latest in the sequence of paying guests. In no time the young couple seemed to all the world to have fallen victim to fancy; romance bloomed, and despite an eleven-year difference in their ages (George was the senior at thirty-three), they became engaged to be married.

It will probably never be ascertained exactly what went wrong. It may have been, as some of their sharp-tongued critics claimed, that the age gap really *did* make a difference. Perhaps, like so many other couples, they simply became disenchanted with each other and the prospect of being manacled together in wedlock "till death you do part". And like so many other couples, they found separation difficult; especially George, who made his exit during a turbulent farewell scene accompanied by loud threats of his imminent suicide.

The following Sunday found Alice back in her accustomed place on her parents' sofa, Mr Pateman senior making up the four; all engaged in earnest discussion of broken hearts and severed ties. It was a dark night, and they talked deep into it, prompting Pateman to do the chivalrous thing and escort Miss Linfold back to the safety of Ryhope House. As he turned to leave the girl at the front gate, Mr Pateman saw a shadowy figure approach and greet Alice as she made her way to the door; though he could not identify the person, it was clearly somebody known to the girl, and he gave it no more thought.

Which was a great pity for Alice. Within minutes the household was awakened by the unfortunate girl staggering and stumbling about in the kitchen, blood pouring from a savage gash across her throat. Unable to utter a single last word, she fell and died.

Early the next morning, the excitable George was brought in for questioning, and subsequently arrested for the murder of his ex-fiancée. During the examination his clothing exhibited what appeared suspiciously like bloodstains, and presented police experts with the opportunity to test a method of biological analysis that had only recently been developed. Compared with modern techniques, the result may seem crude and unimpressive; but for the time it was startling and gave prosecuting counsel the evidence needed to secure a conviction. As a medical witness at the trial summed up: "The science of evidence with regard to bloodstains has taken a step further in this case than any other in my experience. It appears that this was an anaemic girl, and the skilled analyst is able by modern methods to say that the stains on this man's clothes are of human blood. Further, they are of anaemic blood, as were also the stains on the girl's clothes."

A small step forward for forensic science led to a long drop downwards for George Pateman!

[*Adapted from* The Case of the Anaemic Housemaid *by Susan Dunkley.*]

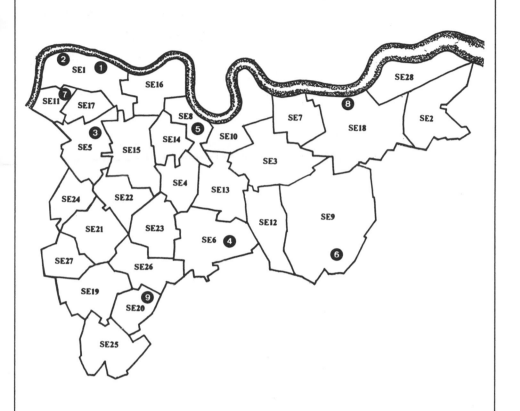

South-East London

1. Frederick George and Maria MANNING...................................... 62
2. Dr Thomas Neill CREAM... 66
3. James GREENACRE... 72
4. Colin LATTIMORE, Ronald LEIGHTON, and Ahmet SALIH.......... 76
5. Alfred and Albert STRATTON...................................... 82
6. David GREENWOOD 85
7. Harry DOBKIN.. 90
8. William COLMAN.. 93
9. Louis and Patrick STAUNTON...................................... 95

"I never liked him very much..."
The Murder of PATRICK O'CONNOR
by FREDERICK GEORGE MANNING and his Wife MARIA
on Wednesday the 8th of August 1849
at 3 Minver (or Minerva) Place (near the present Weston Street), SE1

Maria de Roux was born in Switzerland in 1819. Her early means of livelihood was as a lady's maid, and in 1846, while travelling from England to join her mistress, Lady Blantyre, on the Continent, she first met Patrick O'Connor. O'Connor was a 49-year-old Irishman, a Customs Officer in the London Docks, but earning a considerable second income from money-lending. Shortly afterwards, Maria met Frederick George Manning, a railway guard on the Great Western Railway and a man of somewhat dubious reputation.

In the following year, 1847, Maria married Manning and the couple moved to Taunton, in Somerset, to run the *White Hart*; Maria, though, persisted in her previous close friendship with O'Connor. Manning himself was still working on the railway, but after he was implicated in a £4000 bullion theft, then arrested and later released following a mail robbery, the Mannings decided that a move to London might be advisable, and they opened a beer shop in Hackney Road. Shortly afterwards Maria took it into her head to abscond with O'Connor; in hot pursuit, Manning was able to effect an uneasy reconciliation.

The Mannings' next address was in Minver Place, Bermondsey, where to make ends meet it was necessary to take in a lodger in the person of a medical student named Massey. Manning suddenly developed a previously undeclared interest in medicine, and seemed anxious to question Massey about various matters related to that youth's intended profession; the effects of chloroform, for example, and whether a person could sign cheques under the influence of narcotics. He wanted to know the effects of shooting somebody with an airgun, and the weakest point of the skull. These were prominent among the queries which began to arouse Massey's suspicion; Massey's suspicion in its turn resulted in the unfortunate man being put out of the house. It was about this time that Manning took delivery of a crowbar and a quantity of quicklime.

O'Connor had throughout continued to be on terms of some intimacy with Mrs Manning, and on August the 8th, 1849, he was invited to tea; it was on the same day that Manning bought a shovel.

O'Connor was never seen alive again.

Mrs Manning had shot him through the head, and according to Manning's final confession, "I found O'Connor moaning in the kitchen. I never liked him very much, and battered in his head with a ripping chisel." He was then buried under the flagstones in the kitchen, well covered with the quicklime.

On the following day Maria Manning visited O'Connor's lodgings and removed a quantity of money and shares, and two gold watches. William was sent out to sell the shares, on which he raised £110. At this point Mrs Manning decided to ditch her husband and, after putting her belongings in the left-luggage at London Bridge Station, she fled to

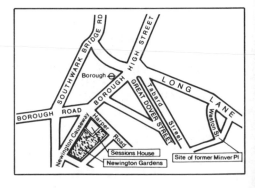

Maria and Frederick Manning

Edinburgh. Manning sat it out at Minver Place for a couple more days and then he also fled; to the Channel Islands.

O'Connor's acquaintances quickly noticed his disappearance and contacted the police, and an official search of the house at Minver Place revealed two newly cemented slabs in the kitchen floor; Patrick O'Connor's remains were beneath them. Mrs Manning was speedily arrested in Edinburgh, but Manning was able to lay low until August the 21st, when he was recognized and taken near St Helier, in Jersey.

The trial of Frederick and Maria Manning opened on October the 25th, 1849, before Mr Justice Cresswell, with the Attorney-General prosecuting. The case aroused huge public interest, with Frederick and Maria each trying to put the blame one upon the other for the murder. It was all to no avail, and both were duly sentenced to death. At the end, just before the day of execution,

Police unearth the remains of Patrick O'Connor from the kitchen at Minver Place

Patrick O'Connor, the victim

Public executions, in the middle of the nineteenth century, were considered a great public spectacle, providing an excuse for entertainment to the populace, the middle classes and the gentry alike. Large crowds were drawn to the site of the scaffold, sometimes arriving as much as a day before the deed to be sure of a good view of the proceedings.

Maria and Frederick Manning were executed on the 13th of November, 1849 in front of Horsemonger Lane Gaol. A crowd of fifty thousand spectators witnessed the hanging, including Charles Dickens, who complained to *The Times* about the levity of the crowd and the barbarity of the scene [see below].

By the day of the execution – which was set for eight o'clock in the morning – a crowd of ten thousand had gathered at the scene, with eight hundred policemen in attendance to maintain order. This gathering was serviced by all manner of hawkers, street traders and entertainers, pickpockets and prostitutes. Broadsides and ballad sheets about the crime sold in great numbers. In all, Henry Mayhew estimated that a quarter of a million copies of broadsides about the Mannings were produced. Many souvenirs and trinkets commemorating the impending event were also on sale.

At the appointed hour Frederick Manning was led out, head bowed and unsteady on his feet, accompanied by Calcraft, the executioner. The white hood was placed over his head and the rope positioned around his neck. Then, it was Maria's turn to appear, dressed in respectable black satin, with a black silk veil and blindfolded, at her own request. Her demeanour was proud and steady as she was led to the scaffold and the preparations made. A warder brought their two hands together as they stood over the trapdoor, awaiting their fate. The chaplain asked the unrepentant Maria one last time if she had anything to say concerning her guilt. "Nothing, but thank yu for your kindness", she replied; and two callous and calculating murderers were launched into eternity.

Manning confessed; but Maria still maintained her innocence, claiming "There is no justice and no right for a foreign subject in this country."

Maria's wearing of a black satin dress on the scaffold is said to have put the material out of fashion for ladies' dresses for a period of at least twenty years.

To the Editor of *The Times*

Sir – I was a witness of the execution at Horsemonger Lane this morning. I went there with the intention of observing the crowd gathered to behold it, and I had excellent opportunities of doing so, at intervals all through the night, and continuously from daybreak until after the spectacle was over.

I do not address you on the subject with any intention of discussing the abstract question of capital punishment, or any of the arguments of its opponents or advocates. I simply wish to turn this dreadful experience to some account for the general good by taking the readiest and most public means of [advertising] to an intimation given by Sir G. Grey in the last session of Parliament, that the Government might be induced to give its support to the measure making the infliction of capital punishment a private solemnity within the prison walls (with such guarantees for the last sentence of the law being inexorably and surely administered as should be satisfactory to the public at large), and of most earnestly beseeching Sir G. Grey as a solemn duty which he owes to society, and as a responsibility which he cannot for ever put away, to originate such a legislative change himself.

A sight so inconceivably awful as the wickedness and levity of the immense crowd collected at the execution this morning could be imagined by no man, and presented by no heathen kind under the sun. The horrors of the gibbet, and of the crime which brought the wretched murderers to it, faded in my mind before the atrocious bearing, looks, and language of the assembled spectators. When I came upon the scene at midnight, the shrillness of the cries and howls that were raised from time to time, denoting that they came from a concourse of boys and girls already assembled in the best places, made my blood run cold...

When the day dawned, thieves, low prostitutes, ruffians, and vagabonds of every kind, flocked onto the ground, with every variety of offensive and foul behaviour. Fightings, faintings, whistlings, imitations of Punch, brutal jokes, tumultuous demonstrations of indecent delight, when swooning women were dragged out of the crowd by the police, with their dresses disordered, gave a new zest to the general entertainment...

I am solemnly convinced that nothing that ingenuity could devise to be done in this city, in the same compass of time, could work such ruin as some public executions, and I stand astounded and appalled by the wickedness it exhibits. I do not believe that any community can prosper where such a scene of horror and demoralisation as was enacted this morning outside Horsemonger Lane Gaol is presented at the very doors of good citizens, and is passed by unknown or forgotten. And when, in our prayers and thanksgivings for the seasons, we are humbly expressing before God our desire to remove the moral evils of the land, I would ask your readers to consider whether it is not time to think of this one, and to root it out.

November 13th, 1847.

[*see* Murder Club Guide No.2 *for a discussion of the early Abolitionist movement*]

The Poison Pen
The Murder of MATILDA CLOVER by Dr THOMAS NEILL CREAM
on Wednesday the 21st of October 1891 at 27 Lambeth Road, SE1

Not a very great deal is known about the early life of Thomas Neill Cream, beyond his having been the eldest of eight brothers and sisters, born of William and Mary Cream on May 27th, 1850. Four years after this event the family left their home at 61 Wellington Lane, Glasgow for the new land of opportunity – Canada; here both William and young Thomas became actively involved in the shipbuilding trade, the father managing one firm, the son being apprenticed to another.

By November 1872 Thomas had forsaken trade for a profession, and on the 12th of the month registered at M'Gill College, Montreal as a student of medicine. Apart from a rather extravagant life-style (at the expense of his father), and the fact – extraordinary in hindsight – that he taught in Sunday School, little is recorded of significance in this period of Cream's development, but that he graduated with merit on March 31st, 1876.

This is the point at which Thomas Cream set his sights on notoriety.

He had already, in the month of September 1874, been provident enough to insure the contents of his lodgings at 106 Mansfield Street for the sum of $1000 with the Commercial Union of Montreal. Little more than a fortnight after graduation, Cream clearly decided that it was time to cash in on his investment. At any rate, there was a mysterious fire resulting in a claim from Cream for $978.40, this despite the fact that almost no damage had been done. The Company smelled a rat and refused to part with a single cent. Eventually a mutually face-saving compromise was reached, and Cream pocketed $350. The career of Thomas Neill Cream, crook, had begun.

It was around this same time that he met the daughter of a prosperous Waterloo (Canada) hotelier, Miss Flora Eliza Brooks. Miss Brooks shortly became pregnant, was aborted by Cream, and nearly died as a result. The furious Brooks senior would settle for nothing less than marriage, and on the 11th of September Thomas was dragged, unenthusiastic, down the aisle to wed his Flora. However, avoiding the wrath (and shotgun) of Brooks was one thing; bestowing all his worldly goods, etc., was quite another, and on the day following the wedding Cream walked out of the house bound for England. The Brooks family were to hear no more of their errant son-in-law until the unfortunate Flora died of consumption just short of a year after her wedding. Then Thomas Cream got in touch; he got in touch to demand the sum of $1000 – claimable, he insisted, under the marriage contract. In the end he settled for $200!

In this intervening year, Cream had enrolled as a post-graduate student at St Thomas's Hospital, London, and rounded off his education with a degree from the Royal College of Physicians and Surgeons at Edinburgh. Thus did Thomas Neill Cream become one more qualified medic to turn murderer.

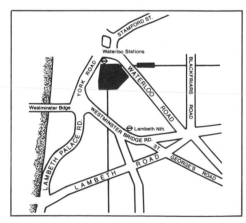

The killing, though, began in a comparatively modest and clumsy manner. Cream had returned to Canada, and was acquiring a lucrative, if unsavoury, reputation as an abortionist, operating out of Dundas Street, London, Ontario. It was during this occupancy that a young chambermaid named Kate Hutchinson Gardener was found dead in the privy behind Cream's rooms; beside her body was a bottle of chloroform. The girl was known to have been visiting Cream for the purpose of securing an abortion, and despite the strength of evidence offered against him, the doctor avoided prosecution for murder. His odious practice, though, was ruined, at least in Ontario.

Chicago fared little better from Cream's attentions, and his newly opened abortion surgery at 434 West Madison Street claimed its first fatality in August 1880. On the 23rd of that summer month, Cream was taken into custody on a charge of causing the death of Julia Faulkner; but luck was with him, and the slippery rogue again escaped his just reward. In December a Miss Stack died after taking medicine prescribed by Dr Cream; the latter's response was the first manifestation of an utterly incomprehensible need to draw unfavourable attention to himself by writing abusive, libellous letters. In this case a series of letters trying to blackmail Frank Pyatt, the perfectly innocent chemist who made up the Stack prescriptions.

A comparatively profitable sideline undertaken by Cream to supplement abortion was the marketing of a quack remedy for epilepsy. Whether the treatment did any good or not is debatable, but it appeared to do no harm, attracting a number of faithful 'patients'. One such was a railway agent named Daniel Stott, who was so impressed with the improvement in his health that he sent his pretty young wife in person to Chicago, to Thomas Cream, for regular supplies. The inevitable happened, and Cream availed himself of the favours of Julia Stott while taking her husband's money. When Stott became an inconvenience to the liaison his medicine was pepped up with an additional ingredient. On the 14th of June 1881 Daniel Stott died in great agony, the sudden seizure being attributed to his epilepsy, so that Cream's nostrum would never have been suspected had it not been for the mad medic's inexplicable

Women were his preoccupation, and his talk of them far from agreeable. He carried pornographic photographs, which he was too ready to display. He was in the habit of taking pills, which, he said, were compounded of strychnine, morphia, and cocaine, and of which the effect, he declared, was aphrodisiac. In short he was a degenerate of filthy desires and practices...
('The Prisoner Neill', by "one who knew him", St James Gazette, 24 October 1892)

communication to the coroner of Boone County, claiming that Stott's death had been the result of a blunder on the part of the pharmacist in overdoing the strychnine, and demanding an exhumation. The coroner dismissed the letter as the fantasy of a madman (which at least was true), and paid it no attention. Not so the recipient of Cream's next letter. The District Attorney did order an exhumation, did find strychnine in the stomach of Daniel Stott, and did eventually send prisoner 4374 Thomas Neill Cream to spend the rest of his life at the Illinois State Penitentiary at Joliet.

On 12th May, 1887 Thomas's father died at Dansville, New York, and the family began to agitate for the son's release from prison, with the result that the sentence was commuted to seventeen years and, with allowance for good behaviour, Cream was released on July 31st 1891. Diverting to Canada only for as long as it took to collect his inheritance of $16,000, an unchastened Cream boarded the *Teutonic* for Liverpool. Four days later, on October 5th, 1891, the deadly doctor was in London, a guest of Anderton's Hotel at 162 Fleet Street.

Having arrived, Cream wasted no time in acquainting himself with the seedier activities that London had on display. On Tuesday October 6th, he met a prostitute – Elizabeth Masters – at Ludgate Circus. After drinking wine at the *King Lud* they went back to her rooms in 9 Orient Buildings, Hercules Road (a turning off Lambeth Road), and thence to Gatti's Music Hall, Westminster Bridge Road.

On the following day, Wednesday the 7th, Cream took lodgings at 103 Lambeth Palace Road, in the heart of South London's slums, an area in which he was to commit a series of indiscriminate murders which were to rival Jack the Ripper's reign of terror in the East End three years before.

On the 9th of October Cream acquainted himself with the talents of Matilda Clover, a follower of the same calling as Elizabeth Masters, and ironically they were seen by Masters and her friend Elizabeth May entering No.27 Lambeth Road. At about this date, possibly the following day, Thomas Cream purchased from Mr Priest's chemist shop at 22 Parliament Street a quantity of *nux vomica*, of which one constituent is the alkaloid strychnine. He subsequently bought a box of empty gelatine capsules and a further supply of *nux vomica*.

Things were about to take a dramatic turn.

The evening of October 13th found James Styles standing outside the *Wellington* in Waterloo Road doing nothing in particular when he saw a young prostitute who had been patrolling her beat stagger and collapse onto the pavement. Styles managed to carry her to the address she gasped out (8 Duke Street, now Duchy Street), whence her condition made necessary her removal to a hospital. On the journey poor Ellen Donworth confided that a man she had met in the *York Hotel* in Waterloo Road, "A tall gentleman with cross eyes, a silk hat and bushy whiskers" had given her a

Title page of a contemporary 'penny dreadful'

couple of draughts from a bottle of "white stuff". She died before reaching the hospital; of strychnine poisoning. Thomas Cream – or "Fred" as he was known to Ellen Donworth – was away clear. Out of the limelight that is, until he chose (for what reason God only knows) to make himself obvious in an extraordinary pair of letters. The first was addressed to George Wyatt, who in his position as deputy coroner had presided over the inquest on Donworth: "I am willing to say that if you and your satellites fail to bring the murderer of Ellen Donworth, alias Ellen Linnell, to justice, I am willing to give you such assistance...provided your Government is willing to pay me £300,000 for my services." It was signed "A. O'Brien, detective." The second letter, dated the 6th November, was received by Mr W.F.D. Smith, one of the newsagenting family of W.H. Smith and Son, at their offices at 186 Strand. The letter was signed "H. Bayne, barrister", and the contents read to the effect that Ellen Donworth had been found in possession of two notes that incriminated Smith in her murder. 'Bayne' was willing to be retained as "counsellor and legal adviser".

But this is to take events out of their strict chronology; for on the 20th of October, Matilda Clover met once again with the man she had been seen with on the 9th. Now the encounter had a less happy conclusion. On this second evening Matilda brought her client "Fred" back to 27 Lambeth Road, where he was seen by the maid, Lucy Rose, as he was leaving. Some hours later Matilda died, writhing and screaming with agonized convulsions. She was buried in a pauper's grave in Tooting on October 27th; believed cause of death: delirium tremens as a result of alcoholism. Cream was in the clear again. Indeed, there was not even a suspicion of murder attached to Matilda Clover's death. Not, that is, until Thomas Cream sent a letter to the Countess Russell, at her suite in the Savoy Hotel, accusing her husband Lord Russell of poisoning Clover. Nor was his Lordship the only one to have a finger pointed at him. Dr William Henry Broadbent, an outstanding physician, received a letter dated 28th November, and signed by "M. Malone"; it opened, "Miss Clover, who until a short time ago lived at 27 Lambeth Road, S.E., died at the above address on

Ellen Donworth's Death

To the Guests,

      of the Metropole Hotel.

Ladies and Gentlemen,

   I hereby notify you that the person who poisoned Ellen Donworth on the 13th last October is to-day in the employ of the Metropole Hotel and that your lives are in danger as long as you remain in this Hotel.

        Yours respectfully,
           W. H. MURRAY.

London April   *1892*

The extraordinary letter addressed by Cream to the residents of the Metropole

20th October (last month) through being poisoned with strychnine". 'Malone' went on to accuse Dr Broadbent of the murder outrightly, and threatened to expose him if £2,500 did not change hands.

Dr Thomas Neill Cream now took a brief – albeit very brief – respite from the rigours of murder and correspondence. In fact he found the time to fall in love (at least in his version of that emotion), and become engaged to be married. The object of these affections was Laura Sabbatini, a highly respectable young woman who lived with her mother at Berkhamstead. On January 7th 1892 he sailed for Canada, leaving Laura waiting.

While in Canada Cream committed one of the most totally gratuitous acts in the annals of crime. He had printed 500 copies of what came to be known as the 'Metropole leaflet'. They were acknowledged by Cream in writing, but never circulated.

Cream embarked at New York bound for Liverpool on March the 23rd, a passenger aboard the *Britannic*. He reached London on April 2nd, and arrived back at Lambeth Palace Road via Edwards' Hotel, 14 Euston Square. The brief respite was over.

It was over most specifically for 21-year-old Alice Marsh and 18-year-old Emma Shrivell, two street girls up from Brighton, and currently lodging at 118 Stamford Street. At about 1.45am on 12th April, PC George Cumley was on his Stamford Street beat when he saw a man being shown out of the door of No.118 by a young woman. The picture was to remain in his head, for not two hours later behind those same doors, two young women died with great suffering from strychnine poisoning.

Thomas Cream's madness must have struck him again now, for he lapsed into a series of unaccountable and slanderous attacks upon the reputation of one of his neighbours. There happened to be lodged at 103 Lambeth Palace Road Walter Joseph Harper, a medical student at nearby St Thomas's and son of the respected Dr Joseph Harper of Barnstaple. To their mutual landlady, Miss Sleaper, Cream suddenly broke the news that young Harper was the author of the Stamford Street atrocities. Miss Sleaper's reaction was that Cream was a lunatic (how close she was to the truth would probably have frightened the good woman half to death!), and the matter lapsed. Until the 26th of April, when Dr Joseph Harper received a letter (accompanied, inexplicably, by a newspaper cutting relating to Ellen Donworth's death) declaring that the correspondent, "W.H. Murray", held incontestible proof that his son Walter had poisoned the Misses Marsh and Shrivell, and that for the consideration of £1,500 the writer was prepared to suppress it. 'Murray' further made it plain that if Harper was unwilling to find the money, the 'evidence' would be offered to the police on the same terms. Quite rightly, the doctor ignored this ludicrous threat and so apparently Cream lost interest in the possibility of a transaction.

We now find Thomas Cream returning to Miss Sabbatini in Berkhamstead, where he persuades her – without a word of explanation – to write three letters for him. Had she known even a fraction of the true reason, she would have run a mile; as it was, love prevailed over her apprehensions and she sat down with pen and paper. The missives themselves, signed "W.H. Murray", were all accusations against Walter Harper, and were sent to Coroner Wyatt, presiding over the Marsh/Shrivell inquest, to the foreman of the jury sitting on the same inquest, and to Mr George Clarke, a detective of Cockspur Street.

Whether driven by a clinical insanity or by a desperate, illogical desire to be associated with his own crimes, Cream began now to boast about his familiarity with the murders. To one man, John Haynes, he not only revealed far more than he should reasonably have known of the events, but actually took Haynes on a guided tour of the murder spots. To another acquaintance, McIntyre, Cream's uncommon knowledge proved of even greater interest – his full title was Police Sergeant McIntyre – and he promptly set a watch on the doctor's movements. On May 12th, and quite by chance, Constable Cumley saw Cream and recognized him as the man he saw leaving the scene of the Stamford Street murders, and he too put a tail on Cream.

May 26th; Cream complained through his solicitors to the Chief Commissioner of Police, saying that his business was being adversely affected by the very obvious police shadow. But time was running out for Thomas Cream, and it was not very many more days before he had talked himself into police custody. The attempt to blackmail Dr Harper came to light, and with Harper's cooperation in pressing charges, Cream was picked up.

At 5.25pm on June 3rd, Inspector Tonbridge confronted Cream in Lambeth Palace Road and put him under arrest. Cream's response was typical of the irritating arrogance that was to tell so heavily against him at his trial: "You have got the wrong man", he said, "but fire away!"

By the time Cream was ready to be charged with attempted blackmail, Matilda Clover's body had been lifted from the soil and analysed. At the inquest on her death, the jury brought in the following verdict: "We are unanimously agreed that Matilda Clover died of strychnine poisoning and that the poison was administered by Thomas Neill with intent to destroy life."

Cream stood upon his trial at the Old Bailey on October 17th 1892 before Mr Justice Hawkins charged with the murder of Matilda Clover. Three days later 'The Hanging Judge'* added another capital sentence to his long record:

> "...The jury...have felt it their bounden duty to find you guilty of the crime of wilful murder, of a murder so diabolical in its character, that one dare hardly trust oneself to speak of the details of your wickedness. What motive could have actuated you to take the life of that girl away, with so much torture I know not. For the crime of which you have been convicted our law knows but one penalty – the penalty of death."

Still unable to believe that he could be so badly used, Thomas Neill Cream stepped on to the scaffold at Newgate on the 15th of November to drop into eternal infamy, leaving behind one of the greatest enigmas of crime – What was the motive?

[*For a discussion of the powers and properties of Strychnine see* Murder Club Guide No.2]

---

* "No human being has the right to take the life of another human being and my business is to make this abundantly clear in the cases that come before me in court."

(Mr Justice Hawkins, 'The Hanging Judge')

On the 4th July 1892, I received in person from John B. Tonbridge, Inspector of Police, a case of pills; a box containing several kinds of coated pills and other medicines; and a single separate pill in paper. I have carefully examined and analysed all these pills and medicaments, with the following results:

The case contained 54 bottles of pills, all in bottles to which I assign numbers. Of these, 7 kinds contained strychnine, viz.,

No.2 $\frac{1}{22}$nd grain strychnine per pill (marked as containing $\frac{1}{16}$th grain in each pill). Of these pills, 9 would form a minimum fatal dose, and 22 an ordinary fatal dose for an adult
No. 8 $\frac{1}{16}$th grain strychnine per pill
No.20 $\frac{1}{130}$th grain strychnine per pill
No.23 $\frac{1}{60}$th grain strychnine per pill
No.32 $\frac{1}{100}$th grain strychnine per pill
No.48 $\frac{1}{60}$th grain strychnine per pill
No.51 $\frac{1}{60}$th grain strychnine per pill

Five of the kinds of pills contained *nux vomica*, which is a substance containing the alkaloids strychnine and brucine. The quantities of alkaloids in these pills were:

No. 6 $\frac{1}{27}$th grain per pill
No.10 $\frac{1}{13}$th grain per pill
No.16 $\frac{1}{60}$th grain per pill
No.19 $\frac{1}{13}$th grain per pill
No.35 $\frac{1}{20}$th grain per pill

Of these alkaloids rather less than one-half was strychnine, and rather more than one-half was brucine, which is a much less potent poison than strychnine. It thus appears that No.2 pills were the only pills which when taken in anything short of immoderate quantities would be likely to kill by strychnine poisoning.

...

(*signed*) Thomas Stevenson

July 11th 1892

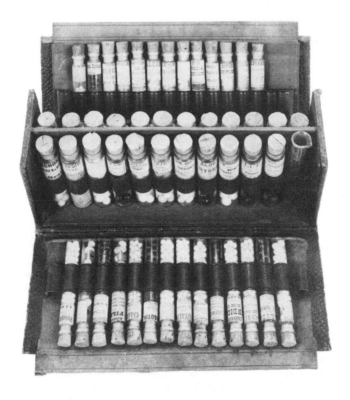

A London-Wide Distribution
The Murder of Mrs HANNAH BROWN
by JAMES GREENACRE
on Christmas Eve 1837
at Carpenter's Buildings (near today's Bethwin Road), SE5

THE
PADDINGTON TRAGEDY.

A
CIRCUMSTANTIAL NARRATIVE
OF THE
LIVES AND TRIAL
OF

JAMES GREENACRE,
AND

THE WOMAN GALE,
FOR THE MURDER OF

MRS. HANNAH BROWN,

HIS INTENDED WIFE,

WHICH WAS BROUGHT TO LIGHT
BY THE
DISCOVERY OF HER

MUTILATED REMAINS;

HIS ATTEMPT AT SUICIDE;
EXAMINATION AND CONFESSION.

THE WHOLE COLLECTED FROM
PRIVATE AND AUTHENTIC SOURCES.

LONDON:
ORLANDO HODGSON, 111, FLEET STREET.

In the annals of crime, for many years past, no act is related that has created such a universal thrill of horror, and sensation of detestation, as that of the Paddington Tragedy.

The discovery of portions of the body of a female, dreadfully mutilated, in the opposite extremities of London, at different periods, showed that some barbarous and bloody deed had been perpetrated; and that this strange and venturous mode was had recourse to as an attempt to escape from detection. The event caused an alarm and consternation, throughout the metropolis, altogether unparalleled. A long lapse, however, of three months, occurred before the slightest clue was gained, as to who the unfortunate victim of this foul act was, notwithstanding the exertion of the immense and practised Police force in London. Thus mystery, for a considerable period added its darkness to the feeling of horror at the awfulness of the crime.

LIFE OF JAMES GREENACRE

James Greenacre was born in 1785, in Norfolk; his parents were farmers. He received a liberal education, and displayed, in his youth, considerable mental talent. At the age of 19, he commenced business as a wholesale grocer and tea-dealer, in the London Road; and in the same year married the daughter of Mr Charles Wear, who formerly kept the *Crown and Anchor Tavern*, at Woolwich.

His next wife was the daughter of John Romford, Esq, a farmer, and considerable landowner, in Essex; by this wife he had three children; she died of a brain fever.

Fifteen months after the death of his second wife, he married a Miss Simmonds, of Long-lane, Bermondsey, who died of Cholera three weeks after his departure for America; by her he had seven children, two only are now living. In all his matrimonial speculations he had the precaution to secure from his intended partners a provision for any issue.

After his failure in the grocery business [due to the exposure of his fraudulent dealing], he went to New York, where he obtained a patent for a washing machine, and commenced business as a manufacturer of this article and as a carpenter. This speculation in about a year failed.

He introduced himself to Mrs Brown through the medium of an advertisement, and after a short acquaintance he proposed marriage, and to all appearance every arrangement for their mutual happiness was agreed upon.

Hannah Brown the unfortunate victim was a native of Norwich, and was about 50 years of age when she met her untimely fate. She was a tall and rather good looking woman, but possessed a most unfortunate temper.

On the 24th of December, he went and brought her boxes and herself to his house in Carpenter's Buildings, Camberwell, and it was in this place, and upon that day, the fatal and awful tragedy was acted. The parlour shutters of his house were noticed to be closed for a few days after Christmas, and he was observed to go out with a blue bag, not very heavy. A month after this time the house was to let.

FINDING OF THE BODY

Shortly after 2 o'clock, in the afternoon of Wednesday December 28th 1836, as a labouring man, named Robert Bond, residing at 45 Edward-st., Dorset-square, Marylebone, was proceeding along the Edgware-road, in the direction of Kilburn, he discovered, behind a large flag stone on the south side of the road, near the toll gate, a package enveloped in a coarse sack, or bag, tied with cord, which he was horrified to find contained the trunk of the body of a female, the head and legs having been severed therefrom. The body was carried to Paddington poorhouse. The spot where the discovery was made is situated about a mile and a half from Cumberland-gate, at the end of Oxford-street, and on the high road to Edgware.

On the west side of the road, and within about 150 yards of Pineapple-gate, nine detached villas, called Canterbury Villas have recently been erected by a gentleman named Biers residing there. Five of them are finished, and four of them

inhabited; but the remainder are in an unfinished state, and the workmen had suspended their labours on account of the severity of the weather. The front gardens are separated from the footpath by a wall about 10 feet high which, however, has not yet been carried up beyond the first six villas. Within 10 feet of the end of the wall a flag-stone about four feet long and three feet wide, had been placed in a leaning position by some of the workmen, and it was behind this stone that the trunk of the unfortunate female was found. Bond, who was one of the workmen employed upon the building, states that, as he was passing the stone, he observed something dark behind it, which on a nearer inspection, he found to be a wrapper of coarse canvas sewed together, and resembling a bag used for bran. On removing the stone, he perceived a pool of blood of about nine inches in diameter, which had apparently oozed through the canvas wrapper. Alarmed by the discovery, he instantly called two men who had the care of the unfinished buildings, who, on their arrival, advised him to open the package, which he then did. In addition to the human trunk it contained a child's frock, made of the commonest printed cotton and in very tattered condition from much wearing. It was in an extremely dirty state, and did not appear larger than to fit a child from nine months to twelve months old. There was also an old huckaback towel, much patched, and marked J.C.B.2, in red cotton and a piece of an old white cotton shawl with a blue border. Both were very dirty. The blood had a fresh appearance.

Immediately on the remains being deposited at the poor-house, the parochial authorities sent for Mr Girdwood, the parish surgeon, to examine them…Mr Girdwood considered that the mutilations had been committed subsequent to death. The head had been severed close from the shoulders, and the thighs within about three inches of the sockets. The bones had been sawed through in a very rough manner, and apparently with a common carpenter's saw, and that gentleman gave it as his opinion that it had not been done for the purpose of an anatomical lecture.

FINDING OF THE HEAD

On the 6th of January as Matthias Rolfe, a lock-keeper, at Stepney, was closing the lock-gate at that place, he found an obstruction which prevented the gate shutting, and upon his putting down a hitcher he pulled up the head of a human being.

The flesh was quite perfect, but the jaw-bone broken and protruding through the skin, (but this might have been done by the lock-gate), and one of the eyes seemed to have been quite cut out, by means of a blunt instrument. One ear was slit; and an ear-ring hole pierced above it. The ears had the appearance of the ear-rings having been torn out from the ears.

On being examined by Mr Girdwood, the surgeon, he found the skull was fractured by a heavy blow, and the eye knocked completely out. He believed this to have been done prior to death, but that the throat was not cut until after life was extinct. It had the appearance of having been four or five days in the water.

The head was conveyed to Paddington workhouse, where it was preserved in spirits, and viewed by many individuals who were in search of missing relations or friends. It was found to be the head belonging to the body which was discovered on the 28th of December.

FINDING OF THE LEGS

As a labourer, of the name of James Page, was cutting osiers, in Coal Harbour Lane [now Coldharbour Lane], on the 2nd of February, he found a sack lying in some bushes, and on looking through a hole he perceived a human knee. He immediately called for assistance, and on opening the sack the legs and thighs of a woman were discovered. After an inquest was held upon them they were removed to Paddington workhouse, and the body, which had been buried, being exhumed, the bones and size of flesh were found to correspond with it exactly.

APPREHENSION OF GREENACRE

The brother of the ill-fated Mrs Brown not having seen or heard of his sister for a longer time than usual, became uneasy; especially as she had left her lodgings with an intention which, as he was informed by a message from Greenacre, was not fulfilled, and, as he reasonably thought, must have been hurtful to her feelings. He therefore prosecuted his enquiries after her, and became impressed with an idea that unfortunately proved too true. He applied for a warrant against Greenacre, and after a long, tedious search, traced him to where he was apprehended.

Upon the policeman knocking on the door of the apartment, where he was in bed, Greenacre told him to wait until he could find the tinder-box, and hearing him groping about burst the door open. He denied at first having any knowledge of Mrs Brown, afterwards he said he had been called to church to a woman of that name, but that he knew not where she was now. Gale was in his bed and was detected attempting to conceal a watch. In Greenacre's pocket book were two pawn-broker's tickets for silk gowns, and in Gale's two for shoes, which in the evidence, at the trial, were identified as Mrs Brown's property.

Greenacre said it was lucky the policeman had come that day, as the next morning he would have been off for America.

In his room were four boxes, all tightly corded. In the adjoining room, which was called Gale's, was found part of a child's frock patched with nankeen. It exactly corresponded with the rags saturated in blood found near the bag containing the body.

ATTEMPT AT SUICIDE

The policeman in charge of the station-house hearing an unusual noise, went to the cell in which Greenacre had been placed, and found him on the floor, with a handkerchief which by the insertion of his foot in a slip knot at one end, he had contrived to draw tightly round his neck. At the time of this discovery he was black in the face, and life to all appearance was extinct; the handkerchief was cut, and a surgeon sent for, who, by bleeding and other means, succeeded in restoring life. Greenacre then observed to the surgeon, that he did not thank him for what he had done. He was removed to a prison hospital and had a straight-waistcoat put on, and proper guards.

TRIAL

The trial of James Greenacre, and Sarah Gale, took place at the Central Criminal Court, April 10-11, 1837, before the Lord Chief Justice of the Common Pleas [Tindal], Mr Justice Coleridge, and Mr Justice Coltman, who were accompanied by the Recorder and several Aldermen. Messrs Adolphus [see below], Clarkson, and Bodkin prosecuted; Messrs. Price and Payne were for the prisoners.

Mr Price addressed the jury, in defence, in a long able speech, many parts of which were eloquent and feeling; indeed so much so, that both prisoners lost their wonted self-possession, and cried bitterly.

After the jury had been absent a quarter of an hour, they returned to the court, finding both prisoners *Guilty*:

...It now only remains for me to pass upon you the dreadful sentence of the law; and that sentence is, that you be taken from hence to the prison from which you came, and thence to a place of execution, where you shall be hanged by the neck until you are dead, and that your body be then buried within the precincts of the gaol; and may the Lord God Almighty take compassion on your sinful soul.

A MATTER OF FACT

This text is taken from Emily Henderson's biography of her father the eminent barrister and historian John Adolphus (published 1871). The book is based on Adolphus's own diaries, which exhibit a disregard for truth that would have been the envy of Seven Dials.*

"I remember my father's uneasiness when Greenacre was brought up day after day before the magistrate and nothing could go on towards his committal, the head of the wretched victim, Hannah Brown, not having been found. Pieces of cut up flesh could not be identified, and all that could be done was to adjourn over and over in very faint hope. Circumstances were strongly against the prisoner, but the law would not permit a trial unless the body could be identified. A most wonderful circumstance occurred at last and settled the matter. Hannah Brown had lodged some months before at a little shop in Goodge-street, Tottenham-court Road, and the very night of her murder she called to take leave of the people there, saying she was going next day to be married. They soon after, of course, heard of her murder. The woman of the shop said one morning to her husband, 'I have now dreamt for four nights of a place where I know we should find Hannah Brown's head, and if you still refuse to go there with me, I am determined to hire a man to dig there, and I shall find it'. At last she prevailed upon her husband, and took him a long way off (I think in the Bayswater direction), where they were making foundations for houses, a large open space. She looked about, and at last said, 'Dig there'. He did so, and found the head in a sack. This, of course, was all important, and was still further corroborated in this way. A gentleman, hearing where the head was found, applied to the magistrate, saying he travelled in an omnibus with a man who had something in a sack he was very careful of; he looked at him very particularly, and should know him. He thought it a most suspicious circumstance that on getting out he ran across that open place I have described and had a lighted lantern. An order was given for thirty prisoners to be shown to this gentleman, who instantly fixed on Greenacre. He was tried and executed as every one knows. The head was quite perfect, and the features had not been mangled in the least. He had imagined, by burying the head, he should render discovery impossible, and so it would have been, and he must have been discharged, but for this wonderful interposition of Providence."

(Recollections of John Adolphus, Emily Henderson. Publ: T. Cautley Newby)

---

* For a note on the broadsheet printers of Seven Dials see *Murder Club Guide No.4.*

The Full 'Rigor' of the Law

The Murder of MAXWELL CONFAIT
by a Person or Persons Unknown

on Friday the 21st of April 1972
at 27 Doggett Road, SE6

and the Trial and Imprisonment of COLIN LATTIMORE, RONALD LEIGHTON, and AHMET SALIH for that Crime

At 1.21 in the early morning of Saturday, 22nd of April 1972, the Fire Brigade was called to 27 Doggett Road, Catford, the house at the end of a block which ran alongside the railway line near Catford Bridge Station. The basement and ground floor of the house were ablaze and the fire seemed to be spreading upward. Three firemen entered the house to search for occupants; Station Officer Speed went upstairs and, finding the back bedroom locked, broke into the room. It was full of smoke, but Speed felt his way across the room and, just past the bed on the floor, came upon the prone form of a man. There was no pulse. Reaching the window, Speed flung it open to let out the smoke and hurried downstairs to help douse the fire. By 1.31am it was out, and at 1.45 the police arrived, followed at 2.00 by divisional police surgeon, Dr Angus Bain.

The dead man was a half-caste in his twenties and, on physical examination, a 'possible homosexual'. He was wearing tight fawn-coloured trousers and a long sleeved T-shirt with a large ace of clubs motif on the chest. His lips were blue and swollen and there was the mark of where flex or cord had been twisted round his neck. Cause of death was asphyxia from this ligature. Dr Bain did not take the rectal temperature, the normal procedure for calculating the time of death, for fear of destroying any evidence of recent sexual activity. Nevertheless, he noted that rigor mortis was almost complete and estimated that death had occured at between eight and ten o'clock the previous evening. At 3.45am, the distinguished pathologist, Dr James Cameron, arrived to view the body. He also avoided taking the rectal temperature, and noted that the body was

cool to the touch, but that, in his opinion, rigor mortis had only just begun. The time of death he put at between 7.45pm and 11.45pm. By 6.30 in the morning, the body had been removed to Lewisham Mortuary and Dr Cameron proceeded with the post-mortem. During the morning the police began a careful search of the house. The fire

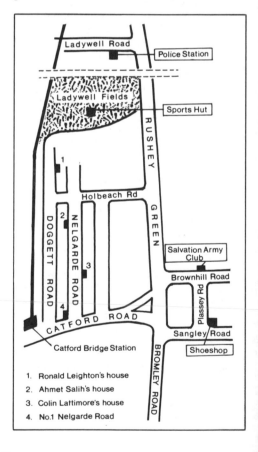

1. Ronald Leighton's house
2. Ahmet Salih's house
3. Colin Lattimore's house
4. No.1 Nelgarde Road

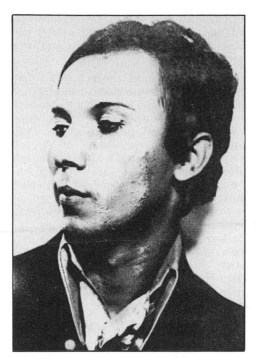 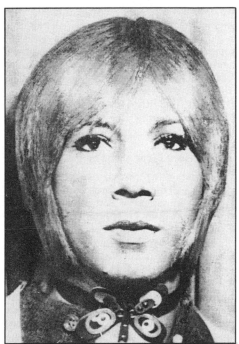

Maxwell Confait and his alter ego 'Michelle'

appeared to have been started deliberately by igniting a petrol can in a cupboard under the stairs in the basement. Just before eleven o'clock a length of electrical flex with a lamp holder at one end and a switch at the other was discovered in a drawer of the dressing table in the dead man's room. There was no sign of a struggle in the room and no fingerprints. Meanwhile Detective Chief Superintendent Alan Jones had been put in charge of the inquiry and a murder HQ had been set up at Lee Road police station.

The First Suspect

The dead man, identified as Maxwell Confait, was twenty-six years old; he was a homosexual prostitute and a transvestite, and preferred to be called 'Michelle'. The first task for Superintendent Jones was to trace and interview Michelle's friends, acquaintances and clients. He began with his landlord, Winston Goode, a West Indian who had been the first person to discover the fire. Goode and Michelle had first met at the *Black Bull* public house, Lewisham, in 1970, when Goode had just broken up with his wife. The two became friends and Goode began to hang about the same haunts

as Confait, even aping Michelle's fondness for wearing women's clothing. In February 1972 Confait moved into a room in Goode's house in Doggett Road at a rent of £2.50 per week. Confait cooked for the two of them, while Goode was out working as a labourer in Charlton. Goode's behaviour on the night of the fire had given the police some reason to view him with suspicion; he had, he said, been asleep in his room in the basement when he was awakened by the crackling of the flames. He ran up to the ground floor to alert his wife and children, who were still living in the house, and then shouted upstairs to Confait. His wife thought he seemed uncommonly wild-eyed and distraught, and after he had set off for Catford Bridge Station to phone the Fire Brigade she sent a neighbour after him. Goode was still fumbling with the dial when the neighbour arrived and had to be relieved of the receiver.

Goode was interviewed by police throughout Saturday the 22nd, and during the course of the interview he let slip that Confait had been intending to leave Doggett Road to live with another lover. Goode admitted to feelings of jealousy, while denying that he had had a homosexual relationship with Michelle. At 5.50pm, samples of hair and semen were taken from Goode, he was then temporarily released. He was interviewed again on the Monday, but by then the police were changing their approach to the inquiry. Some days later, Goode was admitted to Bexley Psychiatric Hospital, confused and unable to remember the traumatic events of the previous few days.

Three More Fires and Three Confessions

On Monday, the 24th of April, there was a rash of small fires in the area around Doggett Road. A minor fire was started on a grassy railway embankment behind Doggett Road; a small hut containing sports equipment was burnt down in near-by Ladywell Fields; and a blaze was started in No.1, Nelgarde Road, an abandoned house in the next street. At 5.20pm, a young lad of eighteen called Colin Lattimore was stopped by PC Roy Cumming, who was driving his Panda car along Nelgarde Road. He was asked about the spate of fires, and Lattimore (who was educationally subnormal with a mental age of eight) quickly admitted his involvement. PC Cumming then said, "If I mention Doggett Road, last Friday, can you tell me anything about that?" The reply, as reported in his notebook, was, "I was with Ronnie. We lit it, but put it out. It was smoking when we left." Ronnie was fifteen-year-old Ronald Leighton. Lattimore was then accompanied by police officers to Leighton's home in Doggett Road, where they found Ronnie with fourteen-year-old Ahmet Salih. All three were taken to Lewisham police station and after preliminary questioning by Temporary DC Peter Woledge, were driven to the murder HQ at Lee Road to be interviewed by Superintendent Jones and DI Graham Stockwell. Colin Lattimore was interviewed between 6.00pm and 6.55pm, Ronnie Leighton between 7.00pm and 7.35pm and Ahmet Salih between 7.40pm and 8.05pm.

These interviews took place with neither a solicitor nor a parent present, although Judges' Rules clearly state that, "As far as practicable, children (whether suspected of a crime or not) should only be interviewed in the presence of a parent or guardian, or, in their absence, some person who is not a police officer and is of the same sex as the child". Lattimore and Salih also later claimed that they were hit by DC Woledge, so that Lattimore had a nose-bleed and Salih cried. Leighton claimed he had been pushed around.

At 9.00pm Lattimore's parents and Leighton's mother arrived at the police station and were told that their sons were ready to make a statement which they were requested to witness; an irregular procedure. Both lads admitted to the murder of Maxwell Confait and to starting the fire at Doggett Road. A little later Mrs Salih arrived, but, because of her poor command of English there was a delay while a Turkish interpreter was contacted. Ahmet's statement was taken at one o'clock in the morning. He admitted to helping start the fire, but said he only observed the killing of Confait. All three were charged with murder. By early on Tuesday the 25th of April, Detective Chief Superintendent Jones had wrapped up the case to his satisfaction.

Alibis and Experts – The Trial

In May the charge of murder against Ahmet Salih was dropped and he was allowed bail on the lesser charges he faced. On June 2nd, 1972, Lattimore, Leighton and Salih appeared at Woolwich Magistrates Court. At this preliminary hearing the prosecution rehearsed its case, which relied almost entirely on the confessions of the three boys. Nevertheless, this was easily sufficient to commit them for trial. Ahmet was allowed bail again, while Colin and Ronnie were returned to Ashford Remand Centre.

At this stage the boys' parents and their legal representatives were quite confident of gaining an acquittal at the trial. At the Woolwich hearing the medical experts, Dr Bain and Dr Cameron, had restated their early assessment that Confait had been killed between 6.30 and 10.30 on the Friday evening. All three boys had an alibi for this period. Colin had spent the day at the remedial day centre he attended and after going home for his tea had spent the evening with his brother Gary at a Salvation Army Youth Club until 11.30. He had come home with his brother, being seen by several people, and had watched television with his parents before going to bed. Even after this, he had made sufficient noise for his father to shout down to him to be quiet. This was at 12.35am.

Ahmet and Ronnie had spent the day together at Ronnie's house. They were joined there by two girls, Ahmet's sister Perihan and Deborah Ricketts, who they walked to the bus stop outside the ABC Cinema at 9.15pm. While out they had reconnoitred a shoe-repair shop in Sangley Road, with an eye to breaking in. They returned home for a screwdriver, then set about 'doing' the shop, stealing some goods and £4.50 from the till. They arrived back at Ahmet's house and watched television until 12.55am, popping out for a few minutes to buy a hot dog at one point. They then decided to 'do' the shoe shop again, being arrested as they left the shop at 1.30am by two policemen. So how could any of the boys have been responsible for Maxwell Confait's death if the medical experts were right? The defence had reason to feel confident.

The trial of Colin Lattimore, Ronnie Leighton and Ahmet Salih began on November the 1st, 1972, at the Old Bailey. Mr Justice Chapman presided, Mr Richard Du Cann, brother of the politician Edward, led for the prosecution and the defence team consisted of John Marriage QC, Cyril Salmon QC and Brian Watling, representing Lattimore, Leighton and Salih respectively.

The crucial element of the trial was clearly the medical evidence, and the defence team were in for a shock. Dr Bain and Dr Cameron had had second thoughts. They now said that Confait could have died as late as 1.00am. The contention was that the heat of the fire had speeded up the onset of rigor mortis. Then it was suggested that the act of strangulation could add to that process. Alcohol was also mentioned as a contributory factor. The result of this, of course, was to throw the whole question of the time of death into confusion and effectively to invalidate the alibis of the three boys. The defence attempted to introduce the curious behaviour of Winston Goode, but this was quickly squashed by the judge. Mr Justice Chapman finally sealed the matter in his summing-up with a general homily on the evils of hooliganism.

On Friday the 24th of November, the jury retired. They took three and a half hours to reach a verdict. Colin Lattimore was found guilty of manslaughter, on grounds of diminished responsibility, and also guilty of

arson at Doggett Road and Ladywell Fields. He was ordered to be detained under the Mental Health Act without limit of time and was sent to Rampton Hospital. Ronnie Leighton was found guilty of murder and of the lesser charges of arson at Doggett Road and Ladywell Fields and burglary at Sangley Road. He was sentenced to life imprisonment and sent to Aylesbury Prison. Ahmet Salih was found guilty of arson at Doggett Road and Ladywell Fields and burglary at Sangley Road. He was sentenced to four years in prison to be spent at the Royal Philanthropic School, Redhill, in recognition of his age.

Leave No Stone Unturned

On Thursday July the 26th 1973, the three boys were refused leave to appeal. The law had run its course, and for the authorities, the matter was settled. George Lattimore, Colin's father, was not, however, a man to give up easily and he believed in his son's innocence. A complaint against DC Woledge for assaulting his son in Lewisham police station was quickly dismissed. He then began to write letters to the Queen, the Prime Minister, the Home Secretary and anyone else he could think of. Two of these letters bore some fruit. His local MP, Mr Carol Johnson, took up the case in October, writing to the Home Office. Ministers and officials were not over-disposed to reconsider matters which, if proved, involved misconduct by the police and a breakdown of the judicial system. Their replies were unspecific and evasive, citing the need for new evidence to reopen the case. The reaction of the National Council for Civil Liberties was much more hopeful. They were sufficiently interested in the case to contact one of the most experienced and prestigious pathologists in the country, Professor Donald Teare. In April 1974 he forwarded to them his written opinion of the medical aspects of the Confait case. He discounted any appreciable effect on the onset of rigor mortis from the heat of the fire, the effects of strangulation, or of alcohol. He unequivocally stated that, on the evidence presented, Maxwell Confait had died between 6.30 and 10.30 pm.

Meanwhile in February 1974 the General Election brought a change of government. The new Home Office team, Roy Jenkins and Alex Lyons, were committed to reviewing the procedures covering miscarriages of justice. At the same time the new MP for Lewisham, Christopher Price, an educational journalist, became involved in the case and began to mobilize his journalistic contacts. On May 22nd, 1974, Winston Goode, the first suspect in the Confait case, committed suicide by swallowing cyanide which

and ordered the return of the documents. Subsequently he led the investigation in the Kristen Bullen baby snatch case, arresting an epileptic girl and extracting a confession when it was later proved that she had an irrefutable alibi. Then Jones ran the rather eccentric inquiry into the 'Slag Heaps' affair, in which Ronald Milhench was discovered to

Left to right: Ronald Leighton, Ahmet Salih, and Colin Lattimore celebrating their release

he obtained from his new employment as a metal stripper in Catford. Under pressure a police inquiry was set up into the death, led by Detective Chief Superintendent 'Pop' Hemsley.

The appeal committee had also begun to compile a dossier on the controversial Detective Chief Superintendent Alan Jones. Even before his involvement in the Confait case, his name had featured in the law books; he had confiscated the passports of a number of the family of Mastoora Begum, while investigating her disappearance. The Court of Appeal had declared his action illegal

have forged the Prime Minister's signature. His assistant in that inquiry was Inspector Davis, who was simultaneously working on the matter of Goode's death. Unsurprisingly, the inquiry into that death reached no helpful conclusions, but it did add to the growing pressure for action.

Christopher Price had also been active. In March 1974 he had introduced a Ten Minute Rule Bill in the House of Commons, to air the evidence in the case. This was followed by a series of newspaper articles in the *South London Press*, the *Guardian* and the *New Statesman* and an item on BBC2 television news. This was followed, on November 6th 1974, by a full scale half-hour documentary on the issues in the Confait case in the *This Week* slot on ITV television. It was called *Time for Murder*.

The first fruits of a new attitude at the Home Office had been a secret report, commissioned from another great contemporary pathologist, Professor Keith Simpson, on the medical aspects of the Confait case. Simpson's conclusions were broadly in line with those of Donald Teare. One of the problems in getting the case reconsidered by the Court of Appeal was that new evidence was needed to enact the procedure. The death of Winston Goode had been argued as constituting this, but it was a moot point whether it really constituted new evidence. On the 14th of January 1975, however, Home Secretary Roy Jenkins announced that the unspecific phrase "other considerations of substance" had been added to the regulations. It became obvious that the Home Office were at last actively reviewing the case. In fact, during the spring of 1974 the case was unofficially examined by Lord Chief Justice Widgery. On the 18th of June, 1975, Roy Jenkins finally announced in Parliament that the Confait case had been sent back to the Court of Appeal.

The Courts Turned Upside Down

The Court of Appeal case at last opened in the Royal Courts of Justice in the Strand on Monday the 6th of October 1975, with Lord Justice Scarman, Lord Justice Ormond and Mr Justice Swanwick on the bench. Richard Du Cann QC again represented the prosecution and the three boys were this time collectively represented by Lewis Hawser QC. It was immediately clear that the new hearing would be a very different affair from the original trial. Lord Justice Scarman early on insisted that the Court should accept any evidence it felt was relevent to the case, and the judge himself took a very active role in questioning witnesses to clarify the evidence. It was not so much the three boys as the medical experts, the Director of Public Prosecutions, the police and the judicial system itself which were on trial. The fire expert at the original trial, Mr Arthur Craven, was allowed to give evidence which questioning had not previously disclosed. This included his assessment of the heat in Confait's room, which was slight, and some inconsistencies in Winston Goode's account of the fire, which indicated that he cannot have tried to alert Confait when he left the burning house. Then Professor Donald Teare appeared in the witness box and impressively demolished the red herrings which had blurred the medical evidence at the trial. This was underlined by written evidence from Professor Keith Simpson, who was too ill to attend the Court in person. Professor Cameron was then allowed the opportunity to rebut this opinion, but ended up by magnanimously concurring with Professor Teare's assessment.

The Court adjourned for a week, and on Friday October the 17th, Lord Justice Scarman began to read the judgement. The three boys – now young men – Colin Lattimore, Ronnie Leighton and Ahmet Salih, were exonerated from any involvement in the murder of Maxwell Confait. It was also stated that there was insufficient evidence for the main arson charge and that the other minor offences had been only worthy of a probation order. All three were promptly freed.

Postscript

In his judgement, Lord Scarman put forward a theory not previously advanced, that as there were no signs of a struggle, Maxwell Confait must have known his killer. This was further embellished by the comment that his Lordship had known of cases where half-strangling was used as a stimulus to the homosexual act. Was Maxwell Confait killed by a lover in a tragic accident?

The Court of Appeal judgement led to the setting up of an enquiry into the wider ramifications of the case, which was headed by an ex-judge, Sir Henry Arthur Fisher. The whole question of the Judges' Rules on police questioning of suspects, and of children and the educationally subnormal in particular, was palpably in need of review.

This inquiry was itself delayed when lawyers sifting through the papers thought they might have found evidence which could yet lead to a successful prosecution. Another investigation of the original case was carried out by Peter Fryer, Assistant Chief Constable of West Mercia. However, no arrests were made.

Hanged by a Fingerprint

The Murder of Mr THOMAS FARROW and his Wife ANN
by ALFRED and ALBERT STRATTON

on the 27th of March 1905
at 34 Deptford High Street, SE8

The early morning of Monday, March 27th 1905 was characteristic of that season's inclement weather; to one young man named William Jones, already soaked through by the penetrating rain, the oil and colour shop where he worked offered the welcome opportunity at least of warmth and shelter. It was before eight o'clock, but the boy was familiar with old Mr Farrow's habit of opening up early to supply painters and decorators starting their day's work. So he was surprised and not a little irritated to find the shutters still up and the door locked. Even more unusually, Jones could not raise anybody by knocking, and he set off for Greenwich where George Chapman, who owned the small chain of shops of which Farrow managed one, had his own business. Chapman sent one of his assistants back to Deptford with Jones, and together they forced an entry at the back of the shop.

It was a badly shaken pair of lads who rushed back out the door just minutes later and sped through the rain to the near-by police station.

There was nothing at all impressive about No.34 Deptford High Street – indeed, there still isn't; it was a small rather run-down shop, with rooms above in which Thomas Farrow, manager of the business for over fifty years, lived with his wife Ann. Farrow was nearing seventy, Mrs Farrow just a little younger.

It was Mr Farrow that the police found first when they accompanied the shop-boys back to the High Street; found him beaten to death in the shop's back parlour. In the bedroom they found his wife, still alive, but with such dreadful injuries that she died in the Seamen's Hospital at Greenwich three days later without regaining consciousness.

It was clearly a case for Scotland Yard's Murder Squad, and it was no time before Chief Inspector Fox was taking command of a group of experienced detectives in a thorough search of the scene of the crime. This exercise yielded two vital clues; one of them would change the whole course of the criminal identification procedure.

Near the doorway through which the murderers were presumed to have fled were found two crude home-made masks which had been fashioned from the top of a lady's silk stocking. To the experienced reasoning of Fox this indicated that almost certainly the criminals were local men, men whose faces were familiar enough to need hiding.

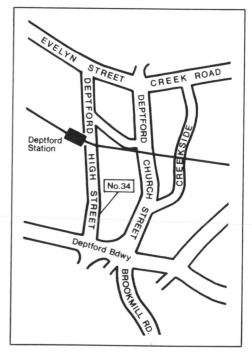

But it was the second clue that was to elevate this simple, sordid crime into national headlines and, more important, to introduce a completely new feature to future crime investigation. The police found a cash box close to the body of Thomas Farrow. The box had obviously been forced by the robber/killer and plundered of its contents, in the course of which, it was discovered, the impression of a right thumb had been left on the metal tray. When comparisons had eliminated those persons known to have handled the cash box it became clear that the print belonged to the killer.

A simple enough deduction, and one which today would bring speedy retribution to the criminal careless enough to leave fingerprints at the scene of his crime. But this was 1905, and Scotland Yard's small Fingerprint Department had been founded only four years previously. Besides, there was no precedent for such evidence being acceptable in a capital case. It had been difficult enough for the pioneers of the new system to convince scientists of the remarkably individual characteristics of fingerprints – what chance with a jury of twelve ordinary people?

With this doubt in mind, the inquiry continued to focus on the finding of Deptford-based criminals with no alibi for the night of 26-27 March. It was not long before the names of Alfred and Albert Stratton began to crop up with sinister regularity. The brothers were already known to the police as housebreakers, thieves with a vicious enough known record to make them suitable candidates for the murderous attack on the Farrows. Subjected to police questioning, Hannah Cromerty, with whom Alfred had shared a room in Brookmill Road, revealed that he and his brother had not been home all night on the 26th, and that when he returned the next morning, Alfred burned the coat that he had been wearing. Albert's partner, Mrs Kate Wade, recalled that he had recently asked her if she had an old pair of stockings he could have.

Both men were arrested and taken to Tower Bridge police station where Detective

Alfred Stratton

Albert Stratton

Inspector Charles Collins of the Fingerprint Department was waiting to take samples of both men's prints. Before long, it was established beyond doubt that the thumb-print on the cash-box tray belonged to Alfred Stratton.

Now, although the police knew with certainty that they had the culprits in custody, it was still necessary to convince a court; and when the case opened at the Old Bailey before Mr Justice Channell in May 1905 it was not only the brothers Stratton that were on trial but the credibility of the technique of fingerprint identification.

It was for this reason that the Crown led with one of the greatest counsels of his time, Sir Richard Muir. It was Muir, in partnership with Collins in the witness box, who patiently inducted the jury in the technicalities of fingerprinting. With the aid of giant enlargements, they were shown how comparisons were made, and in particular the conclusive eleven points of similarity between Alfred's fingerprint and the impression left at the scene of Thomas Farrow's murder. The jury, cleary impressed with their newly acquired information, had one of their own members fingerprinted in order to test the theory in comparison with the prisoner's prints.

For Stratton, Mr H.G. Rooth dismissed the whole principle of fingerprint evidence as "unreliable", and called his own witness, in the person of Dr Garson, to swear that the print on the cash box was not made by Alfred Stratton. When Muir's turn came to cross-examine he was able in a stroke completely to undermine the credibility of this 'expert' witness:

"Did you," he demanded of the witness, "when you read of this case in the press, write two letters offering your services as an expert? Did you, on the very same day write one letter to the defence offering your services and another to the Treasury asking to be retained for the prosecution?"
"Yes," barely audible.
"How, then, do you reconcile the writing of those two letters on the same day? One offering to swear to the infallibility of the system, and the other to its fallibility?"
"I am an independent witness."
Mr Justice Channell: "A very unreliable witness I should think, after writing two such letters."

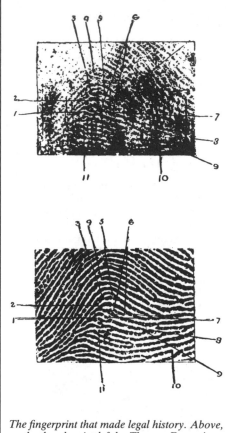

The fingerprint that made legal history. Above, the thumb-print left by Thomas Farrow's murderer on the cash-box that he robbed. Below, the thumb-print of Alfred Stratton. A convincing eleven points of similarity prove beyond any doubt that they were made by the same person.

Even so, it could not be said that the judge himself was entirely convinced by this new-fangled system, going only so far in his summing up as to acknowledge a strong resemblance between the two fingerprints under consideration. The jury entertained no such doubts, and after a brief retirement announced a verdict of guilty against both prisoners. And so the end of Alfred and Albert Stratton – hanged by a fingerprint – was the beginning of a new era in the fight against crime.

[*For a brief history of the fingerprint system of identification see* Murder Club Guide No.3]

The Button and Badge Murder

The Murder of NELLIE GRACE TREW
by DAVID GREENWOOD
on Saturday the 9th of February 1918
on Eltham Common, Well Hall Road, SE9

It is only when it is all over, and any survey of it is tinged with hindsight, that we have the opportunity to 'read' the background and consequences of a recent murder case. For the most part the narrative unfolds piecemeal, some of the aspects remaining isolated until perhaps the very end, when they can be fitted like pieces into a puzzle. This is particularly true of multiple, or 'serial' killings, where a small reported paragraph – perhaps covering the discovery of a body in suspicious circumstances, may require weeks, or months, sometimes years, of patient investigation before the next paragraph can be written, and longer before all the pieces can be assembled for the trial; post-mortem, inquest, magistrate's hearing. After the trial, the appeal. After the appeal, the punishment.

The case of David Greenwood, and his senseless killing of young Nellie Trew, is not a complicated one, but in the course of researching it, the writer became aware of this gradual unfolding of the narrative through the columns of the local newspapers, which reflected the fact that, though not of global importance, every death in such circumstances is a notable local tragedy. It might also serve as a tribute to the contribution made by newspapers to police inquiries; it was, after all, the nationwide co-operation of the Press in publishing illustrations of the 'button and badge' that led to the identification of David Greenwood as the killer.

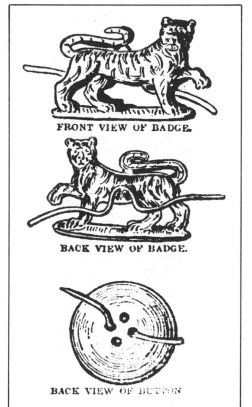

FRONT VIEW OF BADGE.

BACK VIEW OF BADGE.

BACK VIEW OF BUTTON

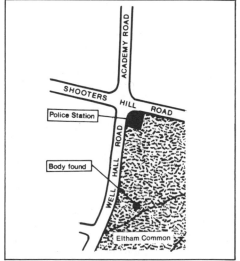

85

SHOCKING DISCOVERY ON ELTHAM COMMON

Young Girl Ill-Treated and Murdered

Seldom has the Woolwich district been so deeply stirred as on Sunday morning, when the news spread that a young girl had been found dead on Eltham Common in circumstances which pointed to outrage and murder. The victim proved to be Nellie Grace Trew, aged 16, who had been living with her parents at 5 Juno Terrace, on the new Government estate at Well Hall. The girl left home on Saturday evening to change a book at Plumstead Library, and as she did not return home her father communicated with the police at Shooters Hill Station. En route, oblivious to the terrible tragedy which had taken place, he passed and repassed the spot where his daughter lay dead.

The scene of the crime is remarkable for the fact that it is a small and lonely area lying between two comparatively busy centres. At the spot where Shooters Hill Road crosses the main thoroughfare, which on the Woolwich side is known as Academy Road, and on the Eltham side becomes Well Hall Road, stands Shooters Hill Police Station, faced on one side by officers quarters and on the other by wings and outbuildings of the Royal Herbert Hospital. A few hundred yards down Well Hall Road is that huge Government estate of houses and many hundreds of hutments. On the left-hand side, proceeding Elthamwards lies a waste of land covered with trees known as Eltham Common, fronted by ample pavement, and as well lighted as the times permit, whilst along the road runs a tramway to Eltham. It was on this waste land that the body was noticed by a tramway worker on Sunday morning, and he at once gave information to the neighbouring police station.

The murdered girl was found on the grass about 40 yards from the roadway, and she had evidently been carried there after succumbing to attack at a different point. A few yards from the pavement, and about 200 yards from Shooters Hill police station, there were signs of a severe struggle, and indistinct footprints in the mud leading to the place at which the body was discovered. The condition of the girl's face showed she had received a severe blow in the mouth, which had probably stunned her, and marks on the neck indicated that she had been strangled, whilst other appearances suggested maltreatment in other directions. It was apparent that as a result of her injuries the girl had lost a considerable amount of blood, which it is hoped will afford one clue to the discovery of the culprit or culprits. The case was at once taken in hand by Divisional Detective Inspector Brown, of Blackheath, who initiated the most vigorous and vigilant enquiries...

(*Kentish Mercury*, 15 February, 1918)

The victim of the murder was a quiet dark-haired girl... She had been employed since July last year in the card index department of the Wages Branch of the Central Office of the Arsenal, where she enjoyed the greatest popularity amongst her colleagues and had won the approval of her superiors by her good behaviour and attention to her duties. A feature of her character which is of interest, as it somewhat deepens the mystery of her death, was her indifference to the society of men; all her acquaintances remark upon the fact that she never associated with men and had not the least suggestion of 'flightiness' in her disposition; she was, on the contrary, a quiet, industrious and home-loving girl, and was in the habit of hurrying home from work to assist her mother whose health is not good.

The prolonged and close search that was instituted by the police for clues that would assist in establishing the identity of the assailant or assailants has not so far been very successful. Two articles were found near the spot at which the initial struggle had occurred, and they may have some association with the tragedy. One was a large overcoat button which had been attached to the garment by wire, and had evidently been torn off as the wire still remained twisted. The other was [a] military badge. The badge is of white metal, fastened with a shank of copper wire, and is believed to be the full dress collar badge of the Gordon Highlanders.

– not worn at the present time.
(*West Kent Argus,* Friday 15 February, 1918)

The police are anxious to know if any member of the public can recognise the badge or button as having been worn by any person known to them. It is possible that persons who let lodgings may have seen a lodger wearing such articles.

Any information to C.I.D., New Scotland Yard, or any police station, will be welcomed.
(*Kentish Mercury*, 15 February, 1918)

At once police made close enquiries regarding leave in all the barracks and billets in the immediate neighbourhood but without tangible result. The murderer, or murderers for it is believed that the outrage was done by two men, must, it is thought, have blood stains on their clothing, as Miss Trew's injuries were terrible.
(*Lewisham Borough News*, 13 February, 1918)

MURDER OF A GIRL AT ELTHAM

Ex-Soldier Arrested and Charged

The police very rapidly carried out their plans for the elucidation of the mystery surrounding the death of Nellie Grace Trew, who, in circumstances related last week, was found strangled on Eltham Common on February 10th. The result was that on the 14th inst., David Greenwood, 21, a turner and discharged soldier, of Jupiter Street, Well Hall, was detained on Friday and was brought up at Woolwich Police Court on Saturday afternoon, to answer the charge of murder...
(*Kentish Mercury*, 22 February, 1918)

[It appears that his workmates in the City, after seeing in the newspapers the photographs of the badge and overcoat button found near the body, noticed that he was no longer wearing a similar badge which he had worn for some time. In reply to their questions he appears to have made a statement to the effect that he had sold the badge to a man on a tramcar for two shillings on Saturday afternoon at Well Hall. His workmates advised him to give the information to the police, which he did, but they were not satisfied and detained him until he could be seen by Chief Inspector Carlin and Divisional Detective Inspector Brown, as a result of whose subsequent enquiries he was arrested and brought to Woolwich]
(*West Kent Argus*, 22 February, 1918)

...The prisoner, who stepped briskly into the dock when the charge was called, is a tall, thin young fellow, with a face that is rather intellectual than otherwise, and he followed the proceedings with a keen interest.

The only witness called was Chief Inspector Carlin of New Scotland Yard, who deposed to the finding of the body of the girl, and proceeded to say that on Thursday morning the prisoner was brought to Scotland Yard by Divisional Detective Inspector Brown, who said in his presence "This is the man who called at Tottenham Court Road police station this morning about the badge." Greenwood said, "I sold it to a man on a tramcar for two shillings." Witness noticed that the buttons of his overcoat were missing, and pieces of thread were sticking out as though the buttons had been recently pulled off. Accused was very agitated whilst witness was making this examination. Witness said, "I would like you to wait in the waiting-room while Inspector Brown and I make some enquiries", and he was left in the charge of Detective Sergeant Crawley. Later that day witness again saw the prisoner in company with Inspector Brown, and said to him: "It is open to you to give an account of your movements on Saturday; you can do so if you like, but you must thoroughly understand that what you do say will be taken down in writing by Inspector Brown and may be used in evidence against you." Accused said, "I should like it taken down," and witness replied, "Very well, you can say what you like, and Mr Brown will write it down." He made the statement and Inspector Brown took it down. It was afterwards read to him, and the accused signed the bottom "I made this statement myself, I made it of my own free will." Witness had the statement there but would rather not read it out at that stage. After making

David Greenwood (centre) under arrest

the statement he picked up the button produced, which was lying on witness's desk beside the badge, and said, "If I say that is my button, what will it mean?" Witness said, "I cannot tell you." He said, "Well, I won't say anything then." Witness told him he should detain him pending enquiries, and he made no reply. He was detained at Cannon Row police station. About 3.30pm. on Friday he saw him there, and said, "I shall charge you with the wilful murder of Nellie Grace Trew, on February 9th, at Eltham Common." He said, "Yes". He then brought him to Woolwich police station. He was charged and made no reply.

Prisoner replied "No, sir", when asked if he had any questions to ask, and was remanded for one week.

FUNERAL

The murdered girl was buried on Saturday at Plumstead cemetery, and a huge concourse of people lined the streets along which the cortege passed. There were many wreaths, including a number sent by employees of Woolwich Arsenal, in which the deceased's father is employed.

(*Kentish Mercury*, 22 February, 1918)

Greenwood was brought up before Mr Hay Halkett at Greenwich police court on Wednesday, and after Chief Inspector Carlin's evidence had been read over he was remanded for seven days. Asked whether he had any objection to this course, prisoner said "None whatever", and so he left the dock. The prisoner's mother, addressing Inspector Carlin as he stepped from the witness box, said, "Can my boy come home with me?" and no reply being given said in pleading tones, "But my boy must come home!" Induced to leave the court, she spoke to a number of persons of her son's good qualities, and his service in the Army, and said he was incapable of such a crime as was alleged against him.

(*Kentish Mercury,* 1 March, 1918)

...Dr Spilsbury, who had made a post-mortem examination, said the girl was apparently healthy and strong. There were marks on the throat as of fingers and finger-nails, and the cause of death was asphyxia from strangulation, presumably by throttling. Considerable violence must have been used, and the girl had offered resistance. Mr Hay Halkett committed the prisoner for trial at the Central Criminal Court.

    (*West Kent Argus*, 22 March, 1918)

At the Central Criminal Court on Wednesday, David Greenwood pleaded not guilty to an indictment charging him with the murder of Nellie Trew.

Mr Travers Humphreys detailed the circumstances, which have been reported.

Dr Spilsbury asked whether a man who had been discharged from the army suffering from disordered action of the heart and subsequent fainting fits, would be likely to have caused such injuries as were found upon the girl, replied that he could not say that such a man would be unable to do so.

The trial was adjourned.

    (*West Kent Argus*, April 26, 1918)

ELTHAM COMMON MURDER
Discharged Soldier Found Guilty

The trial of David Greenwood, the young discharged soldier, on a charge of the murder of Nellie Trew, was concluded at the Central Criminal Court on Friday.

Mr Travers Humphreys for the prosecution, pointed out that his [Greenwood's] evidence was entirely different from that given by him at the inquest on March 6th. Prisoner replied that he remembered the circumstances better now than he did then.

Mr Slesser, for the defence, said that the prosecution had failed to connect the prisoner with the murder. He was a young man of excellent character, and he had never shown any tendency likely to cause him to commit so terrible a crime.

The jury, after an absence of two hours and forty minutes, found Greenwood guilty, but recommended him to mercy on account of his services to his country and of his youth.

Asked if he had anything to say, he replied "I am not guilty of this crime. I know nothing about it. I have never spoken to Nellie Trew in my life. I hope your Lordship will not take any notice of the recommendation of the jury, as it would always be a disgrace for me, and I would rather face the full penalty."

Mr Justice Atkins (addressing the prisoner) said: "You have been found guilty of a most heinous crime. You have taken your unfortunate victim's life, and for that crime there is only one penalty. At the same time I shall forward the recommendation of the jury to the proper authorities where, I have no doubt, it will receive every consideration. It is not right, however, that you should anticipate that the course of the law will necessarily be interfered with on account of that recommendation."

Sentence of death having been passed, prisoner walked out of the dock. His mother, who was in court, collapsed and was removed weeping.

Greenwood has, we understand, made an application for leave to appeal against his sentence.

    (*Kentish Mercury*, 3 May, 1918)

GREENWOOD APPEAL

The Court of Criminal Appeal has dismissed the appeal made by Frederick [sic] Greenwood against the sentence of death for the murder of Nellie Trew at Eltham Common. Mr Justice Darling, in delivering judgement, said there was evidence on which the jury could come to the conclusion at which they had arrived, provided they were properly directed by the learned Judge. The summing-up took a considerable time of a case which had lasted three days, and the Court held that there was no justification for saying that the learned Judge had misdirected the jury. Although the evidence was circumstantial, it was sufficient to justify the verdict.

The execution of Greenwood has been

fixed to take place at Wandsworth Gaol on the 31st.

(*West Kent Argus*, 24 May, 1918)

THE ELTHAM MURDER
Petition for Greenwood's Reprieve

The Rev Frank M. Smith, of Catford Central Hall Mission, 39, Culverley Road, Catford, writes: "Knowing your love of fair play and your sense of justice, I am writing to ask you to insert this letter in your widely-circulated and influential newspaper. I know there are very many of your readers who are convinced that the evidence at the trial of the young ex-soldier David Greenwood – who was discharged from the Army on account of shell-shock – wholly circumstantial, and, as they think, very unsubstantial, is insufficient to warrant the death sentence, and that the strong recommendation to mercy on the grounds of his youth, his blameless character, and his services to his country should have great weight in this momentous decision. I understand that the date of the execution is fixed for the 31st inst., and if this extreme measure be allowed to take effect there will be a large number of the public in the South-East of London, who will feel that justice has been outraged. Petitions to the Home Secretary for the reprieve of David Greenwood are being signed by thousands all over the district. I shall be glad to hear from any who are in sympathy with the case."

(*Kentish Mercury*, 24 May, 1918)

A REPRIEVE

It was announced yesterday that David Greenwood, the ex-soldier and munition worker, who was convicted for the murder of Nellie Grace Trew on Eltham Common and sentenced to be hanged, has been reprieved. The execution was fixed for today.

(*Kentish Mercury*, 31 May, 1918)

Another Victim of the Blitz
The Murder of Mrs RACHEL DOBKIN
by her Estranged Husband HARRY
on or about Friday the 11th of April 1941
and the depositing of the body in the cellar
of the Baptist Church (now demolished), Vauxhall Road, SE11

On July the 17th 1942 a workman who was helping to demolish the badly bomb-damaged Vauxhall Baptist Chapel in Vauxhall Road, Kennington (now Kennington Lane), prised up a stone slab and found beneath it a mummified body. The immediate assumption was that the remains were either of an air raid victim or had come from the old burial ground underneath the church, which had ceased to be used some fifty years before. When the church had been bombed on the 15th of October 1940 more than a hundred people had been killed in the conflagration and the area around the chapel had been the target of a number of Luftwaffe raids between that time and March of 1941. Nor was it the first body that the workers had come upon while demolishing the chapel. Nevertheless, routine was followed, and the police were called in, arriving in the persons of Detective Inspectors Hatton and Keeling, the bones being removed to Southwark Mortuary for examination by pathologist Dr Keith Simpson.

Simpson immediately suspected foul play. In trying to raise the bones, the skull had become detached and Simpson realized that the head had already been cut from the body. In addition to this, the limbs had been severed at the elbows and knees, flesh had been removed from the face, the lower jaw was missing and the bones were partially burnt. An obvious attempt had been made

The cleared cellar at the back of the Vauxhall Baptist Chapel; beneath the arrow is where the remains of Mrs Dobkin were unearthed. The photograph was taken from the point marked on the map. The back of number 302 Kennington Road can be seen in the background

to disguise the identity of the corpse. Dr Simpson obtained the permission of the coroner to take the remains back to his laboratory at Guy's Hospital for a more detailed inspection. Returning to the crypt of the church in a vain attempt to find the missing limbs, Simpson noticed a yellowish deposit in the earth, subsequently analysed as slaked lime. This had been used to suppress the smell of putrefaction, but it also had the effect of preventing maggots from destroying the body. Examining the throat and voice box, Simpson detected a blood clot, strongly indicating death due to strangulation. The

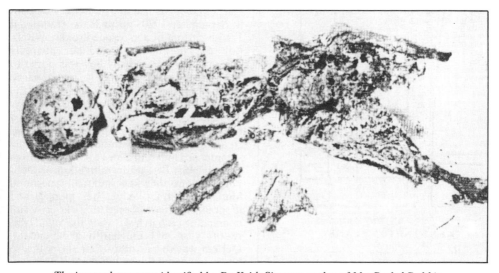

The incomplete corpse identified by Dr Keith Simpson as that of Mrs Rachel Dobkin

next task was to discover the identity of the victim. The body was that of a woman aged between forty and fifty, with dark greying hair, was five feet one inch tall, and had suffered from a fibroid tumour. Time of death was estimated at between twelve and fifteen months prior to discovery. Meanwhile the police had been checking the lists of missing persons, and noted that fifteen months previously Mrs Rachel Dobkin, estranged wife of Harry Dobkin, the fire watcher at the firm of solicitors next door to the Baptist Chapel at 302 Vauxhall Road, had disappeared. An interview with her sister elicited the information that she was about the right age, with dark greying hair, was about five feet one tall, and had a fibroid tumour. She also gave police the name of Mrs Dobkin's dentist, Barnett Kopkin of Stoke Newington, who kept meticulous records and was able to describe exactly the residual roots and fillings in her mouth. They matched the upper jaw of the skull.

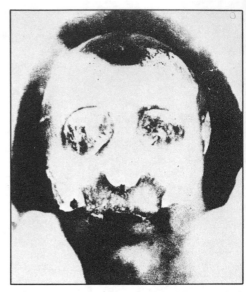

The superimposition of a negative of the unearthed skull on to a known portrait of Mrs Dobkin proving a perfect match

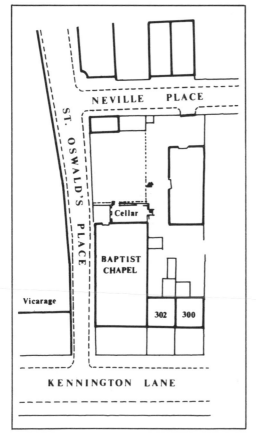

Finally, Miss Mary Newman, the head of the Photography Department at Guy's, superimposed a photograph of the skull on to a photograph of Rachel Dobkin, a technique first used six years earlier in the Buck Ruxton case [see *Murder Club Guide No.3*]. The fit was uncanny. The bones found in the crypt were the mortal remains of Mrs Rachel Dobkin.

Rachel Dubinski had married Harry Dobkin in September 1920, through the traditional Jewish custom of a marriage broker. Within three days they had separated, but unhappily nine months later a baby boy was born. In 1923 Mrs Dobkin obtained a maintenance order obliging her husband to pay for the upkeep of their child. Dobkin was always a spasmodic payer, and over the years had been imprisoned several times for defaulting. In addition, Mrs Dobkin had unsuccessfully summonsed him four times for assault. However, it must be said in mitigation of Dobkin's actions that she habitually pestered him in the street to get her money, and it should be remembered that she was still demanding cash in 1941 when the 'child' was twenty years old and hardly a dependant. Dobkin was to hint later that she was also blackmailing him over some undisclosed indiscretion at work.

On Good Friday, the 11th of April 1941, Dobkin and his wife had met in a café in Kingsland Road, Shoreditch, near to where he lived in Navarino Road, Dalston, E8. They left at 6.30 and she was never seen alive again, though he claimed that she had boarded a No.22 bus to visit her mother. Next day Rachel's sister reported her missing to the police, implicating Harry Dobkin in the process. Because of the priorities of war, Dobkin was not interviewed about the disappearance until April the 16th. On the night of the 14th a small fire had broken out in the ruined cellar of the Baptist Church. This was peculiar, because there had been no air raids and the blaze was only noticed at 3.23am by a passing policeman. When the fire brigade arrived Harry Dobkin was there, pretending to put it out. He told the constable that the fire had started at 1.30am and that he hadn't bothered to inform the authorities because there was little danger of the fire spreading. There was a serious air raid on the next night, so the incident was quickly forgotten. Dobkin was interviewed twice more about his wife's disappearance

and a description and photograph were circulated by the police but no further action was taken.

On the 26th of August 1942, Dobkin was interviewed for the first time by Chief Inspector Hatton, and escorted to the church cellar, where he vehemently denied any involvement in his wife's death. He was then arrested for her murder.

The trial of Harry Dobkin opened at the Old Bailey on the 17th of November 1942, with Mr Justice Wrottesley presiding and Mr L.A. Byrne prosecuting. Dobkin's counsel, Mr F.H. Lawton, spent most of his efforts trying vainly to challenge the identification evidence. The prisoner's appearance in the witness box left the jury unimpressed, and it took them only twenty minutes to arrive at a verdict of guilty. Before his execution Dobkin confessed to his wife's murder, claiming that she was always pestering him for money and he wanted to be rid of her for good. On the 7th of January, 1943, Harry Dobkin was hanged behind the walls of Wandsworth Prison.

Pity the Poor Convict
The Murder of THOMAS JONES
by Fellow-Convict WILLIAM COLMAN
on the 29th of August 1809
on board a Prison Hulk moored at Woolwich, SE18

WILLIAM COLMAN
A Convict on board the Hulks at Woolwich. Executed on Pennington [Penenden] Heath, 26th of March, 1810, for the Murder of a Fellow-Prisoner

At the Lent Assizes for the county of Kent, William Colman was indicted for the wilful murder of Thomas Jones, on the 29th of August 1809, in the parish of Woolwich, by giving him several stabs in the neck and breast with a knife.

The prisoner was a young man, aged only twenty, and both himself and the deceased were convicts on board the hulks at Woolwich. The case was proved by two other convicts, and the facts they stated were as follows:

A brick had a night or two before been thrown at one of the officers of the convicts, and the prisoner suspected the deceased had given the information that he was the man who had committed the offence. Being incensed at the deceased, he repeatedly swore he would be revenged. They were, however, apparently reconciled, shook hands, and drank together; the deceased also helped the prisoner into bed, as he was incommoded by being loaded with very heavy irons. It appeared, however, that the prisoner still cherished his purpose of revenge, for, after remaining in bed some time, when he supposed all about him were asleep, he softly rose and went to the place where he knew a knife was kept, which he got. He then stole to the bed of the deceased and stabbed him in the throat and breast in the most determined manner. The wounds he gave were instantly mortal. He was, however, observed to have got out of bed, and gone to the place where the knife was by the two convicts who gave evidence against him.

The jury instantly pronounced him guilty; and he suffered death on the third day after conviction.

[*See also Appendix Two to this volume,* The Prison Hulks at Woolwich]

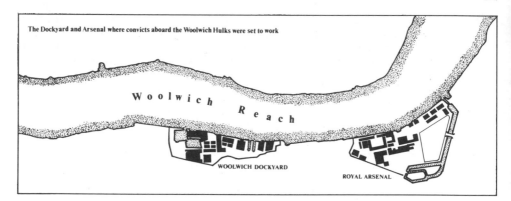

The Dockyard and Arsenal where convicts aboard the Woolwich Hulks were set to work

Woolwich Reach

WOOLWICH DOCKYARD

ROYAL ARSENAL

Starved of Affection

The Death of HARRIET STAUNTON
on Friday the 13th of April 1877
at 34 Forbes Road (now Mosslea Road), Penge, SE20
and the Trial of her Husband LOUIS, his Brother PATRICK, Mrs PATRICK STAUNTON, and ALICE RHODES for her Murder

The following account of what was at the time called The Penge Murder has been adapted from contemporary sources.

There can be no question about the nature of the crime committed by the Stauntons. They murdered by slow degrees their unhappy victim, in a cold, cruel, merciless manner... A more hideous crime has seldom figured in the annals of criminal justice. Nothing is more calculated to rouse indignation than cruelty towards a child or a woman, weak, helpless, and incapable of self-protection. In the present instance, however, the crime, horrible as it is in itself, is aggravated tenfold by the circumstances under which it was committed, and more especially by the motive. While the unhappy Harriet Staunton is being slowly done to death by inches in the abominable den in which she is confined, Louis is living in open adultery, at Little Grays, with Alice Rhodes. He has got his wife's money, and her life is now the only thing that stands in his way, and Patrick is but too ready to help his brother... Nothing, they argued among themselves, can possibly be easier than to starve the wretched woman to the point of death, and then, while the breath is still just within her body, to take her to some out-of-the-way place and get a medical man suddenly called in without any particular knowledge of the case, to give a certificate of death from natural causes...

On the 16th of June, 1875, Louis Staunton, an auctioneer's clerk, married Miss Harriet Richardson, the lady's mother having tried to prevent the marriage by applying to the Court of Chancery to place her daughter under control as a person of weak intellect. That, however, the Court refused to do, and, as we have said, the marriage took place,

Louis Staunton being twenty-four years of age and his wife thirty-five, and as there was no settlement he ultimately came into possession of £3000 – her property. The newly married couple went to live at 8 Loughborough Park Road, Brixton, and near them [at No.29] lived the husband's brother Patrick and his wife. In March, 1876, Mrs Louis Staunton was delivered of a son, and prior to that event Alice Rhodes, a girl of eighteen and a sister of Mrs Patrick, came to live with Louis Staunton. During the month that followed Harriet Staunton's confinement it was said on the evidence of a servant and a cousin of Mrs Patrick's, Clara Brown, that there were undue familiarities between Alice Rhodes and Louis Staunton, who had undoubtedly known her before. In the May following Louis and his wife removed to Gipsy Hill [No.6 Colby Road], Norwood, and it must be noted that she was then, according to the evidence of the doctor who attended her in her confinement, a well nourished and healthy woman. Mr and Mrs Patrick Staunton had, in the latter part of the same year gone to live at the Wood-

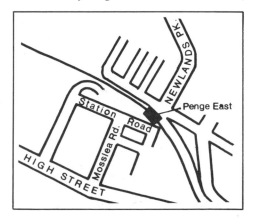

lands [now Firth Cottage] – a lonely house near Cudham, Kent – and in their charge was placed Louis Staunton's child. Not long afterwards Harriet Staunton was also placed with them by her husband, much altercation and many painful scenes having previously taken place between them. When Harriet Staunton went to the Woodlands her husband took a place called Little Gray's Farm, and there he and Alice Rhodes lived together. That was the condition of affairs until April 1877. During the time Harriet Staunton was at Woodlands she was occasionally visited by her husband. In April, Louis Staunton's child died, after a somewhat suspicious fashion, in a hospital, and

Mosslea Road], Penge, not being able at the time to walk without assistance, and being in a very feeble and emaciated condition, and there, about one o'clock the next day, she died. A certificate was given by a Dr Longrigg stating the cause of death to be apoplexy supervening upon cerebral disease, but he had only seen her when in a dying condition, and that certificate was afterwards very properly withdrawn, and an inquest being held, competent medical testimony assigned her death to starvation.

On Wednesday, September 19th, at the Old Bailey, before Mr Justice Hawkins, the prisoners, Louis Staunton, twenty-six, des-

MISS ALICE RHODES

LOUIS STAUNTON

was buried by the father, who gave an assumed name; whilst about that time Mrs Harriet Staunton's mother, who had not been on good terms with her daughter on account of her marriage, began to be uneasy and make enquiries about her, and she was thwarted and treated with much brutality by the Stauntons. It was said by them that up to that time Harriet was quite well, while the prosecution urged that, according to the evidence of Clara Brown, she had been slowly starved during nearly the whole of her residence at Woodlands. On the 12th of April Harriet Staunton was removed from the Woodlands to 34 Forbes Road [now

cribed as a farmer; Patrick Staunton, twenty-four, an artist; Elizabeth Ann Staunton, twenty-eight, married; and Alice Rhodes, twenty, spinster, were put upon their trial, on an indictment charging them with the wilful murder of Harriet Staunton...

...The trial continued from day to day, and did not conclude till a late hour on Wednesday night.

THE SCENE IN COURT

At five minutes past eleven o'clock on Wednesday night the Penge Mystery became the Penge Murder. Before ten minutes more had passed Mr Justice Hawkins had assumed the black cap, and the two brothers and the two sisters had been sentenced to death. The court had assembled at half-past ten in the morning, and from that time until thirty-eight minutes past nine, with slight intervals for refreshment on two occasions, nothing had been done but the summing-up of evidence which nearly everyone in the court knew by heart. The morning faded into the afternoon, the afternoon grew gloomy with the dusk, the night came on, and still no sound echoed through the building but the single voice of the Judge. On this seventh day of the trial the court was more crowded than ever, and strange to say more ladies

Alice Rhodes, her head bowed, never looking upon the court, and, like Louis Staunton, appearing to be stupefied with terror. There had been occasions during this miserable trial, when it required the best fortitude of all the prisoners to prevent their giving way to their pent-up feelings, and we know that on the last day but one those ladies who were present were pained to hear the hysterical shrieks of Mrs Patrick Staunton and the convulsive sobs of Alice Rhodes. But as Wednesday wore wearily along there was no such scene. Whenever any of the audience looked towards the dock with the grave Governor of Newgate Gaol in one corner, and the background of male and

than usual had taken places to gratify their curiosity. It was a strange contrast. On one side of the court, in that broad pen under the clock, sat the four miserable prisoners. Louis Staunton, pale as death, cast his eyes up at the distant window and appeared to be in a trance or a daze. He did not speak; he did not write; he did not move. In the centre of the dock, side by side, sat the husband and wife, Patrick and Mrs Patrick Staunton. Those unhappy people could scarcely have been closer, and throughout the terrible day they occupied themselves in constantly writing and conversing with desperate earnestness. At the further end of the dock was placed

female warders, their curiosity was gratified no further than to see the pale, startled face of Louis, the centre group of the unhappy husband and wife, probably conversing for the last time on earth, and at the opposite corner the bent head of Alice Rhodes. All was sad and solemn. No shrieks, or sobs, or hysterical outbursts interrupted the steady voice of the persistent Judge.

But contrast the depressing picture under the clock with that which faced the prisoners. The great sword of justice stood out against a background of crimson. The scarlet and black robes of the Judge, the blue silk and dark fur on the gowns of the Sheriffs, the gold chain of office, the bouquets of chrysanthemum lying idly on the desks, the court suits, lace ruffles, and glittering swords of the Under-Sheriffs, made, with the jewels and dresses of the ladies, young and old, who had come to see the trial, a strangely different picture from the gloomy sorrow beneath the clock. On one side shivering despair, on the other gaiety and life. This is not the place to comment on the form of curiosity which prompts women to take a deep interest in such scenes as these, to come in their Sunday best, their bracelets and their bonnets, to gaze for hours on fellow creatures trembling between life and death. There may have been no worse fault than thoughtlessness, but would it not have been well on Wednesday to hide the number of that day's *Punch*, to keep the opera glasses in the background, if they were necessary at all, and certainly to endeavour to support exhausted nature without foaming glasses of champagne, which were actually consumed in open court at luncheon time?

The day seemed interminable during the long summing up. Sometimes there came through the open window the shouting voices of the newsboys selling the various editions of the evening papers. At half-past eight o'clock the shouts became like the roar of a mob outside the prison walls; but the day wore sadly on, the clock struck hour after hour, the daylight went out, and with an illumination of gas in court Mr Justice Hawkins at six o'clock began a new series of evidence and comment.

It was not until twenty minutes to ten that the jury had retired to consider their verdict. The jury were taken out of court, the four prisoners were escorted below by their warders, the Judge went out with the Sheriffs, and the anxious ladies who had remained bravely at their posts were prepared to discuss with their companions the probabilities of the verdict. All who are familiar with the procedure of criminal courts know the buzz of relief which occurs after the suspension of a long sitting. There is a chattering in the court, the members of the Bar stretch themselves and talk to their friends, and those curious people who make it a point to attend at every *cause célèbre* have an opportunity of airing their strangely acquired information. So the time wears away until

Mrs Harriet Staunton (née Richardson)

the clock strikes eleven. But at five minutes past eleven young Mr Poland of the Treasury, bustles into court, and instinctively everyone feels that the jury are coming back. A buzz of expectancy passes along the bar benches. Seats are resumed. The Judge is fetched into court. "Silence" is emphatically proclaimed, and once more the two brothers and the two sisters are in the front row of the dock. There is no sitting now. They must all stand and hear the verdict pronounced upon them. Louis, still ashy pale, looks as if he were in a stupor and gazes unmoved. Patrick trembles like a leaf, and, as he has done on every day of the trial, looks behind him pitifully and pleadingly for his wife. Once she is by his side he seems more consoled. The two women, half stooping and shrinking from the look of the court and the eyes of the women round and about them at every corner, stand by the side of the men. The dock is now full. The warders have been doubled and trebled, and it requires all the kindly assistance of the Governor, Mr Smith, and all the attention of every one concerned, to prevent Patrick and his wife from falling. It is a dreadful moment, and the suspense is painful. Once again the names of the jurymen are called over, and each one answers. Then, after another "Silence!", the Clerk of the Arraigns speaks: "How say you, gentlemen, is Louis Staunton guilty of the murder with which he stands charged?" The Foreman's voice trembles, "Guilty."

"Is Patrick Staunton guilty of the murder with which he stands charged?" "Guilty." "Is Elizabeth Ann Staunton guilty of the murder with which she stands charged?" "Guilty." There was a shudder at this announcement. "Is Alice Rhodes guilty of the murder with which she stands charged?" "Guilty." At the last sentence there is an exclamation of "Oh!" a sudden sharp murmur of pity which runs instantly round the court. All eyes are fixed on the miserable creatures in the dock. The murmur of commiseration grows so loud that the recommendation to mercy of the women is scarcely heard. And now Alice Rhodes has fainted in the dock. With a piteous moan she has fallen into the arms of the attendants, and has been gently placed on a chair. "I will, I will," murmurs Mrs Patrick Staunton to her husband. He has implored her for his sake

to be firm, and she is acting bravely. Still Louis Staunton gazes upon the Court as if in a dream. Still Patrick Staunton positively shivers. How long will that unhappy woman bear up? Her sister is moaning in a fainting fit, and smelling salts are being administered; and whilst the old-fashioned cry of the usher, "Oyez, oyez, oyez," asks why sentence of death should not be pronounced, and the Judge sternly comments on the enormity of the offence, the two brothers and the sisters stand at the bar. Patrick Staunton grasps his wife's hand; he presses it intensely and affectionately. Again she murmurs she will be firm, but at the mention of death her strength succumbs, and with one pitiful cry, "O, give me a chair," she sinks by the side of her sister in a swoon. And now the two brothers are left standing to hear the sentence of death pronounced. Before the

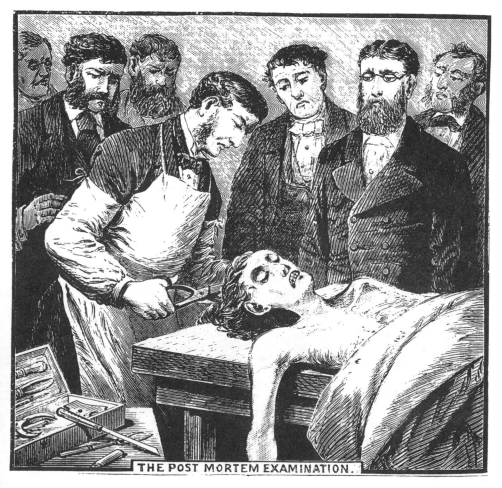

THE POST MORTEM EXAMINATION.

dreadful words are over, Patrick, remembering, no doubt, their old affection, has slipped his hand into his brother's as much as to say that if "they were not lovely and pleasant in their lives," still that in "death they are not divided," but Louis Staunton, pale as hewn marble, neither trembles nor falters, nor looks at his brother, nor turns towards poor Alice Rhodes as she lies fainting in the corner, but simply gazes across the crowded court into vacancy. As we look amid the huddled crowd of warders, fainting women, and pale men condemned to death, they are asked if they have anything to say against the coming execution. Mr Sidney Smith, the Governor of the gaol, answers for the women, No; but Alice Rhodes, recovered for an instant, answers for herself, "Only that I am innocent." Louis and Patrick Staunton say nothing.

Outside the court a dense crowd remained for several hours, in anxious expectancy to know the result. The appearance was precisely such as used to be presented on the eve of an execution of some notorious murderer in times gone by, when such scenes were public.* The thoroughfare was almost

* The last public execution, that of Michael Barrett [see this volume], took place on the 26th of May, 1868.

MAIDSTONE GAOL

blocked by the vast throng, which was only dispersed when, at a few minutes past eleven o'clock, tidings came from the court that all four prisoners had been found guilty of murder and sentenced to death.

At about six o'clock on the following morning, the prisoners were removed to Maidstone gaol where the brothers were at once placed in the condemned cell, and the two women were removed to the female wards.**

** But this was not the end of the Staunton Case. The trial – which had consisted mostly of medical evidence – was to continue long after Mr Justice Hawkins's death sentence and the removal of the prisoners to Maidstone Gaol.

The medical controversy, begun in the Old Bailey and resumed now in a wider arena, revolved around the two possible causes for Harriet Staunton's death. The first was the initially accepted view of the post-mortem doctors, that Harriet had succumbed to neglect and starvation – her emaciated body giving eloquent confirmation of this opinion. However, Mr (later Sir) Edward Clarke defending Patrick Staunton, put on the witness stand Dr J.S. Bristowe, an expert on morbid anatomy, who deposed that Harriet Staunton's symptoms were also shared by tuberculosis, an opinion endorsed by a Dr Payne who agreed that the state of Harriet's body could be due either to starvation or to tubercular meningitis.

Despite the judge's clear summing up in favour of starvation, and the jury's concurrence, there was sufficient agitation in medical circles to cause a petition to be drawn up by some seven hundred doctors headed by no less a celebrity than Sir William Jenner, one of the Queen's physicians. They stated clearly their belief that Drs Bristowe and Payne were correct; the post-mortem findings were consistent with tubercular disease.

In October 1877 the Home Secretary bowed to this eminent pressure, and the Stauntons' sentences were commuted to various terms of imprisonment; Alice Rhodes was released.

But even that did not completely close the Staunton file. In 1921, Sir Bernard Spilsbury had the last word on the case; with the benefit of forty years' hindsight and the dramatic development of the science of pathology, he stated categorically to a meeting of the Medico-Legal Society: "The findings [of the post-mortem] were overwhelmingly in favour of *starvation* being the cause of Harriet Staunton's death".

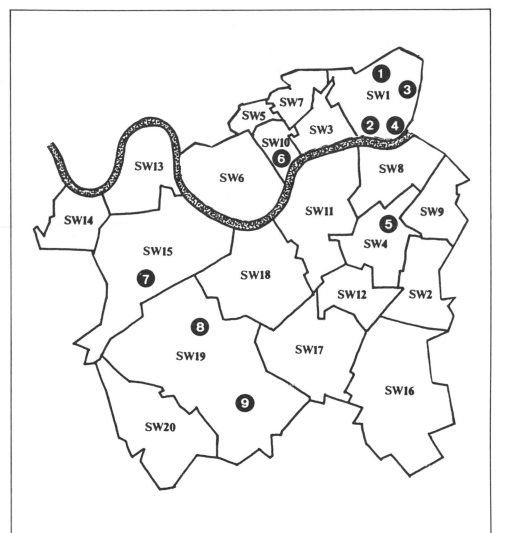

South-West London

1. PHILIP, Earl of Pembroke and Montgomery.................................. 102
2. John BELLINGHAM 104
3. Adelaide BARTLETT 107
4. John ROBINSON 111
5. Stinie MORRISON 113
6. Ronald TRUE 118
7. Daniel GOOD... 121
8. Dr George LAMSON 124
9. George BRAIN 126

One Law for the Rich...

The Murder of NATHANIEL CONY, Gentleman
by PHILIP HERBERT,
EARL OF PEMBROKE AND MONTGOMERY
on the 4th of February 1678
in *Long's House* (now demolished) in the Haymarket, SW1

PHILIP, EARL OF PEMBROKE AND MONTGOMERY

Tried for the Murder of Nathaniel Cony by his Brother Peers in 1678 and found guilty of Manslaughter later

An indictment for murder against a peer which necessitated his being tried by his brother peers occurred in 1678, the accused being Philip, Earl of Pembroke and Montgomery, and the dead man Nathaniel Cony, gentleman.

The Lords came from their House above, in their usual order, to the court erected for them in Westminster Hall; and the Lord High Steward's commission being read, as also the certiorari to the commissioners, before whom the indictment was found, and the return thereof, the Constable of the Tower being a peer, Sir John Robinson, his lieutenant, brought the Earl of Pembroke to the bar; after which the Lord High Steward made a speech to the prisoner, wherein he acquainted him that he stood charged with no less a crime than murder by the grand jury of the county of Middlesex, who were all men of quality; but that this was no more than an accusation, upon which their Lordships should not prejudge him, the examination of the grand jury having been but partial. That his lordship was now to be tried in full Parliament, and not by a select number of Lords. That he being made a spectacle to such august assembly, and having his faults and weaknesses exposed, must be very mortifying; and it behoved his lordship to recollect himself, and use the utmost caution in his defence, but advised him not to let the disgrace of standing as a felon at the bar too much deject him,

or the terrors of justice amaze him; for whatever might lawfully be hoped for, his lordship might expect from the peers; and if he were dismayed, when he considered how inexorable the rule of law was in the case of blood (which their Lordships indeed could not depart from) yet it might be a support to him to consider that nothing but plain and positive proof, and such as deserved to be called evidence, would be received against him. That their Lordships thought themselves bound in honour to be counsel for him in matters of law; and that, though there were counsel to plead against him, no skill or arguments could pervert their Lordships' justice. He should not fall by the charms of eloquence, or be depressed by anything but the burden of his crime and even as to that all candid allowances would be made.

Then the prisoner was arraigned and held up his hand.

Mr Richard Savage deposed that, being in company with my Lord Pembroke at Mr Long's in the Haymarket on 4th of February 1678, and Mr Cony making a great noise at the bar, my lord looked out at the door of the room where they were and seeing Mr Cony invited him and his friend Mr Goring into the room, and after some time falling into discourse, Mr Goring used some impertinent language to my lord, and told his lordship he was as good or a better gentleman than he; upon which my lord threw a glass of wine in Goring's face, and stepped back and drew his sword; and Goring being about to draw his, the deponent [Richard Savage] took it from him and broke it, and persuaded my lord to put up his sword again; but to prevent more words, the deponent shoved Mr Goring out of the room, and while the deponent was thrusting him out he heard a bustle behind him, and, leaving the drawer to keep Mr Goring out, he turned, and saw my Lord Pembroke strike Mr Cony, who immediately fell down, and then my lord gave him a kick; and then, finding Mr Cony did not stir, my lord and the deponent took him off the ground and laid him on the chairs, and covered him up warm.

The Attorney-General: Did my lord kick him but once?
Savage: My lord kicked him but once that I saw, and that was on the body, and not with a very great force. We chafed his temples, and he opened his eyes, but did not speak; when I asked him if he knew me he shook his head as if he did, and then closed his eyes again.
The Attorney-General: What condition was he in before the accident?
Savage: He was very drunk, and, I think, proposed something about play to my lord; but how my lord came to strike him I cannot tell, for I was putting Goring out of the room.

Similar evidence and evidence as to the dead man's internal injuries having been given, the Lord High Steward asked: Will your lordship say anything for yourself?
Earl of Pembroke: I have nothing more to say, my Lord.

Mr Solicitor having summed up the evidence for the King, the Lords went to their House above, and after two hours' debate returned, and having taken their places, the Lord High Steward, beginning with the puisne baron (my Lord Butler), demanded of their Lordships severally in their order if Philip, Earl of Pembroke and Montgomery, were guilty of the felony of murder whereof he stood indicted, or not guilty. And my Lord High Steward having numbered them, declared that six of their Lordships had found the prisoner guilty, eighteen had found him not guilty, and forty had found him guilty of manslaughter. Then the prisoner was commanded to be brought to the bar again, and the Lord High Steward acquainted him that the judgement of the Lords was, that he was guilty of manslaughter; and demanded what he could say why judgement should not pass upon him to die, according to law.

The Earl of Pembroke answered that he claimed the privilege of the statute.

The Lord High Steward told him he must have it; for as by the Act of Clergy was allowed to a commoner by reading and burning in the hand*, a peer convicted of such felony was to be delivered without either; but his lordship would do well to take notice that no man could have the benefit of that statute but once.

_____
* See Appendix Four

A Chronology of the Life and Infamies of Philip Earl of Pembroke and Montgomery

Jan 1653	Born, the son of Philip Herbert, 5th Earl of Pembroke & Montgomery and his second wife, Catherine Villiers.
1661	Created a Knight of the Bath.
June 1674	Succeeded his half-brother as 7th Earl.
July 1674	Nearly died after being run through twice in a duel with Bernard Howard.
Dec 1674	Married Henriette Mauricette, sister of the Duchess of Portsmouth, the King's mistress.
April 1675	Took his seat in the House of Lords.
May 1675	Appointed Lord Lieutenant of Wiltshire, a post usually offered to the Earls of Pembroke.
Sept 1675	Threatened with the wrath of the King by the Duchess of Portsmouth for neglecting his pregnant wife, who later gave birth to a daughter.
April 1676	Attacked in a tavern by Sir Francis Vincent after threatening members of a jury which had just given judgement in a lawsuit against a kinsman. Wounded Sir George Hewitt in the arm during a duel.

May 1676	Accosted Lord Duras in St James Park and ran his sword twice through the drapes of his Sedan chair, just missing his Lordship.
Nov 1676	Quarrelled with a Mr Vaughan at *Locketts*, a fashionable eating place. Ran Vaughan through with his sword in a duel after the unfair intervention of his henchmen. Vaughan's fate unknown.
25 Dec 1677	Terrorised a clergyman into getting drunk. Committed to the Tower of Lond for blasphemy.
30 Jan 1678	Released by a warrant of the House of Lords on the grounds of insufficient evidence.
3 Feb 1678	Attacked Nathaniel Cony after an argument in *Long's House*, a tavern in the Haymarket. [See text above.]
5 Feb 1678	Philip Ricault reported an attack on him by Pembroke to the House of Lords. Pembroke bound over to keep the peace for a year on a recognizance of £2000.
10 Feb 1678	Nathaniel Cony died.
4 Apr 1678	Tried for murder before the House of Lords. Found guilty of manslaughter. Pleaded Benefit of Clergy to avoid punishment. All lands and money automatically forfeited.
5 Apr 1678	Lands and money restored by a warrant of King Charles.
Nov 1678	Attacked the Earl of Dorset in *Locketts*. Confined to his country seat, Wilton, for a short period.
5 Dec 1678	Murdered a man in Aylesbury. Went unpunished because of influence.
Jan 1680	Unsuccessful attempt made on Pembroke's life with a pistol at the Haymarket Theatre. Another man killed.
19 Aug 1680	Killed a constable, William Smeeth, with a sword after a fight at Turnham Green, while travelling from Windsor to London with three companions in a Hackney coach. Indicted for murder by a Middlesex jury. Fled to Paris.
8 May 1681	A petition for a royal pardon presented by 22 Whig peers to the King.
22 June 1681	A royal pardon granted by the King.
May 1683	Wife fled abroad to escape Pembroke. Entered a monastery in Paris.
Aug 1683	Died of excessive drink and debauchery. Buried in Salisbury Cathedral.

The Abhorrent Alternative
The Assassination of Prime Minister SPENCER PERCEVAL by JOHN BELLINGHAM
on the 11th of May 1812 in the Lobby of the House of Commons, SW1

On the evening of the 11th of May 1812 a furtive figure took up position in the House of Commons just behind the folding-doors which lead into the body of the House. At five o'clock the Right Honourable Spencer Perceval, Prime Minister and First Lord of the Treasury, advanced up the lobby; as he did so the shadows parted and a hidden assassin stepped out and aimed a pistol squarely at Perceval's heart; his aim had been perfect and the Prime Minister staggered and fell, moaning in a low tone, "Murder!" Just behind him were Lord Osborne, and Mr W.Smith, Member for Norwich, who lifted their fellow into the office of the Speaker's secretary, where the injured man expired.

The shot had attracted a strong body of people into the Lobby, and a cry rose "Shut the door; let no one out!", "Where's the murderer?" "Who was the rascal that did it?"

At that moment the stranger, still holding a pistol in his hand, advanced through the crowd and calmly announced, "I am the unfortunate man", and surrendered himself into the hands of a group of Members, who searched his person to reveal another pistol, loaded and primed, and a bundle of letters and papers.

When he had been conveyed to the bar of the House before the Speaker and Members for interrogation, it was General Gascoyne, Member for Liverpool, who identified the villain: "Is your name not John Bellingham?" The man nodded assent, and continued in his silence. The inquiry discovered that Bellingham had lately been a frequent visitor to the Commons, lurking in the corridors and public galleries, making inquiries as to the names of various Members, and scrutinizing

The Right Honourable Spencer Perceval; a portrait painted from his death-mask

the assembled House through a pair of opera glasses. Gascoyne gave evidence that his knowledge of the prisoner was as the result of receiving a number of petitions and memoranda from him, outlining a catalogue of grievances against the Government as the result of some real or imagined injustices suffered in Russia.

In his early working life, Bellingham had travelled in the service of a Russian merchant to the town of Archangel, where he remained for three years. On his return he married a Miss Nevill and, being a man ambitious for his future, he shortly afterwards, in 1804, removed once again to Archangel on business, taking his new bride with him. As the result of a complicated commercial dispute – for which he appears to have carried no special blame – Bellingham's anticipated short-term trip ended with the confiscation of his exit visa, and his virtual imprisonment during the succeeding five years. To complicate matters, the unlucky man also had an award made against him of two thousand roubles to be paid to the other party in the dispute. Whether at the request of the British ambassador, or whether the Russians finally gave up the prospect of ever getting their two thousand roubles, Bellingham was repatriated in 1809. Back in Liverpool he commenced in the

John Bellingham

business of insurance-broker; it appears, however, that his experiences in Russia would not leave him, and eventually unbalanced his reason. He began to write letters of accusation to the Privy Council, demanding compensation for what he saw as the misconduct of Lord Granville Leveson Gower, the ambassador in Russia, for not defending his rights as a British subject. These letters were ultimately passed on to the Treasury and the attention of Spencer Perceval. That gentleman presumably detected a hint of madness in the matter and, unwisely for him as it turned out, decided to ignore it. Bellingham's next line of attack was via General Gascoyne, his local MP, who took his lead from the Chancellor and refused to have anything to do with it. The Prince Regent referred *his* correspondence back to the Treasury, and it was once more made clear that neither the government nor the Crown were inclined to positive action.

These futile fusillades had now occupied three years, so Bellingham decided upon a singular and unprecedented mode of attack;

he wrote to the police magistrates at Bow Street:

> Sirs, – I much regret it being my lot to have to apply to your worships under most peculiar and novel circumstances. For the particulars of the case I refer to the enclosed letter of Mr Secretary Ryder, the notification from Mr Perceval, and my petition to Parliament, together with the printed papers herewith. The affair requires no further remark than that I consider his Majesty's Government to have completely endeavoured to close the door of justice, in declining to have, or even permit, my grievances to be brought before Parliament for redress, which privilege is the birthright of every individual. The purport of the present is, therefore, once more to solicit his Majesty's Ministers, through your medium, to let what is right and proper be done in my instance, which is all I require. Should this reasonable request be finally denied, I shall then feel justified in executing justice myself – in which case I shall be

ready to argue the merits of so reluctant a measure with his Majesty's Attorney-General, wherever and whenever I may be called upon to do so. In the hopes of averting so abhorrent but compulsive an alternative I have the honour to be, sirs, your very humble and obedient servant,

John Bellingham

9 New Millman Street,
March 23, 1812.

And indeed, John Bellingham did feel compelled to the abhorrent alternative, and did have his opportunity to argue the merits of his case. It took place at the Old Bailey on the 15th of May, 1812, before Lord Chief Justice Mansfield. In terms of the quantity and quality of attendance at the Court, Bellingham could not have asked for better; a contemporary describes how "The judges at ten o'clock took their seats on each side of the Lord Mayor; and the recorder, the Duke of Clarence, the Marquis Wellesley and almost all the aldermen of the City of London occupied the bench. The Court was crowded to excess, and no distinction of rank was observed, so that Members of the House of Commons were forced to mingle with the throng. There were also present a great number of ladies, all led by the most intense curiosity to behold the assassin, and to hear what he might urge in defence or palliation of his atrocious act".

But Bellingham's cause was, as it always had been, a lost one; even his counsel's last-ditch defence of insanity was dismissed by a judge who – interestingly anticipating the McNaghten Rules a generation away – asked the jury to consider whether the prisoner possessed the facility to distinguish good from evil, right from wrong. [see *Murder Club Guide No.3* for a discussion on the McNaghten Rules]

After only fourteen minutes the jury came to the conclusion that John Bellingham knew quite well what he was about when he assassinated Spencer Perceval; and he was ordered for execution on the following Monday.

It is recorded that Bellingham ascended the scaffold "with rather a light step, a cheerful countenance and a confident, calm, but not exulting air"; he descended with rather more speed and a little less grace, and his body was carried in a cart, "followed by a crowd of the lower class", to St Bartholomew's Hospital for private dissection.

The Most Intimate Relations of Men and Women

The Death of EDWIN BARTLETT
on the First of January 1886
at 85 Claverton Street (now demolished), SW1

And the Trial of his Wife ADELAIDE
and her Lover the Reverend GEORGE DYSON for his Murder

The cruel exposure of private lives and intimate relationships that occurs when a murderer is brought before the courts has always been a source of fascination to the watching public. The revelation of what goes on behind the door across the street, especially if it is behind the façade of outward respectability, is irresistible. The Victorians, who are held (for no very good reason) to have been the guardians of popular morality were neither better nor worse than we are today in this respect.

The Bartlett case contained all the ingredients of a classic scandal in plentiful measure, for the relationship that developed between Edwin Bartlett, his wife Adelaide, and the young Methodist minister George Dyson was a truly curious one.

Adelaide Blanche de la Tremouille was born in Orléans in 1856, the natural daughter of a wealthy Englishman then living in France, and was brought over to England as a child. The year 1875 found her lodged in

Kingston, in the same house as a young man named Frank Bartlett. There she and her father met Frank's elder brother, Edwin, a grocer who owned a chain of six shops in South London. Within a very short time a marriage had been arranged by Adelaide's father between herself and Edwin, who was ten years her senior; the prospective husband being offered financial help with his business as a part of the settlement. Like many self-made men, Edwin Bartlett had an over-developed respect for the value of education and determined that his young wife should have the benefits that he had lacked. Consequently, Adelaide was dispatched to a school in Stoke Newington for the next three years and thence to a convent in Belgium for twelve months; at the same time undertaking the duties of a wife during the holidays.

Adelaide's education completed, at least temporarily, the Bartletts moved into a flat above one of Edwin's shops in Station Road, Herne Hill, being joined there by the husband's recently widowed father. It transpired that this combination did not lead to a happy household, Mr Bartlett senior considering Adelaide rather too forward in her behaviour, even accusing her of being over-familiar with Edwin's brother, Frank. The outcome of this was Frank's departure for America, a formal written apology from the old man to Adelaide at Edwin's insistence, and a change of accommodation to a flat above another grocer's shop in Lordship Lane, Dulwich, where there was no room for the father.

On the face of it, the Bartletts seemed a happy couple, with Edwin an indulgent, even doting, husband. From the evidence that later came out in court, it seems that Edwin held rather eccentric views on marriage. He believed, for example, that a man should have two wives, one for intellectual companionship and the other for what he termed 'use'. Adelaide, it seemed, served the first function and claimed that she only had sexual contact with her husband on one occasion, this led to an uncomfortable pregnancy and miscarriage in 1881, and she was not encouraged to try the experiment again.

In 1883 the couple decided to move to what was then the country, to a house in

Phipps Bridge Road, Merton. There they met the young minister of the local Wesleyan Chapel, the Reverend Mr George Dyson. All three seemed to get on famously and it was soon decided that Dyson should visit the house to give Adelaide some further tutoring in history, geography, mathematics and Latin. Adelaide and Dyson were thus thrown together alone for large parts of the day, with the predictable result that an inappropriate degree of affection soon grew between the two of them. Dyson was even moved to compose sentimental verses to send to his love.

> Who is it that hath burst the door
> Unclosed the heart that shut before
> And set her queenlike on its throne
> And made its homage all her own –
> My Birdie.

Edwin Bartlett for his part seemed positively to encourage the relationship, going so far as to write to thank Dyson for sending his wife a love letter. It seemed to please him that the pair should kiss in his presence, go for walks together in public and spend long hours in one another's company. In August 1885 the Bartletts took a holiday at Dover. Mr Bartlett paid for a first-class return ticket for Dyson to join them. During the holiday Edwin went up to London and made a will. Dyson was a joint executor, Adelaide the main beneficiary with no stipulations – which were then common – about her remarriage. Bartlett told them both what he had done, and that he would be pleased to think they might marry if anything should happen to him. They were, it would seem, more or less engaged.

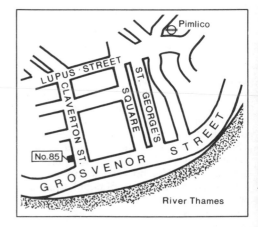

In October the Bartletts decided to move again, this time back into the centre of London, taking rooms in the house of Mr and Mrs Dogget at 85 Claverton Street, Pimlico. Though it was more difficult for Dyson to visit from Merton, he was still in fairly regular attendance. Soon after this, however, Dyson moved his ministry to a Methodist church in Putney, a far more convenient location, and Edwin Bartlett paid for his season ticket up to Pimlico.

Edwin had always been blessed with the most robust health, apart from a little tooth trouble, but on December the 8th, 1885, he

to gradually improve and Leach arranged for him to visit a dentist for the removal of several abscessed teeth, which could not have been helping his condition.

During this period Adelaide had been nursing her husband with the utmost devotion, staying by his bedside, sleeping in a chair next to him at night and holding his toe, a curious comfort which seemed to calm Mr Bartlett. The Rev. Dyson continued to call regularly, each time dropping in to pay his respects to the patient. On one visit Mrs Bartlett made the unusual request that he should obtain some chloroform for her,

Adelaide Bartlett

The Reverend George Dyson

was taken ill and the local medic, Dr Alfred Leach, was summoned. The symptoms were perplexing; he had a pain in his side, intermittent diarrhoea and intestinal haemorrhaging and, most curiously, a blue line round the edge of his gums. He was also very exhausted and depressed. This caused the perceptive doctor to consider mercury poisoning, but after learning that his patient had taken a mysterious pill a week previously he concluded that, if toxic it was, then Bartlett must have been poisoned accidentally. Over the next few days Edwin seemed

which she said she used to relieve her husband's pains and was embarrassed to ask the doctor for. This Dyson agreed to, obtaining the drug in small quantities from three chemists in Putney and Wimbledon, with the excuse that he needed it to remove some stains from clothes, he then poured the supply into one large bottle to give to Adelaide.

On Thursday, December 31st, Edwin Bartlett again visited the dentist and seemed generally to be in better spirits. At four o'clock the next morning, however, Adelaide was knocking wildly on the door of her landlord, Mr Dogget – who by coincidence was the local Registrar of Deaths – explaining that she thought her husband had expired. The doctor was called and the fact confirmed. Edwin Bartlett had been dead for more than two hours. Adelaide's story was that she had fallen asleep at his bedside and awoken to find him lying face down and apparently dead. She had turned him over and tried to revive him with brandy, then ran for help. Edwin's father was sent for, and took an understandably suspicious view of developments, demanding of the doctor that a post-mortem be carried out.

The results left little doubt as to the cause of death. Edwin Bartlett had been murdered; poisoned with a large dose of chloroform.

Now chloroform is a strong poison, but it has rarely been the cause of death, and certainly not of murder, because it so inflames and burns the internal organs that it would be excruciatingly painful, not to say impossible, to drink. The inexplicable fact about Edwin Bartlett's death was that while his stomach reeked of chloroform, his throat and digestive passages were not in the least inflamed. To this day no satisfactory explanation has been put forward as to how this could be achieved; it remains the enigma of the Bartlett case.

At this point the activities of Adelaide and George Dyson became highly suspicious. She took the bottle of chloroform that Dyson had obtained for her from where it had stood on the bedside table at Claverton Street and tipped its contents out of the window of a train between London Bridge and Peckham Rye. Dyson disposed of the three small bottles in his possession somewhere on Wandsworth Common.

At the inquest into Edwin Bartlett's death the jury, no doubt scandalized by what they would have seen as the immoral goings on within the Bartlett household, were predisposed to take a stern view of events, and returned a verdict that Bartlett had died of chloroform administered by his wife for the purpose of taking his life, and that George Dyson had been an accessory before the fact.

The trial of Adelaide Bartlett and the Rev. George Dyson opened at the Old Bailey on

ESOTERIC

ANTHROPOLOGY

(THE MYSTERIES OF MAN):

A COMPREHENSIVE AND CONFIDENTIAL TREATISE ON THE
STRUCTURE, FUNCTIONS, PASSIONAL ATTRACTIONS, AND
PERVERSIONS, TRUE AND FALSE PHYSICAL AND
SOCIAL CONDITIONS, AND THE MOST INTIMATE
RELATIONS OF MEN AND WOMEN.

ANATOMICAL, PHYSIOLOGICAL, PATHOLOGICAL,
THERAPEUTICAL, AND OBSTETRICAL;

HYGIENIC AND HYDROPATHIC.

From the American Stereotype Edition, Revised and Rewritten.

By T. L. NICHOLS, M.D., F.A.S.,

Principal of the American Hydropathic Institute; Author of "Human
Physiology the Basis of Sanitary and Social Science."

MALVERN:
PUBLISHED BY T. L. NICHOLS.

The sex manual found at the Bartlett house in Claverton Street. Until well into the second quarter of the present century such books were obliged to masquerade as 'Anthropology', and were invariably credited to a medical doctor

the 12th of April 1886, before Mr Justice Wills. The prosecution was led by the Attorney-General, Sir Charles Russell. Dyson was defended by Mr Frank Lockwood, and Adelaide had a team of counsel led by Mr Edward Clarke. There was an immediate sensation. The Crown offered no evidence against George Dyson and he was formally acquitted. It is true that the evidence against him was weak and circumstantial, but the main consideration had been that a defendant could not at that time give evidence; and the prosecution badly needed Dyson's evidence to convict Adelaide Bartlett.

The trial, predictably, created much public interest, mainly due to the curious relationship between Edwin Bartlett and his wife. Much was made of the only book that was found in the flat in Claverton Street, a medical manual on the sexual relations between man and wife and family planning. Then there was the discovery of six contraceptive devices in Edwin Bartlett's trousers pocket and Adelaide Bartlett's quite desperate last-gasp explanation that she had obtained the chloroform to cool her husband's unwelcome ardour. This was to say nothing of her unconventional relationship with the Reverend Mr Dyson, over which the judge seemed particularly outraged.

Nevertheless, there were many inconsistencies in the Crown's case. They could not explain, for example, how the poison could have been administered. Mrs Bartlett had been more than devoted in nursing her husband and he was aware of, and seemed to approve of, all the so-called scandalous goings on in the household. Edward Clarke made a memorable six-hour speech in Adelaide Bartlett's defence which seemed to seal the matter. When the jury returned the foreman did not answer yea or nay to the clerk's traditional inquiry, but read a statement –

"Although we think that there is the gravest suspicion attaching to the prisoner, we do not think there is sufficient evidence to show how or by whom the chloroform was administered."

Adelaide Bartlett had been found not guilty.

In popular fiction, Adelaide would no doubt have married George Dyson; but she did not. She changed her name, and was heard of no more. The epitaph was left to the celebrated surgeon Sir James Paget, who attended the trial. "Mrs Bartlett", he declared, "was no doubt properly acquitted. But now it is to be hoped that, in the interests of science, she will tell us how she did it!"

[See Appendix Two to this volume for a note on Chloroform as a poison.]

The Charing Cross Trunk Murder
The Murder of MINNIE ALICE BONATI
by JOHN ROBINSON
on Thursday the 5th of May 1927
at 86 Rochester Row, SW1
and the depositing of her Body in a
Trunk at Charing Cross Station

It was a common enough transaction. An everyday occurrence; all in a day's work for Mr Glass. The trunk that was passed to him across the counter of the left-luggage office at Charing Cross station was ordinary enough as well – round-topped, of wickerwork covered with black canvas, and bound with a business-like leather strap.

The date was May 6th, a Friday in 1927; the respectable-looking owner of the trunk, who looked as though he might have seen military service abroad, had arrived in a taxi-cab, and in a taxi-cab he had departed, leaving strict instructions for the safe keeping of his piece of luggage.

By Monday morning the trunk was seeming less ordinary, more – noticeable. It became difficult to escape the offensive, all-pervading smell that seemed to originate from within it. And when a policeman was summoned to oversee the investigation of the trunk and its contents, it was found to be a very unusual item of baggage indeed. Unlike most of its kind, this trunk had, wrapped up in the usual clothing, five brown paper parcels. Each of these five parcels contained a dismembered part of a female body.

According to strict – though in this case rather inappropriate – procedure, a police surgeon was summoned to certify that the woman was dead before her remains could be removed to the mortuary, and thence into the capable hands and experienced analytical mind of Sir Bernard Spilsbury, pathologist to the Home Office. Despite the onset of putrefaction, when Spilsbury had pieced together the remains in the trunk he had most of the body of a short, plump woman of about thirty-five. She had been dead for perhaps a week, and the cause of death had been asphyxia. Extensive bruising on the body suggested that she had been beaten unconscious before being suffocated.

Armed with such clues as they could gather from the trunk and its grisly contents, the police began their laborious search – first for the identity of the victim, and then for that of her killer. The initials "FA" and the label "F Austin; to St Leonards" referred to a previous – and quite innocent – owner of the luggage. There was more success, though, with the name-tag "P. Holt" on a pair of knickers found in the trunk.

Although Mrs Holt clearly had no personal connection with the tragedy, there was some likelihood that one of her many previous employees had stolen the undergarment; and so proved to be the case. Mrs Holt identified the remains as a woman known to her as Rolls, in reality Minnie Alice Bonati, thirty-six years old, a prostitute, and last seen alive in Chelsea in the late afternoon of May the 4th.

Meanwhile the publicity which such cases inevitably attract was now beginning to produce favourable results in terms of hard evidence. The trunk itself had been recognized by a Brixton second-hand dealer who remembered selling it to a well-dressed mili-

The round-topped trunk deposited by John Robinson at Charing Cross left-luggage counter

tary-looking gentleman. A shoe-shine boy had turned up with a left-luggage ticket which he had seen dropped out of a taxi window; and the taxi driver himself came forward to add the information that some time after mid-day on Friday the 6th he had deposited two young men at Rochester Row police station, SW1, and on the return had been hailed by a gentleman standing with a heavy trunk in the doorway of No.86 Rochester Row, just opposite the police station. Both man and trunk were destined for Charing Cross station.

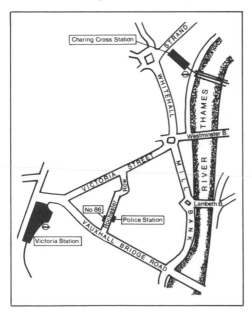

A routine investigation of the offices at 86 Rochester Row revealed that one of the occupants of the rather run-down office suites – John Robinson, trading as "Edwards and Co. Business Transfer Agents" – had not been seen around for several days. He had disappeared from his lodgings in Kennington too, though by one of those pieces of luck on which even the most experienced detectives rely, they found a telegram addressed "Robinson, *Greyhound Hotel*, Hammersmith". The Robinson named was not John but his bigamously married wife (the bigamy was a fact of which she was unaware, and understandably not overjoyed to find out) from whom he was now estranged, and who worked at the *Greyhound*. The man who accompanied 'Mrs Robinson' when she next met her husband was Chief Inspector George Cornish; the same gentleman who took Robinson back to Scotland Yard with him to stand in an identity parade.

Thirty-six-year-old Robinson, of course, denied all knowledge of Minnie Bonati let alone of her murder, and as if to lend credence to his story, neither the taxi driver, the railway porter, nor Ward, the second-hand dealer from Brixton, were able to pick him out of the identity parade.

However, the police had not left the Robinson trail yet. In the wake of the senior officers, the more painstaking job of combing the Rochester Row office was taking place, and the search produced a bloodstained match caught in the wicker-work of the waste basket. It proved to be the one clue necessary to break Robinson's confidence; enough to force him to make a statement which, however untrue it was in detail, associated him with the death of Minnie Bonati. Minnie, he told the police, had propositioned him at Victoria station; back at the office, she had become abusive, demanding money and threatening violence, they struggled, the woman fell, knocking herself unconscious on a coal-bucket and in a panic Robinson fled the building. No-one was more shocked next morning, he said, to find the body of Minnie Bonati still lying where it had fallen the previous afternoon. He now realized that she must be dead, and that he must do something to get rid of the corpse. He made no denial at all of the trunk business, of the dismembering, only of the killing.

John Robinson's trial at the Old Bailey began on Monday 11th of July. It was not one of the spectacular trials; the defence, though ably led by Mr Lawrence Viney, failed to convince judge and jury that Minnie was the victim of an unfortunate, and in many senses self-provoked, accident. When Mr Justice Swift asked Robinson why he did not seek help for the unconscious woman lying on his office floor, why, when he realized that she was dead he did not summon the police to explain matters, the prisoner replied "I did not see it in that light."

He was sentenced to death on July 13th; he was executed at Pentonville Prison one month later.

A Murder from the 'Yiddisher' District
The Murder of LEON BERON
by STINIE MORRISON (alias MORRIS STEIN)
in the early hours of Sunday the 1st of January 1911
on Clapham Common, SW4

A Body on the Common

On Sunday, the 1st of January, 1911, PC Joseph Mumford was patrolling his regular beat on Clapham Common. At 8.10am, he was walking along a path leading north-west from the bandstand when he noticed, about twelve feet from the path in the bushes, what appeared to be a body. It was a short, stocky, middle-aged man, smartly dressed in an overcoat with an astrakhan collar and patent leather boots. He was undoubtedly dead, and not from any natural cause. A black silk handkerchief had been folded over his face and tucked into his collar and the top of his coat and his sleeves were splattered with blood. Stretching back to the path, was a pool of blood and a trail across the ground from where he had evidently been dragged. Near by lay a bowler hat, and there were footprints in the soft earth. PC Mumford carefully left the body undisturbed and ran to Cavendish Road police station to summon help.

Later that morning the body was removed to Battersea Mortuary, stripped and photographed and a post-mortem carried out. The cause of death was immediately obvious, a large horseshoe-shaped wound on the forehead, the result of a blow with a blunt instrument (a jemmy was later suggested). There were further blows to the head, three stab wounds in the chest and a number of superficial scratches and cuts on the face, including a curious 'S'-shaped cut on either cheek. The victim was noted as being Jewish in appearance and in his pocket was a small account book containing a list of Polish and French women's names with sums of money placed against them. In the front of the book was an address and the name 'Mr Israel Inglazer'. Divisional Detective Inspector Alfred Ward, who had been put in charge of the inquiry, quickly decided to call in Detective Inspector Frederick Porter Wensley of the Whitechapel Police, the area in which the address was situated.

Wensley was at that time involved in the 'Houndsditch' inquiry; three policemen had been shot dead during a robbery by what was believed to be East European anarchists. Just two days after the discovery of the body on Clapham Common, this case was to culminate in the notorious 'Siege of Sydney Street'. Frederick Wensley was an experienced officer, with an unsurpassed knowledge of the local Jewish immigrant underworld, and it did not take him long to locate the mysterious 'Mr Inglazer'. By that evening the two detectives had burst into a shabby second-floor room at 133 Jubilee Street, Stepney, which the dead man – real name Leon Beron – shared with one of his brothers.

The 'Quaint Little Jew'

Leon Beron was a 48-year-old Polish Jew who had first arrived in the East End from Paris in 1894. In the seventeen years he had lived in London he had never held down a legitimate job. He was, nevertheless, a

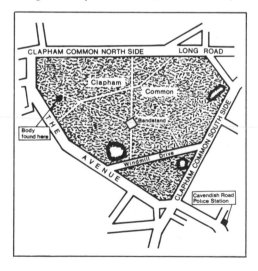

man of some means. He owned some slum property which was mainly rented by prostitutes, and he was known as a womanizer and a regular client himself of the oldest profession. It was further rumoured that he was a financial backer of burglaries and a fence for stolen goods. Beron had come to the attention of the police two years previously when two men had attempted to rob him of his gold watch, which he wore on a chain with a £5 gold piece, and of a leather pouch containing twenty sovereigns. These same coveted articles were noticeably missing from the battered body on Clapham Common.

The police were here confronted with a delicate situation. Since the Houndsditch Murders the Press had generated a widespread and irrational fear of anarchist revolution, so that there existed considerable popular feeling against the immigrant Jewish community which was popularly supposed to spawn such 'excesses'. The previous week a Stepney councillor had declared that... "the borough has been inundated by a swarm of people fitly described as the scum of Central Europe". If the murder on Clapham Common were to be connected in the public mind with this agitation there was no knowing where it might end. The early press reports had already made the inevitable connection with the Houndsditch murders and had gleefully suggested that the 'S'-shaped scratches on Beron's face stood for *szpieg*, *spic* or *schlosser* and were an anarchist device to brand an informer publicly. The police badly needed to damp down any rumours of this sort. The scratches were dismissed as the figment of a lurid imagination. Beron's criminal connections were also carefully avoided; he was calculatedly portrayed as an eccentric, a figure of amusement and pity, a 'mad landlord' and 'a quaint little Jew'.

A Most Convenient Suspect

The first priority of the police investigation was to learn more about Beron's daily habits and his movements up to the date of the murder. They discovered that he spent a great deal of his time at Snelwar's Warsaw Restaurant at 32 Osborn Street in Whitechapel. At Snelwar's, Polish immigrants were served, for eighteen pence a day, with lunch, dinner and as many drinks as they required to carry out their business, reminisce about the old country and generally while away the day. Beron had been seen frequently in the previous month with a tall, elegantly dressed stranger who variously called himself Moses Tagger, Morris Stein and Stinie Morrison. Beron's brother Solomon and other regulars at Snelwar's Restaurant had all pointed the finger of suspicion in this direction, and a glance at Morrison's past record justified the police interest.

Stinie Morrison was born in the Ukraine in 1879 and had journeyed to England at the age of eighteen in 1898. Within a few months of his arrival he received his first prison sentence – one month's hard labour for theft. This was followed by further periods in prison, culminating in a sentence of five years' hard labour for burglary in 1901. On being released on licence in 1905, he once again fell in with a gang of burglars. In 1906 he was arrested and sentenced to five years on Dartmoor. Morrison proved a moody and uncooperative prisoner, and during his time became involved in a brawl and was given twenty strokes of the 'cat', a humiliating experience which left a permanent impression on him. In September 1910 he was again released on licence, and seemed to be making a genuine attempt to go straight. He got a job in Pither's Bakery at 213 Lavender Hill, close by Clapham Common, using the skill in bread-making he had learned in prison; the bakery was directly opposite Lavender Hill Police Station. After just six weeks he was warned off by the local police who, knowing his record, wanted him off their patch. From here, Stinie Morrison returned to his old haunts and his old friends in Whitechapel.

On New Year's Eve, the day leading up to the murder, Beron had left his lodgings at mid-day and spent the afternoon collecting his rents. At just after seven o'clock he entered Snelwar's Restaurant in the company of Stinie Morrison. Stinie held under his arm a brown-paper parcel containing, he said, a flute, which he entrusted to the waiter, Joe Mintz, to store behind the counter. Mintz subsequently told the police that the parcel was heavy and could have been an iron bar. Stinie and Beron were talking through the evening, though each left the restaurant at some point, Beron being seen

Modern site of the 'Body on Clapham Common'

by his brother Solomon outside Cohen's restaurant in Fieldgate at 10.45pm. Beron and Morrison finally left Snelwar's at a quarter to twelve, Stinie having repossessed his brown-paper parcel. They then parted, Stinie returning to his lodgings at 91 Newark Street, where he was seen by his landlady, Annie Zimmerman, who locked up after him. This, however, would have been no barrier to an experienced burglar like Stinie if he had wanted to go out again. The police also found a witness, Mrs Deitch, a brothel keeper, who claimed to have seen Morrison and Beron together in Commercial Road at 2.15am.

Stinie's behaviour on the morning after the murder was no less suspicious. Setting out from his lodgings, he deposited a package in the left-luggage office at St Mary's Station, Whitechapel, under the name 'Banman', before crossing the river to exchange £10 in gold sovereigns for banknotes with a disreputable Jewish jeweller called Max Frank, in the Walworth Road. After this he went to stay with a prostitute of his acquaintance, Florrie Dellow, in York Road, Lambeth, for the next few days, well away from the attentions of the police.

"You Have Accused Me of Murder"

The police now followed two lines of inquiry. First, they placed a discreet watch on Stinie's lodgings and his regular haunts. Secondly, there was the question of how Beron and Morrison (if he was the murderer) had reached Clapham Common and how Stinie had returned. Police visited likely taxi ranks to interview cab drivers, and a reward of £1 was offered for useful information.

The Press had begun to sniff out that the police had a suspect and, following several broad hints that his name began with an 'S' or an 'M', pictures of Stinie appeared in the newspapers of the 6th of January. At the same time the offer of a reward began to bear fruit. A hansom-cab driver, Edward Hayman, had picked up two passengers at 2.00am on the corner of Sidney Street and taken them to Lavender Gardens, Clapham. This would have taken Beron and Morrison to the scene of the crime. A second hansom-cab driver, a shady character called Alfred Stevens, claimed to have taken a tall man whom he identified as Morrison from Clapham Cross to the *Hanover Arms* near Kennington Church at 3.10am. A taxi-cab driver, Alfred Castling, then stated that he had transported two men, one of them tall, from Kennington, back across London, to Finsbury Gate at 3.30am. The weakness of this evidence was that Stinie Morrison's picture had already been published in the newspapers by the time he was identified by the witnesses.

On the 8th of January the patient vigilance of the police finally paid off. Stinie reappeared at his lodgings and, after asking his landlady to take his washing to the public laundry, strolled down the street to Cohen's Restaurant. At 9.30am he was arrested inside the restaurant, initially on a charge of failing to register his address as a prisoner on licence, and bundled out and dragged down the road to Leman Street police station, pursued by a cat-calling, rowdy mob. In the police station, confronted by Inspector Wensley, he was reported as saying "You have accused me of serious crime. You have accused me of murder." This was taken to be an unprompted admission of knowledge of a crime which had not yet been mentioned, though he seems unlikely not to have heard the shouts of the crowd which had surrounded him in the street, even if he had not seen a newspaper containing his own photograph.

The police next visited his temporary abode in Lambeth, where they discovered the left-luggage ticket in the lining of a billycock hat. At St Mary's Station they recovered a parcel containing a pistol and 44 rounds of ammunition. Sorting through his washing, they also found a shirt with spots of blood on

Stinie Morrison at the time of his trial

the collar, cuffs and sleeves, though why he should keep such supposedly incriminating evidence for a week is difficult to understand.

On the 9th of January, Stinie Morrison was charged with murder and appeared at the South-West London Police Court at Lavender Hill to be remanded to Brixton Prison until his trial.

The Palace of Varieties

The trial of Stinie Morrison opened at Court No.1 at the Old Bailey on the 6th of March, 1911. It must stand as one of the most curious and chaotic dramas to be acted out in that celebrated courtroom. Stinie stood throughout the trial, sharply dressed and erect, with one hand on his hip, affecting an attitude of disdain and moral outrage towards the proceedings going on around him. Many of the witnesses were East European immigrants, with an unsteady grasp of English and little understanding or respect for the rituals of the court. To the judge, Mr Justice Darling, who delighted in impressing any court with his clever witticisms, this was a heaven-sent opportunity. Solomon Beron, the deceased's brother, was particularly wild-eyed, excitable and incoherent, and shortly after giving evidence had to be removed to Colney Hatch Lunatic Asylum, where he remained for the rest of his days. The foreman of the jury also continually interrupted the testimony to ask questions, an almost unprecedented break with the etiquette of the court that juries should hear but not be heard from.

The prosecution was pressed strongly by Sir Richard Muir, though its weakness was that the evidence was entirely circumstantial, and Sir Richard used every opportunity to blacken Stinie's character and bring out his criminal past. The defence, led by Mr Edward Abinger, sought to impugn the honesty of many of the witnesses and the victim of the crime. Beron, it was hinted, could have been a police spy who had 'shopped' the Houndsditch murderers. The greatest disaster for the defence, however, was Stinie's appearance in the witness box with a plainly preposterous account of his movements on the night before the murder. He claimed he had been selling imitation jewellery during the day, before dining in Snelwar's Restaurant at eight o'clock. He had then visited the Shoreditch Empire bet-

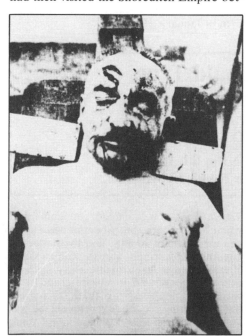

Leon Beron's body showing the controversial 'S' cuts on his cheeks

ween 8.45 and 11.10pm to watch Gertie Gitana, Harry Champion and Harry Lauder. After this he returned to the restaurant to pick up his flute, where he saw Beron but didn't talk to him, leaving at 11.45pm to return to his lodgings. He added that he had passed Beron on the corner of Sydney Street on his way home. One of Stinie's many girlfriends, 16-year-old Janie Brodsky, and her sister Esther were called to verify Stinie's jaunt to the Varieties. This was all a patent fabrication, though why Morrison should go to such trouble to fix an alibi for a time that was irrelevant to the crime is difficult to explain. It certainly cannot have made a good impression on the jury.

It was evident from his summing up on the 15th of January that Mr Justice Darling, while he might have thought Stinie guilty, was very unhappy about the reliability of some of the prosecution evidence. Unfortunately, the effect of his rather confusing remarks and the fact that he sent the jury out to consider their verdict at the unusually late hour of eight o'clock in the evening was the opposite of his intention. The jury took just thirty-five minutes to reach a verdict of guilty. When Mr Justice Darling intoned the infamous words ending "and may God have mercy on your soul" Stinie replied, "I decline such mercy. I do not believe there is a God in Heaven either." He was then taken down and removed to the condemned cell in Wandsworth Prison.

Reprieved but Tortured

Stinie's appeal was heard on the 27th of April, 1911. Although there was some criticism of the prosecution's presentation of the case, this was insufficient to declare a mistrial and the appeal was dismissed. Stinie did, however, have determined supporters and a petition for a reprieve containing 75,000 signatures was sent to the Home Secretary. One person who refused to sign it was Stinie Morrison. Nevertheless, the unease felt by the trial judge was shared by others and, on April the 13th, the Home Secretary, Mr Winston Churchill, commuted the death sentence to one of life imprisonment.

Stinie Morrison was transported to Dartmoor by train. At Waterloo station, as he was being transferred from a police van to the train, he momentarily shook himself free of the warders and shouted to the crowd of curious onlookers, "This is the way they treat a prisoner. I am a gentleman. You see how they treat me. Leave me alone!"

After his arrival at Dartmoor the volatile Ukrainian proved no more cooperative. He was surly, often violent and at once began a hunger strike, the first of many during the ten turbulent years of his imprisonment. He further occupied his time with a volley of letters and appeals. He still insisted on his innocence, but his persistent demand was to be allowed the death penalty rather than continue the hopeless rigours of prison life. One petition was even composed in rather undistinguished verse:

I had enough of convict life,
My heart is getting chilly
Enough of bread-and-water strife
And officers to knock me silly.

Rt. Hon. Sir, I beg you hear my
    humble plea
And send – 'Granted' – in reply!
If you will not give me my liberty
I pray you let me die.

My Freedom or my Death
Nothing else will Satisfy me!

While Stinie was petitioning for his own death, his supporters on the outside were still pressuring for his release. The committee was now led by Baroness Hilda Von Goetz, a wealthy society lady with a passion for penal reform, with the ever faithful Janie Brodsky, the defence lawyers at the trial and a number of radical journalists providing strong support. In 1913 they managed to organize another petition, this time with 42,000 signatures, and published a number of pamphlets airing the facts of Stinie's trial and imprisonment. The issue was only pushed aside by the understandable distraction of the First World War, though Stinie, isolated in his prison hell, continued his protests. In December 1912 he had been transferred to Parkhurst Prison, on the Isle of Wight, but the petitions, the fits of violence, the suicide attempts and the hunger strikes continued, gradually sapping his physical strength and his reason.

At the beginning of 1921 Stinie was again on hunger strike and being force fed with a feeding cup. At 2.15pm on the 21st of January the warders entered his cell to find that he had suffered a heart attack. At 4.30pm he died. Stinie Morrison was finally laid to rest in Carisbrooke Cemetery on the 27th of January, 1921.

The Real Ronald True
The Murder of GERTRUDE YATES
(also known as OLIVE YOUNG)
by RONALD TRUE
on Monday March the 6th 1922
at 13a Finborough Road, SW10

Insanity has always been a difficult condition to define legally and the question of criminal responsibility in the issue of murder has been a continuing cause for controversy. The McNaghten Rules, developed by the Law Lords during the nineteenth century provided a conservative definition which had become considerably out of line with medical opinion [see *Murder Club Guide No.3*]. The case of Ronald True in 1922 provided an opportunity for many of the main arguments in this controversy to be aired.

True's mother was sixteen and unmarried when he was born, but when he was eleven she married into wealth, and thereafter his circumstances were always comfortable. Ronald showed inescapable early signs of delinquency – petty theft, cheating, and lying, which did not seem to abate as he got older. Leaving school at seventeen, he was sent abroad, to New Zealand, Argentina, Canada and then Mexico, in the hope that this would improve his behaviour, but successive employers dismissed him once his

The real Ronald True?

dishonesty, boastfulness and incompetence became apparent. It was during this period that he first became addicted to morphia.

The start of the First World War gave him an opportunity to return to England, and in 1915 he somehow gained a commission in the Royal Flying Corps, where his eccentricity and incompetence were again evident, resulting in a serious flying accident while still training at Farnborough. This eventually led to his being invalided out of the service in 1917. He then went to New York for a period, where he posed as an injured air ace, and married Frances Roberts, an actress. Though True's behaviour was never less than peculiar, and often complicated by bouts of depression, he could nevertheless be charming – the life and soul of a party; especially when he had access to morphia. Returning to England with his new wife, Ronald was again dispatched abroad by his family, this time to the Gold Coast. The results were predictable, and inside six months he was back in England and palpably unemployable.

The family now decided that something needed to be done, at least to curb his morphia addiction, and he was sent to various nursing homes. The treatment met with little success, though this is unsurprising as he would periodically absent himself to London on a morphia binge, leaving a string of unpaid bills, gambling debts, forged cheques and petty thefts in his wake. To complicate the syndrome, his bouts of moodiness had become increasingly violent, and he had begun to take against his wife. The family had finally approached the conclusion that he must be permanently institutionalized when he disappeared for one last time, claiming that he had found a job in Bedford. He was of course on another binge in London, moving from hotel to hotel as the time came to pay the bill. He became friendly with a man called James Armstrong and contrived to buy a pistol from him, the bullets for which he proceeded to file down. He needed the gun, he said, to protect himself from a man, also calling himself Ronald True, who followed him around issuing cheques in his name and was bent on killing him. This had begun as a harmless delusion to rationalize the thefts and debts. These were all the doing of 'the other Ronald True'. It was now, however, developing into full-scale paranoia. True had also developed a fixation for a call-girl called Gertrude Yates, who worked under the name of Olive Young. He had visited her once at her basement flat at 13a Finborough Road, Fulham, distinguishing himself by stealing £5 from her purse. She was clearly scared and wanted nothing more to do with him, but he continued to pester her with phone calls. At this time True began to drop garbled hints about a final showdown with 'the other Ronald True' at Finborough Road and mentioned a girl called Olive, who was somehow involved.

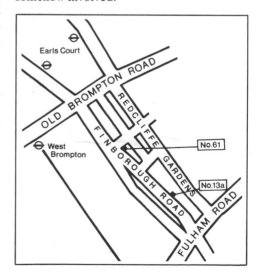

True had hired a car and chauffeur, and for three nights running he drove with James Armstrong and parked at the end of Finborough Road, saying that he wanted to see if some friends were in. Each time he returned to the car and drove Armstrong home. On the third night, Sunday, March the 5th, 1922, he returned and, dismissing the car and chauffeur, was let into the flat by Olive Young.

All went well until the morning. True rose at 7.30 to make a cup of tea and, returning to the bedroom, unexpectedly hit Olive Young three times over the head with a rolling pin as she innocently sipped her tea. He then stuffed a towel down her throat, strangled her with the girdle of her dressing gown and dragged her body into the bathroom. Returning to the blood-spattered bedroom, he put two pillows under the bedclothes to simulate her body, took £8 from her handbag and selected the best of her jewellery. He then sat down and waited for her domestic servant, Emily Steel, to arrive at nine o'clock. As Emily was preparing her breakfast of fried sausages, 'Major' True appeared, asked her not to disturb Miss Young as they had bedded down rather late and, pressing a half-crown into her hand, left. Minutes later, Emily Steel discovered the body of her mistress in the bathroom.

True's next extraordinary action was to visit a gents' outfitters, where he bought an off-the-peg suit and had his own bloodstained clothing tied into a bundle. He explained their state as being the result of a flying accident. He had, it seemed, just flown over from Paris! He then pawned the jewellery he had stolen and set off for an afternoon's drive to Hounslow with Armstrong.

In his deluded state, True had made no attempt at all to cover his tracks, and it was with no expenditure of effort that the police located and arrested him that evening in the Hammersmith Palace of Varieties.

Ronald True was later lodged in the prison hospital at Brixton, where medical staff lost little time in concluding that he was insane.

Ronald True cheerfully taking notes at his committal hearing. To onlookers in the court he appeared to continue this meticulous practice throughout his trial at the Old Bailey. Only the warders behind him could see that he was actually playing with a small plastic duck, continuously propelling it back and forth along the shelf of the dock, completely oblivious to the struggle for his life that was being played out in front of him.

At one point, he escaped into the next ward, where the murderer Henry Jacoby was housed [see this volume]. Slapping him on the back, True quipped, "Here's another for our Murderer's Club. We only accept those who kill outright!"

At True's trial at the Old Bailey, his counsel, Sir Henry Curtis-Bennett, sought to prove that he could not be held responsible for his actions. Opposing, Sir Richard Muir contended that, while the prisoner might be deranged, he knew the difference between right and wrong. Mr Justice M'Cardie's summing-up was favourable to the prosecution and True was found guilty.

From the evidence, the Home Secretary was bound to appoint the customary panel of three medical men to judge on True's sanity and, as a result of their findings commuted the sentence to life imprisonment, committing True to Broadmoor Criminal Lunatic Asylum. A great furore arose in the Press because two days previously Jacoby, a pathetic criminal from a far less exalted background, had been hanged. It was suggested that influence had been used to secure True's reprieve, and the Home Secretary was eventually forced to defend his position in the House of Commons before the matter was allowed to rest.

Ronald True remained in Broadmoor for twenty-nine years, eventually dying of natural causes in 1951. He was said to be a popular inmate and very active in all sports and social activities.

"A Daniel Come to Judgement!"
The Murder of JANE JONES
by DANIEL GOOD
on or about Tuesday the 5th of April 1842
in the stables of Granard Lodge, Putney Park Lane, SW15

The following account of the discovery of the horrific crime of Daniel Good and his subsequent trial derives from *The Life and Recollections of Calcraft the Hangman*, which was published in London in 1880.

Daniel Good was a middle-aged Irishman in the employment as coachman of Mr Shiell, East India merchant, residing at Granard Lodge, Roehampton.

On the 6th of April, 1842, Good called in a chaise at the shop of Mr Collingbourn, a pawnbroker, in Wandsworth [High Street], and bought a pair of black knee-breeches, which he took on credit. The shop-boy saw him at the same time put a pair of trousers under his coat skirt, and place them with the breeches in the chaise. Mr Collingbourn followed him out, and charged him with the theft, but he denied it and hurriedly drove off.

---

* *Merchant of Venice*, Act IV, Sc. 1.

The pawnbroker sent a policeman, William Gardner, after the thief, and with the officer went the shop-boy and Robert Speed, a neighbour. Good lived at the stables, about a quarter of a mile from Mr Shiell's house, and the boy went and rang the bell, whilst Gardner, the policeman, kept in the background. Good answered the bell, and the policeman stepped forward and told him that he had orders to arrest him for stealing a pair of trousers.

Good positively denied having done so, but the policeman said he must come in and search the place. He then pushed his way in, and the boy and Mr Speed followed. Having searched some portion of the place, they proceeded to search the stable, but Good put his back against the door, and tried hard to hinder them. While searching one of the stalls, they pulled out some hay, and then found what they at first thought was part of the carcase of a pig. The boy, who was the first to see exactly what it was exclaimed:

"Why, it's part of the body of a woman!"

When they got it into the light, they discovered that it really was the trunk of a female, with the head, the legs, and the arms chopped off.

As soon as the discovery was made Good, though under arrest for the robbery of the trousers, slipped out of the stable door, the key of which, by the policeman, had thoughtlessly been left in the lock outside. Having thus got them safe inside Good shut the door, and locked Mr Speed, the boy, and the policeman in. He then took the key and made good his escape.

As it was a strong door, and the stable was a considerable distance from the house, they were some time trying with a stable fork to open it, during which time Good got miles away.

On examining another of the stalls, they discovered a large quantity of blood, and also a heavy axe, and a saw all covered with gore. In fact the place looked like a slaughter-house, and it was very apparent that a dreadful murder had only recently been committed. They next went to the coach-house, attracted by the dreadful smell emanating from the place. Here they found a large fire laid, and on the ground a quantity of charred bones, the remains of which led to

"Here they found a large fire laid..."

the supposition that the head, legs, feet and hands, and arms of the unfortunate victim had already been burnt.

Information, in the meantime, had been conveyed to the police at Wandsworth, and an immediate search for Good was commenced. All efforts to find him, however, were for some time fruitless.

The next obstacle in the case was the difficulty of identification as no one could recognise the body, and for some time no one knew who she was. From enquiries made, however, it was found that Good had been renting a kitchen at 18 Southampton Street, Manchester Square, where he formerly had in keeping a woman named Jane Jones, whom he at one time professed to be courting, but to whom afterwards he was said to be married and who had recently passed as Mrs Good.

There was also living with her an intelligent boy, about ten years of age, who was said to be a son of Good by a former wife. This boy was always instructed to call her mother, and in his evidence at the inquest he stated that he had always been told that she was his true mother's sister, who had died about seven years previously.

The medical evidence showed that the doctors believed the remains to be those of a finely developed young woman, about 24 years of age, who had never borne a child,

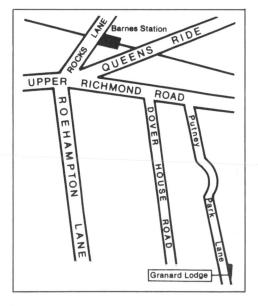

but who would have given birth to one in about five months. It was also shown that Jane Jones, alias the reputed wife of Good, had on the previous Saturday afternoon gone out to meet her supposed husband. She and Good were seen together at Barnes, and they were finally traced together to the stable, where, on the Sunday night, she evidently went to sleep with Good. She was said to be thought forty years of age.

The motive for the murder was supposed to lie in the fact that Good had recently been keeping company with a young woman named Lydia Susannah Butcher, who had formerly been in respectable service at Wimbledon, but who, at the time of the murder, was living with her father at 13 Charlotte Place, Woolwich. Though over fifty years of age, Good was accepted, and engaged to be married to this girl, and he was looked upon as her future husband. He had told her that his wife was dead, and that there was a good deal of clothing, and a mangle of hers, which the girl, Lydia Susannah Butcher, could have.

The coroner's jury found a verdict that the remains were those of Jane Jones, alias Mrs Good, and that she was wilfully murdered by her reputed husband, Daniel Good.

A reward was offered for his apprehension, and another wife of Good was found residing at Flower and Dean Street, Spitalfields. She was an old woman, who kept a stall and was known by the name 'Old Molly Good'. After his escape from the stable, it would appear that Good immediately went to the old woman, and told her that he was sorry he had been a bad husband, and that he wished to come back and live with her. He, however, had previously been and fetched away all the things belonging to Jane Jones from Southampton Street, and also the boy, and had told the landlady that she was not coming back again.

The police, having ascertained that Old Molly Good was Daniel's wife, kept a watch on the place, but instead of going in plain clothes, they went making enquiries about him in uniform. Good, who was in the house, was watching for their coming, and as soon as he saw them, he again made off, and got clear away. The whole of the police who managed this part of the business in such a bungling manner got discharged.

It was now some time before Good was heard of again, and perhaps he would never have been discovered had not the reward

Granard Lodge, Putney Park Lane

offered for his apprehension caused people throughout the country to keep a sharp look-out.

On the 16th April, he was at length recognised at Tunbridge Wells, by a man who had formerly known him, and at which place he had obtained employment as a labourer. When he was first accosted as Daniel Good he denied in the most positive manner that that was his name. He was then passing in the name of Connor, and to all persons who came to see him he declared that Connor was his name. The police were further communicated with, and he was eventually identified beyond a doubt.

He was brought to London and tried at the Central Criminal Court, before Lord Denman, Baron Alderson, and Mr Justice Coltman. The Attorney-General Mr Waddington, Mr Adolphus, and Mr Russell Gurney, the late Recorder of London, were for the prosecution, and Mr Deane was for the prisoner.

The jury found him guilty.

When asked in the usual way whether he had anything to say why sentence of death should not be passed on him he said that he was entirely innocent, that he did not take the life of the deceased, but that she committed suicide herself, by cutting her throat with a knife, because she had found out that he was keeping company with Lydia Susannah Butcher, and she was jealous of her. He added that when he found her dead he consulted a man who used to come round with matches, and asked him what he had best do with the body. The match man said he had better burn it, and he offered, for the sum of a sovereign, to cut the body up and burn some and carry the rest away. He gave the man a sovereign to do this, and the man did part of it, and left the rest.

The learned judges then assumed their black caps, and sentence of death was passed upon him in the usual way...

...the crowd that witnessed the execution was one of the largest that had ever assembled in front of Newgate.

"A slice of cake, young Percy?"
The Murder of PERCY JOHN
by Dr GEORGE HENRY LAMSON
on Saturday the 3rd of December 1881
at Blenheim House School (now demolished),
1-2 St George's Road, SW19

There are not many really intelligent and cunning murderers, but Dr Henry Lamson must be placed among their number. He was caught, though, and some might put this down to his trying to be just too clever by half.

Lamson was born in 1849 and from an early age exhibited an adventurous spirit. At the age of eighteen he chose to study medicine in Paris. On the outbreak of the Franco-Prussian War he volunteered for the French Ambulance Corps and served with distinction. After qualifying in 1874, he worked for two years in a Paris hospital before volunteering again for active service in the Balkans. For this effort he was decorated both by the Serbian and the Romanian

Governments. In 1878, he elected to return to England and in the same year married a wealthy ward of Chancery, Kate John, and in the process inherited £1500.

Unfortunately, while in the Balkans he had developed an addiction to morphine. He invested his wife's money in a series of medical practices, each of which failed, eating up more and more of his capital. He had also begun to develop a dishonest streak in his character as his money problems became more desperate. In Brighton he falsely added the name of a popular doctor to his brass plate, and in London hired locals to call at his surgery to make it seem more successful when he was trying to sell the practice. By 1881 he was in a dire position, with no capital and no practice, and had resorted to issuing false cheques to tide himself over. He was badly in need of some new source of finance, and he found one readily to hand.

His wife's mother, the widow of a Manchester merchant, had left her fortune in trust to her three sons and two daughters until they reached the age of twenty-one. One son, Herbert, had already died, and in 1879 the second son, Henry, also died, of a mysterious stomach complaint. This left the two daughters – Lamson's wife Kate and a married sister, Margaret Chapman – and the youngest son, Percy. Percy John was only fifteen in 1878 and was crippled with a curvature of the spine and paralysis of the lower limbs. If he, too, were to die, Lamson would immediately inherit over £700 through his wife's interest.

Percy, who hero-worshipped Henry Lamson, was invited, with Margaret Chapman and her husband, to spend the summer holiday with the Lamsons on the Isle of Wight. Before they arrived Lamson bought quinine sulphate powder and one grain of aconitine, a highly toxic irritant vegetable poison from a local Ventnor pharmacist. Lamson then announced to Percy and the Chapmans that he must leave that same evening on a trip to America in search of new employment. During the course of the afternoon he administered the quinine sulphate powder to Percy, saying that he didn't look well. That evening, when Lamson was well on his way out of the country,

Dr Henry George Lamson

Percy was taken ill with severe vomiting and did not recover until the next morning.

Returning to England after a fortnight, Lamson continued to run up further debts to the point where another attempt on his nephew's life seemed the only solution. Lamson wrote to Percy John at Blenheim Special School, Wimbledon, where he was a pupil, to inform the boy that he wished to pay him a visit before travelling to Paris on business. The following day, December the 3rd, 1881, he arrived at 7.00pm and was shown up to see the headmaster, Mr William Bedbrook. Percy was carried into the room and Mr Bedbrook offered Lamson a glass of sherry. Lamson inexplicably asked to have sugar in it, and a bowl of caster sugar was brought to the room. From his black bag Lamson now produced three slices of Dundee cake, and selected one each for Bedbrook and Percy; he then turned the conversation to some empty gelatine capsules which he had discovered while he was in America. Filling one with the harmless caster sugar, he offered it to Percy saying "Percy, you are a champion pill-taker, take this. Show Mr Bedbrook how easy it is to swallow." He then quickly took his leave, stating that he had to catch the train for London Bridge to get to Paris that night. On the way out, he remarked to Bedbrook on

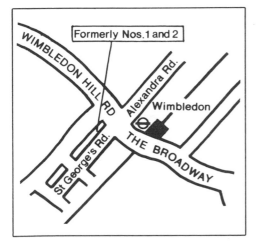

Formerly Nos. 1 and 2

WIMBLEDON HILL RD

Alexandra Rd.

Wimbledon

St George's Rd.

THE BROADWAY

how ill Percy was looking and how he might not last long.

Later that evening Percy was taken by a violent spasm of vomiting, and after lapsing into a coma died at twenty past eleven, despite all the efforts of the school physician. Next morning the police were called, and, the local doctors being unable to ascertain a cause of death, Dr Thomas Stevenson, the premier toxicologist of the day, was brought in to perform an autopsy and test various substances found at the school. Grey patches on the stomach suggested the presence of a vegetable alkaloid poison and a raisin in the stomach contained traces of aconitine, as did a powder sent to Percy from Ventnor. At the inquest Lamson was mentioned by name and this jogged the memory of an assistant at Allen & Hanbury's, a pharmacists in the City of London, who recalled selling aconitine to a Dr Lamson on November the 24th.

From the safety of Paris, Lamson had obviously decided that his crime was unprovable and that he could brazen the matter out. After writing a letter protesting his inno-

cence, he set out for London, arriving at Scotland Yard in the company of his wife to discuss any misconceptions the police might have. To his chagrin, he was immediately arrested and lodged in Wandsworth Prison.

The trial opened at the Old Bailey on March the 8th, 1882 and lasted six days. The defence counsel, Mr Montagu Williams, claimed that nobody knew the exact effects of aconitine poisoning or how it had been administered, and cited Lamson's good relationship with the victim and his family as shedding doubt on any evil intention, but the circumstantial evidence was so strong that it took the jury only thirty minutes to reach a verdict of guilty.

Lamson's demeanour deteriorated dramatically in prison, partly due to the withdrawal of morphine, and, towards the end, he confessed to the cold-blooded crime he had committed. On April the 18th, 1882, he was led in considerable trepidation from his cell in Wandsworth to face righteous retribution at the hands of Marwood, the hangman.

[*See also Appendix Two to this volume*]

The Man in the Green Van
The Murder of 'IRISH' ROSE ATKINS
by GEORGE BRAIN
on Wednesday the 13th of July 1938
in the area of Wimbledon Park,
and the dumping of her Body in Somerset Road, SW19

The last time 30-year-old 'Irish' Rose Atkins was seen alive was at 11.30 on the night of Wednesday 13th July, 1938, when an acquaintance noticed her talking to a man in a green van.

The first time she was seen dead was when a man motoring through Wimbledon in the early hours of the following morning saw her body lying in Somerset Road, a quiet street then and now, just opposite the Common.

Rose Atkins appeared at first to have been the victim of a hit-and-run accident, and there was no denying the tyre marks on her

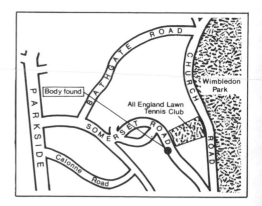

George Brain

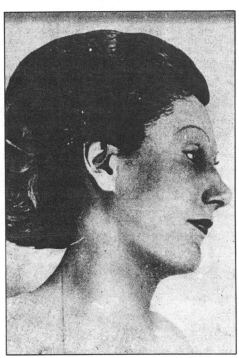

The dead body of 'Irish' Rose Atkins after being made-up for identification

body, but closer examination disclosed that she had been bludgeoned about the head and stabbed to death some time before and in some other place than she was found. Driving over her with a car had been either a gratuitous act of violence or a desperate way of assuring the woman's death. Nevertheless, it provided the police with one vital piece of information to add to the description of the green van – the tyre marks could only have been made by the wheels of an Austin 7 or a Morris 8.

One of the problems facing the investigation team was that Rose had been a professional prostitute, and in that line of business she met not only more than her share of seedy men, but most of them were fly-by-night one-timers. The man in the green van could have been anybody looking for Rose's brand of company.

But by one of those strokes of lucky coincidence without which the lives of policemen would be impossible, a St Pancras firm specializing in wholesale boot-and-shoe repairs reported that one of their drivers had gone missing. They seemed fairly un-

concerned about the whereabouts of the man, but rather anxious about the £32 of theirs which he had taken with him. The embezzler's name was Brain, George Brain, late of Richmond; and he had left his green Morris 8 delivery van in a workmate's garage, stained with the blood of Rose Atkins, also her empty handbag with his fingerprints on it, and, hidden close by, a bloody leather-knife.

An immediate nationwide search was then launched which went on without success for nine days. George Brain had gone to ground. George Brain had gone to ground literally, for the next news came from Sheerness on the Isle of Sheppey, where a schoolboy who had been crawling about in the undergrowth (as schoolboys do), reported coming across Brain crawling about in the undergrowth (which is a thing grown men rarely do). When police arrived to arrest him George Brain was stretched out on the grass reading a book.

In a trial that was unremarkable, Brain, an unremarkable killer (who had already admitted beating Rose Atkins over the head

The site opposite the All England Tennis Club in Somerset Road where the body of Rose Atkins was found

with a starting handle in a panic when she demanded money from him, already admitted robbing her of all her money – four shillings) failed to convince the jury that he had killed during a mental 'black-out'. Perhaps they felt that this might account for the bludgeoning, possibly the stabbing as well, but could they believe that a man in such confusion would make sure of the job by backing his car over the victim?

So George Brain was hanged on the 1st of November at Wandsworth Prison, and the cynical may be forgiven for thinking that four shillings for two lives was very cheap – even for 1938.

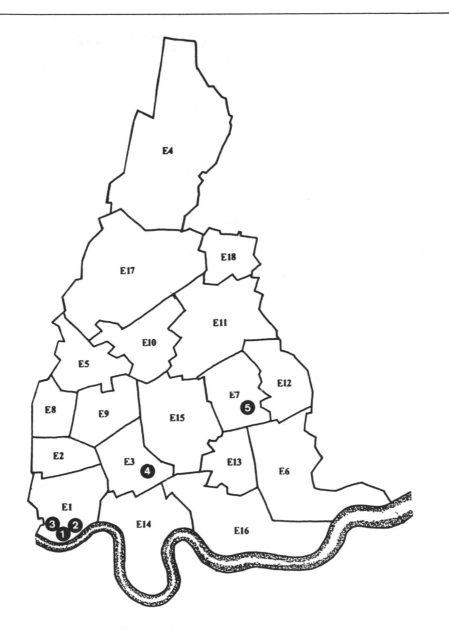

East London

1. John WILLIAMS 130
2. Henry WAINRIGHT 136
3. JACK THE RIPPER 140
4. Franz MÜLLER 145
5. Ronald William BARTON 147

The Ratcliffe Highway Murders

The Murder of the MARR FAMILY and JAMES BIGGS, and the WILLIAMSON FAMILY
by JOHN WILLIAMS
on the 7th and 19th of December 1811
on the Ratcliffe Highway (now The Highway), E1
as recounted by Thomas De Quincey

Never, throughout the annals of universal Christendom, has there indeed been any act of one solitary insulated individual, armed with power so appalling over the hearts of men, as that exterminating murder, by which, during the winter of 1811, John Williams, in one hour, smote two households with emptiness, exterminated all but two entire households, and asserted his own supremacy over all the children of Cain.

Yet, first of all, one word as to the local scene of the murders. Ratcliffe Highway is a public thoroughfare in the most chaotic quarter of eastern, or nautical, London; and at this time, when no adequate police existed except the detective police of Bow Street, admirable for its own peculiar purposes, but utterly incommensurate to the general service of the capital, it was a most dangerous quarter. Every third man, at the least, might be set down as a foreigner. Lascars, Chinese, Moors, Negroes, were met at every step.

And apart from the manifold ruffianism, shrouded impenetrability under the mixed hats and turbans of men whose past was untraceable to any European eye, it is well known that the navy of Christendom is the sure receptacle of all the murderers and ruffians whose crimes have given them a motive for withdrawing themselves for a season from the public eye...

Williams was a man of middle stature (five feet seven-and-a-half to five feet eight inches high), slenderly built, rather thin, but wiry, tolerably muscular, and clear of all superfluous flesh. A lady, who saw him under examination, assured me that his hair was of the most extraordinary and vivid colour, viz., a bright yellow, something between an orange and a lemon colour.

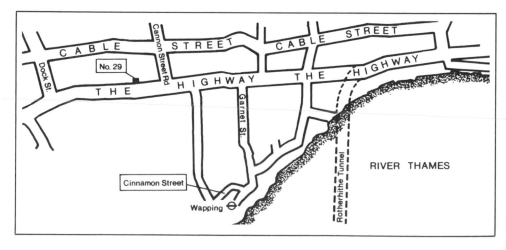

In other respects, his appearance was natural enough; and, judging by a plaster cast of him, which I purchased in London, I should say mean, as regarded his facial structure. One fact, however, was striking, and fell in with the impression of his natural tiger character, that his face wore at all times a bloodless ghastly pallor...

Into this perilous region [Ratcliffe Highway] it was that, on a Saturday night in December, Mr Williams forced his way through the crowded streets, bound on business...He carried his tools closely buttoned up under his loose roomy coat...

Surely he could never be so indiscreet as to be sailing about on a roving cruise in search of some chance person to murder? Oh, no: he had suited himself with a victim some time before, viz., an old and very intimate friend. For he seems to have laid it down as a maxim – that the best person to murder was a friend; and, in default of a friend, which is an article one cannot always command, an acquaintance: because, in either case, on first approaching his subject, suspicion would be disarmed: whereas a stranger might take alarm, and find in the very countenance of his murderer elect a warning summons to place himself on guard...

Marr was the name of that unhappy man who had been selected for the subject of this present Saturday night's performance... The minutes are numbered, the sands of the hour-glass are running out, that measure the duration of this feud on earth. This night it shall cease. Tomorrow is the day which in England they call Sunday, which in Scotland they call by the Judaic name of "Sabbath". To both nations, under different names, the day has the same functions; to both it is a day of rest; so it is written; thou, too, young Marr, shalt find rest – thou, and thy household, and the stranger that is within thy gates. But that rest must be in the world which lies beyond the grave. On this side of the grave ye have all slept your final sleep.

The night was one of exceeding darkness; and in this humble quarter of London, whatever the night happened to be, light or dark, quiet or stormy, all shops were kept open on Saturday nights until twelve o'clock, at the least, and many for half an hour longer...

Marr's position in life was this: he kept a little hosier's shop, and had invested in his stock, and the fittings of his shop, about £180. At this time he was a stout, fresh-coloured young man of twenty-seven.

The household of Marr, consisting of five persons, is as follows: First, there is himself, who, if he should happen to be ruined, in a limited commercial sense, has energy enough to jump up again, like a

Thomas De Quincey

pyramid of fire, and soar high above ruin many times repeated. Yes, poor Marr, so it might be, if thou wert left to thy native energies unmolested; but even now there stands on the other side of the street one born of hell, who puts his peremptory negative on all these flattering prospects. Second in the list of this household, stands his pretty and amiable wife, who is happy after the fashion of youthful wives, for she is only twenty-two, and anxious (if at all) only on account of her darling infant. For, thirdly, there is in a cradle, not quite nine feet below the street viz., in a warm, cosy kitchen, and rocked at intervals by the young mother, a baby eight months old. Nineteen months have Marr and herself been married; and this is their first-born child. Grieve not for this child, that it must keep the deep rest of Sunday in some other world; for wherefore should an orphan, steeped to the lips in poverty, when once bereaved of father and mother, linger upon an alien and murderous earth? Fourthly, there is a stoutish boy, an apprentice, say thirteen years old; a Devonshire boy, with handsome features, such as most Devonshire youths have; satisfied with his place; not overworked; treated kindly, and aware that he was treated kindly. Fifthly, and lastly, is a servant girl, a grown-up young woman; and she, being particularly kindhearted, occupies (as often happens in families of humble pretensions as to rank) a sort of sisterly place in her relation to her mistress.

To this young woman it was that suddenly, within three or four minutes of midnight, Marr called aloud from the head of the stairs – directing her to go out and purchase some oysters for the family supper. Hastily, therefore, receiving money from Marr, with a basket in her

Crossroads at Cable Street and Cannon Street Row where Williams was buried with a stake through his heart

hand, but unbonneted, Mary tripped out of the shop. It became afterwards, on recollection, a heart-chilling remembrance to herself – that, precisely as she emerged from the shop-door, she noticed, on the opposite side of the street, by the light of the lamps, a man's figure; stationary at the instant, but in the next instant slowly moving. This was Williams...

It was indispensable that the [shop's] shutters should be accurately closed before Williams could safely get to work. But as soon as ever this preliminary precaution had been completed, once having secured that concealment from the public eye, it then became of still greater importance not to lose a moment by delay, than it had previously been not to hazard anything by precipitance. For all depended upon going in before Marr should have locked the door.

Williams waited, of necessity, for the sound of a passing watchman's retreating steps; waited, perhaps, for thirty seconds; but when the danger was past, the next danger was, lest Marr should lock the door; one turn of the key, and the murderer would have been locked out. In, therefore, he bolted, and by a dextrous movement of his left hand, no doubt, turned the key, without letting Marr perceive this fatal stratagem...

[*Mary returns from her errand. . .*]

Mary rang, and at the same time very gently knocked. She had no fear of disturbing her master or mistress; them she made sure of finding still up. Her anxiety was for the baby, who being disturbed might again rob her mistress of a night's rest. And she well knew that, with three people all anxiously awaiting her return, and by this time, perhaps, seriously uneasy at her delay, the least audible whisper from herself would in a moment bring one of them to the door. Yet how is this? To her astonishment, but with the astonishment came creeping over her an icy horror, no stir or murmur was heard ascending from the kitchen.

One person might have fallen asleep, but

two – but three – that was a mere impossibility. And even supposing all three together with the baby locked in sleep, still how unaccountable was this utter, utter silence! Most naturally at this moment something like hysterical horror over-shadowed the poor girl, and now at last she rang the bell with the violence that belongs to sickening terror. Listen therefore, poor trembling heart; listen, and for twenty seconds be still as death. Still as death she was: and during that dreadful stillness, when she hushed her breath that she might listen, occurred an incident of killing fear, that to her dying day would never cease to renew its echoes in her ear. She, Mary, the poor trembling girl, checking and overruling herself by a final effort, that she might leave full opening for her dear young mistress's answer to her own frantic appeal, heard at last and most distinctly a sound within the house. Yes, now beyond a doubt there is coming an answer to her summons. What was it? On the stairs, not the stairs that led downwards to the kitchen, but the stairs that led upwards to the single storey of bed-chambers above, was heard a creaking sound. Next was heard most distinctly a footfall: one, two, three, four, five stairs were slowly and distinctly descended. Then the dreadful footsteps were heard advancing along the little narrow passage to the door. The steps – oh heavens! *whose* steps? – have paused at the door. The very breathing can be heard of that dreadful being, who has silenced all breathing except his own in the house. There is but a door between him and Mary. What is he doing on the other side of the door? A cautious step, a stealthy step it was that came down the stairs, then paced along the little narrow passage – narrow as a coffin – till at last the step pauses at the door. How hard the fellow breathes! He, the solitary murderer, is on one side of the door; Mary is on the other side. Now suppose that he should suddenly open the door, and that incautiously in the dark Mary should rush in, and find herself in the arms of the murderer... But now Mary is upon her guard. The unknown murderer and she have both their lips upon the door, listening, breathing hard; but luckily they are on different sides of the door; and upon the least indication of unlocking, or un-

FIFTY POUNDS
REWARD.

Horrid Murder!!

WHEREAS,

The Dwelling House of Mr. TIMOTHY MARR, 29, Ratcliff Highway, Man's Mercer, was entered this morning between the hours of Twelve and Two o'Clock, by some persons unknown, when the said Mr. MARR, Mrs. CELIA MARR, his wife, TIMOTHY their INFANT CHILD in the cradle, and JAMES BIGGS, a servant lad, were all of them most inhumanly and barbarously Murdered!!

A Ship Carpenter's Pen Maul, broken at the point, and a Bricklayer's long Iron Ripping Chisel about Twenty Inches in length, have been found upon the Premises, with the former of which it is supposed the Murder was committed. Any person having lost such articles, or any Dealer in Old Iron, who has lately Sold or missed such, are earnestly requested to give immediate Information.

The Churchwardens, Overseers, and Trustees, of the Parish of St. George Middlesex, do hereby offer a Reward of FIFTY POUNDS, for the Discovery and Apprehension of the Person or Persons who committed such Murder, to be paid on Conviction.

By Order of the Churchwardens, Overseers, and Trustees,

JOHN CLEMENT,
VESTRY CLERK.

Ratcliff-highway,
SUNDAY, 8th, DECEMBER, 1811.

SKIRVEN, Printer, Ratcliff Highway, London.

latching, she would have recoiled into the asylum of general darkness.

What was the murderer's meaning in coming along the passage to the front door? The meaning was this: separately, as an individual, Mary was worth nothing at all to him. But, considered as a member of a household, she had this value, viz., that she, if caught and murdered, perfected and rounded the desolation of the house. The case being reported, as reported it would be all over Christendom, led the imagination captive. The whole convey of victims was thus netted; the household ruin was thus full and orbicular; and in that proportion the tendency of men and women, flutter as they might, would be helplessly and hopelessly to sink into the all-conquering hands of the mighty murderer. He had but to say – my testimonials are dated from No.29 Ratcliffe Highway, and the poor vanquished imagination sank powerless before the fascinating rattlesnake eye of the murderer.

Mary began now to ring the bell and to ply the knocker with unintermitting violence. And the natural consequence was, that the next door neighbour, who had recently gone to bed and instantly fallen asleep, was roused.

The poor girl remained sufficiently mistress of herself rapidly to explain the circumstance of her own absence for an hour; her belief that Mr and Mrs Marr's family had all been murdered in the interval and that at this very moment the murderer was in the house.

The person to whom she addressed this statement was a pawnbroker; and a brave man he must have been; for it was a perilous undertaking, merely as a trial of physical strength, singly to face a mysterious assassin. A brick wall, 9 or 10 feet high, divided his own back premises from those of Marr. Over this he vaulted; and at the moment when he was recalling himself to the necessity of going back for a candle, he suddenly perceived a feeble ray of light already glimmering on some part of Marr's premises. Marr's back door stood wide open. Probably the murderer had passed through it one half minute before. Rapidly the brave man passed onwards to the shop, and there beheld the carnage of the night stretched out on the floor, and the narrow premises so floated with gore, that it was hardly possible to escape the pollution of blood in picking out a path to the front door.

By this time the heart-shaking news involved in the outcries of Mary had availed, even at that late hour, to gather a small mob about the house. The pawnbroker threw open the door. One or two watchmen headed the crowd; but the soul-harrowing spectacle checked them, and impressed sudden silence upon their voices, previously so loud. The tragic drama read aloud its own history...

Vain would be all attempts to convey the horror which thrilled the gathering spectators of this piteous tragedy... Suddenly some person appeared amongst the crowd who was aware that the murdered parents had a young infant; this would be found either below stairs, or in one of the bedrooms above. Immediately a stream of people poured down into the kitchen, where at once they saw the cradle - but with the bed-clothes in a state of indescribable confusion. On disentangling these, pools of blood became visible; and the next ominous sign was, that the hood at the head of the cradle had been smashed to pieces. It became evident that the wretch had found himself doubly embarrassed – first, by the arched hood at the head of the cradle, which accordingly he had beat into a ruin with his mallet, and secondly, by the gathering of the blankets and pillows about the baby's head. The free play of his blows had thus been baffled. And he had therefore finished the scene by applying his razor to the throat of the little innocent; after which, with no apparent purpose, as though he had become confused by the spectacle of his own atrocities, he had busied himself in piling the clothes elaborately over the child's corpse.

On the Sunday se'ennight (Sunday the octave from the event), took place the funeral of the Marrs; in the first coffin was placed Marr; in the second Mrs Marr, and the baby in her arms; in the third the apprentice boy. They were buried side by side; and 30,000 labouring people followed the funeral procession, with horror and grief written in their countenances.

As yet no whisper was astir that indicated, even conjecturally, the hideous author of these ruins – this patron of gravediggers. Had as much been known on this Sunday of the funeral concerning that person as became known universally six days later, the people would have gone right from the churchyard to the murderer's lodgings, and (brooking no delay) would have torn him limb from limb.

De Quincey then treats at length a second bloody multiple murder that appeared to be committed by the same hand. The victims were the elderly publican of the *King's Arms* at 81 Gravel Lane (now Garnet Street), his wife Catherine, and their ageing maidservant. It happened that the Williamsons had at the time a lodger in the house, 26-year-old John Turner who, having been aroused from his sleep and overseen the intruder crouched over the bodies, had lowered himself from his window by means of knotted sheets, into the arms of a passing watchman:

. . . a short consultation was held by the people assembled, and it was at once resolved that an entry should be forced into the house by way of the cellar flap. . . On looking round the cellar, the first object that attracted their attention was the body of Mr Williamson, which lay at the foot of the stairs, with a violent contusion on the head, his throat dreadfully cut, and an iron crow by his side. The proceeded upstairs into the parlour, where they found Mrs Williamson also dead, with her skull and throat cut, and blood still issuing from the wounds, and near her lay the body of the servant-woman, whose head was also horribly bruised, and her throat cut in a most shocking manner.

(*The Newgate Calendar*)

This time the police found a vital clue at the scene of the carnage, a sailor's maul, which eventually led to the *Pear Tree* tavern in Cinnamon Street and one of its habituees, John Williams. Williams aroused sufficient suspicion under interrogation at Shadwell police station that he was remanded to Coldbath Fields prison pending further investigation.

On December 28th, John Williams cheated justice and the executioner by hanging himself from a beam in his cell:

On the last day of this fatal year [1811] the remains of this sanguinary assassin were privately removed, at eleven o'clock at night, and conveyed to St George's watch-house, near the London Docks, preparatory to interment.

The procession advanced slowly up Ratcliffe Highway, accompanied by an immense concourse of persons . . . When the cart came opposite the late Mr Marr's house a halt was made for nearly a quarter of an hour. The procession then moved down Old Gravel Lane, along Wapping, up New Crane Lane, and into New Gravel Lane. It then proceeded up the hill, and again entered Ratcliffe Highway, down which it moved into Cannon Street, and advanced to St George's Turnpike, where the new road is intersected by Cannon Street. Here a grave, about six feet deep, had been prepared, immediately over which the main water-pipe runs. Between twelve and one o'clock the body was taken from the platform and lowered into the grave, immediately after a stake was driven through it; and, the pit being covered, this solemn ceremony concluded.

VIEW OF THE BODY OF JOHN WILLIAMS the supposed Murderer of the families of Marr and Williamson, and self-destroyer, approaching the hole dug to receive it, in the Cross Road, at Cannon Street - Turnpike.

"Come to see a man die have you, you curs?"

The Murder of HARRIET LANE
by HENRY WAINWRIGHT
in the month of June 1874
at 215 Whitechapel Road (backing on to Vine Court), E1

When Henry Wainwright and Harriet Lane launched into their roles as man and mistress it was with little anticipation of the tragedy that was to be their *liaison dangereuse*.

Henry was a sociable and socially popular man, to be found always at the centre of a group of educated, cultured friends. He was fond of giving readings of Dickens and Thomas Hood, and he could always be sure of an enthusiastic audience for his lecture 'The Wit of Sidney Smith'. The Wainwrights were a prosperous family, Henry inheriting from his father not only the trade of brush-making but also a share of the latter's considerable fortune. This enabled him to set up in the brush business on his own account, in a shop at No.215 Whitechapel Road, and to provide a comfortable residence in Tredegar Square for himself and the woman whom he had married in 1862.

He had been married for nine years when he met an attractive milliner's apprentice named Harriet Lane at the Broxbourne Gardens pleasure resort. Harriet was then twenty, and in wit, education and background every bit Henry's equal. Before long she had been set up in a house in Mile End, in St Peter's Street, and was in receipt of a weekly stipend of £5 from Wainwright, in addition to the clothes, jewellery, and other costly gifts with which she was showered. In August 1872 Henry and Harriet became the proud parents of a baby daughter; it was a happy event that was repeated in December the following year when, for the sake of propriety, Harriet had published the announcement of her marriage to "Mr Percy King of Chelsea" (in reality, Henry Wainwright).

Inevitably, perhaps, the situation of supporting two homes and a business, of living two domestic lives, began to sour for Henry; frictions began to arise. Whether the real

Mrs Wainwright contributed to the disagreements – if she knew of Harriet's existence at all – we do not know. Certainly one of the first and most crushing blows delivered to Henry Wainwright was his brother's withdrawal from their business partnership. It is at least credible that the regular tapping of company profits to provide Harriet's comforts provided some provocation to brother William. In consequence of some subsequently unwise commercial associations, Henry found himself not only in serious debt, but facing the financial humiliation of bankruptcy. But a life of indulging and being indulged had also begun to leave its mark on Harriet; not least in her increasing dependence upon the liquid joy that she found inside a gin bottle.

To help meet financial needs Harriet's allowance was dramatically withdrawn, with predictable result, and between them Henry and a brother named Thomas hatched the complicated plot that was to remove the in-

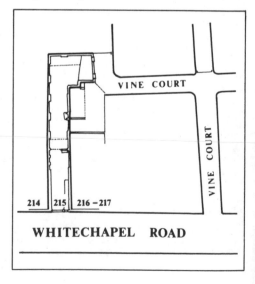

Henry Wainwright

convenience of a fractious, demanding, and by this time alcoholic, mistress.

Henry now visited Harriet always in company with Thomas; Thomas, however, had adopted the name Edward Frieake, and posed as Henry's close friend. (In fact the real Edward Frieake *was* a close friend of Henry's, and was a reputable auctioneer in the City.) Between them, the two brothers sought to effect the transfer of Harriet's affections from one to the other. This done, Harriet announced to the world at large that she was going off with Edward Frieake, and that they intended settling on the Continent. Despite inquiries from family and friends, this was the last ever heard from Harriet.

This did not entirely solve Henry's problems, for while he had disposed of the major drain on his finances, it had done nothing to stop the persistent clamouring of his creditors. In June 1875, almost a year since Harriet had gone 'abroad', Henry Wainwright was declared bankrupt. On September 11th, the possession of his brush warehouse passed into the hands of a Mr Beterend. On this date Henry retained the sevices of a youth named Stokes to help clear the few remaining possessions from the warehouse to Thomas's house; and he made the mistake of leaving the lad in charge of a number of wrapped packages while he went to summon a cab. It was a pity for Wainwright that he did not send Stokes on the errand; a pity for Wainwright that he did not choose a less inquisitive assistant. As it was, as soon as the master was out of sight Stokes was prodding around the foul-smelling bundles, from one of which fell, to the lad's alarm and understandable disgust, a severed human hand in an advanced state of decomposition.

Nosy he may have been, but Stokes was a cool-headed boy, and when Wainwright returned he gave no intimation of his discovery, but declared that he would prefer not to travel in the cab with Henry and the parcels, but would follow on foot and help unload at the other end of the journey.

By the time Stokes had persuaded a couple of policemen that he really had seen what he had seen, and that what he had seen was now travelling in the back of a cab in the charge of Henry Wainwright, Wainwright had a head-start in the direction of brother Thomas's house near London Bridge. And with perfect timing was overtaken by the police while lifting the offending parcels from the back of the cab.

The trial of Henry and Thomas Wainwright opened at the Old Bailey on November 27th 1875; and the grisly story that unfolded, the

Henry Wainwright's brushmaking business at 215 Whitechapel Road

story of the two bullets found in Harriet Lane's severed head; of her burial in the warehouse, and of the ultimate exhumation and dismemberment, put Thomas in prison as an accessory, and sent the murderous Henry to the scaffold.

THE SENTENCE

Lord Chief Justice (Sir James Alexander Cockburn: Prisoner at the bar, you have been found guilty, in my opinion upon the clearest and most conclusive evidence, of the murder of Harriet Louisa Lane, which has been laid to your charge. No one, I think, who has heard this trial can entertain the slightest shadow of doubt of your guilt, and I can only deplore that, standing as you surely are on the brink of eternity, you should have called God to witness the rash assertion which has just issued from your lips.

Wainwright has just protested his innocence of the crime.

There can be no doubt that you took the life of this poor woman, who had been on the closest and most intimate terms of familiarity and affection with you, who had been the mother of your children. You enveigled her into the lone warehouse. The revolver was not there before but it must have been taken there for the purpose, and with that she was slain. The grave was dug there for her remains, which were those you were moving when you were arrested; and about that no one can entertain the shadow of doubt. It was a barbarous, cruel, inhuman, and cowardly act.

I have now only to pass upon you the dreadful sentence of the law, which is that you be taken from hence to the place whence you came, thence to a legal place of execution, to be there hanged by the neck till you shall be dead; and your body be buried within the precincts of the gaol in which you shall last confined after your conviction; and may the Lord have mercy upon your soul.
(Wednesday, 1st December 1875.)

Before the assembled multitude outside Newgate, Henry Wainwright stood and snarled "Come to see a man die, have you, you curs?" They were his last words.

The back of Henry Wainwright's store-room in Vine Court in 1987

NEWGATE – TUESDAY MORNING

"The last act of the Whitechapel tragedy has been played out. The closing scenes took place within the strong walls of Newgate. In the grey hours of the early dawn, Death hovered around the couch of Henry Wainwright. The guilty man awoke on the morning of the 21st, to meet Death face to face. Our artist has endeavoured to realise the situation by the aid of his graphic pencil."

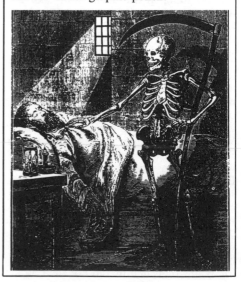

THE WHITECHAPEL TRAGEDY

PLAYING AT WAINWRIGHT

"On Tuesday a ludicrous, but what might have proved fatal, case of hanging occurred at Bedworth. A number of youths joined in a game called 'Wainwright' and drew for the characters represented in the late tragedy. After a trial of three hours, the one whose part it was to enact Wainwright was found guilty and sentenced to be hanged. The youth who represented the Hangman pinioned the prisoner who was then marched to a place of execution. They took leather belts from their waists, fastened them together and placed the noose round his neck, and the other end of the strap was fastened to the iron projecting from the lamp-post. They ran off, leaving him hanging to the lamp-post. Fortunately the strap gave way at the buckle, so what might have been a tragedy ended as a farce."

PLAYING AT WAINWRIGHT

Catch Me When You Can

The Murder of MARY ANN NICHOLS, ANNIE CHAPMAN, ELIZABETH STRIDE, CATHERINE EDDOWES, and MARY (or MARIE) JANE KELLY by an Unknown Assassin called JACK THE RIPPER during the months of August to November 1888 in the Whitechapel area of East London

For the three months from the end of August to the beginning of November in the year of 1888, the Whitechapel area of the East End of London was witness to a series of vicious – and still unsolved – murders. The slayings were characterized by an unparalleled savagery; each of the five victims – all prostitutes – had been attacked from behind and their throats cut; the bodies were afterwards subjected to such mutilation and dissection as to suggest a perverted sexual motive.

The enduring mystery of these, probably the world's most celebrated crimes, has resulted in a Ripper bibliography* itself a bulkier tome than most of the volumes it lists, and this Guide is not an appropriate place in which to enter the forum on Jack's true identity.

There follows instead a graphic, if gruesome, account of the murders themselves, described with texts and illustrations contemporary with the gaslight times of the Ripper's London. And though the capital's East End has changed dramatically in the past hundred years, there are still desolate corners to be found in which lurk the vestiges of Jack's reign of terror.

---

* *Jack the Ripper: A Bibliography and Review of the Literature*, Alexander Kelly.

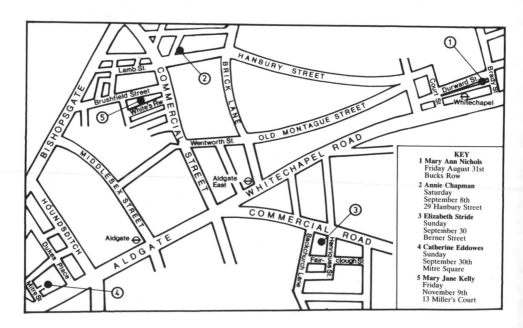

KEY
1 **Mary Ann Nichols** Friday August 31st Bucks Row
2 **Annie Chapman** Saturday September 8th 29 Hanbury Street
3 **Elizabeth Stride** Sunday September 30 Berner Street
4 **Catherine Eddowes** Sunday September 30th Mitre Square
5 **Mary Jane Kelly** Friday November 9th 13 Miller's Court

1. Friday 31 August 1888
Buck's Row (now Durward Street)

MARY ANN 'POLLY' NICHOLS, aged 42

No murder was ever more ferociously and more brutally done. The knife, which must have been a large and sharp one, was jabbed into the deceased at the lower part of the abdomen, and then drawn upwards, not once but twice. The first cut veered to the right, slitting up the groin, and passing over the left hip, but the second cut went straight upward, along the centre of the body, and reaching to the breast-bone . . . The throat is cut in two gashes, there is a gash under the left ear, reaching nearly to the centre of the throat. Along half its length, however, it is accompanied by another one which reaches around under the other ear, making a wide and horrible hole, and nearly severing the head from the body.

(The Star)

The shell of Essex Wharf, Durward St., opposite the spot on which Polly Nichols was slain

2. Saturday 8 September 1888
29 Hanbury Street

ANNIE CHAPMAN
called 'Dark Annie', aged 47

The revolting tale of the Whitechapel murders has been further embellished by the astounding statements which the coroner [Mr Wynne Baxter] deemed fit to make public at his summing up of the case of the unfortunate woman Chapman. The public have supped full of horrors, and now there is added thereto a suggestion which, in spite of its plausibility, is almost too horrible to be credited...it supplies a motive for the deed.

Mr Phillips [Dr George Bagster Phillips, surgeon], being recalled to add further facts to his previous evidence, he stated that the mutilation of the body was of such a character as could only have been effected by a practised hand. It appears that the abdomen had been entirely laid open; that the intestines, severed from their mesenteric attachments had been lifted out of the body, and placed by the shoulder of the corpse; whilst from the pelvis the uterus and its appendages, with the upper part of the vagina and the posterior two-thirds of the bladder, had been entirely removed. No trace of these parts could be found, and the incisions were cleanly cut, avoiding the rectum, and dividing the vagina low enough to avoid injury to the cervix uteri. Obviously the work was that of an expert – of one, at least, who had such knowledge of anatomical or pathological examination as to be enabled to secure the pelvic organs with one sweep of a knife, which must therefore, as Mr Phillips pointed out, have been at least five inches long.

The theory based on this evidence was coherent enough. It suggested that the murderer . . . had committed the crime for the purpose of possessing himself of the uterus. The similarity between the injuries inflicted in this case and those upon the woman Nichols, whose body was found in Buck's Row a few days before, gave from the first the idea that they were the work of the same hand. But in the

Buck's Row case the mutilation did not extend so far, and there was no portion of the body missing. Again, this is explained by those who think that the possession of the uterus was the sole motive, by assuming that the miscreant had not time to complete his design in Buck's Row . . . In the face of these facts, the statement made by Mr Wynne Baxter [the coroner] presents a great *prima facie* probability, but we must deprecate strongly any tendency to jump at a conclusion in a matter which may admit of another interpretation. Mr Baxter said:

"Within a few hours of the issue of the morning papers containing a report of the medical evidence given at the last sitting of the Court, I received a communication from an officer of one of our great medical schools that they had information which might or might not have a distinct bearing on our enquiry. I attended at the first opportunity, and was informed by the sub-curator of the Pathological Museum that some months ago an American had called inquiring of the organ [uterus] that was missing from the deceased. He stated his willingness to give £20 apiece for each specimen. He stated that the object was to issue an actual specimen with each copy of a publication on which he was then engaged. He was told that his request was impossible to be complied with, but he still urged his request. He wished them preserved not in spirits of wine, the usual medium, but in glycerine, in order to preserve them in a flaccid condition, and he wished them sent to America direct."

Although this statement seems to afford a satisfactory explanation of the motive for the deed and mutilation of the corpse, it is impossible to read it without being struck with certain improbabilities and absurdities that go far to upset the theory altogether...

(*The Lancet*, 30 September 1888)

3. Sunday 30 September 1888
Berner Street (now Henriques Street)

ELIZABETH STRIDE
called 'Long Liz', aged 45

4. Sunday 30 September 1888
Mitre Square

CATHERINE EDDOWES, aged 43

Two more murders must now be added to the blacklist of similar crimes of which the East End has very lately been the scene. The circumstances of both of them bear a close resemblance to those of the former atrocities. The victim in both has been a woman. In neither can robbery have been the motive, nor can the deed be set down as the outcome of an ordinary street brawl. Both have unquestionably been murders deliberately planned, and carried out by the hand of some one who has been no novice to the work. It was early yesterday morning that the bodies of the two women were discovered at places within a quarter of an hour's walk of one another, and at intervals of somewhat less than an hour. The first body was found lying in a yard in Berner-street, a low thoroughfare running out of the Commercial-road. The discovery was made about 1 o'clock in the early morning by a carter who was entering the yard to put up his cart. The body was that of a woman with a deep gash on the throat, running almost from ear to ear. She was quite dead, but the corpse was still warm, and in the opinion of the medical experts who were promptly summoned to the place, the deed of blood must have been done not many minutes before. The probability seems to be that the murderer was interrupted by the arrival of the carter, and that he made his escape unobserved, under the shelter of the darkness, which was almost total at the spot...The body has been identified as that of Elizabeth Stride, a widow according to one account, according to another a woman living apart from her husband, and by all accounts belonging to the 'unfortunate' class. Her movements have been traced up to a certain point. She left her house in Dean-street, Spitalfields, between 6 and 7 o'clock on Saturday

evening, saying that she was not going to meet anyone in particular. From that hour there is nothing certainly known about her up to the time at which her body was found, lifeless indeed, but not otherwise mutilated than by the gash in the throat, which had severed the jugular vein and must have caused instantaneous death...

...Not so the corpse of the second victim. In this case the purpose of the murderer had been fulfilled, and a mutilation inflicted of the same nature as that upon the body of Annie Chapman. It was in the south-western corner of Mitre-square, in Aldgate, that the second body was found. It was again the body of a woman, and again death had resulted from a

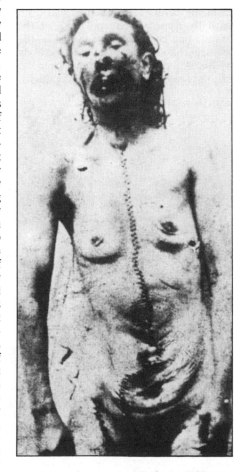

Mortuary photograph of Catherine Eddowes showing post-mortem suture

deep wound across the throat. But in this instance the face had also been so slashed as to render it hard for the remains to be identified, and the abdomen had been ripped up, and a portion of the intestines had been dragged out and left lying about the neck...The deed of blood had been the work of a practised hand. The body bore clear proof of some anatomical skill, but the murderer had been in a hurry, and had carried out his design in a more rough fashion that that with which Annie Chapman's body had been mutilated. The best chance of identification seems to be from the victim's dress, of which a minute description has been put out...Beyond this we are unable at present to go."

(The Times, 1 October 1888)

5. Friday 9 November 1888
13 Miller's Court (now demolished)

MARY (or MARIE) JANE KELLY
aged 25

The throat had been cut right across with a knife, nearly severing the head from the body. The abdomen had been partially ripped open, and both of the breasts had been cut from the body, the left arm, like the head, hung to the body by the skin only. The nose had been cut off, the forehead skinned, and the thighs, down to the feet, stripped of the flesh. The abdomen had been slashed with a knife across and downwards, and the liver and entrails wrenched away. The entrails and other portions of the frame were missing, but the liver, etc., it is said, were found placed between the feet of this poor victim. The flesh from the thighs and legs, together with the breasts and nose, had been placed by the murderer on the table, and one of the hands of the dead woman had been pushed into her stomach."

(Illustrated Police News)

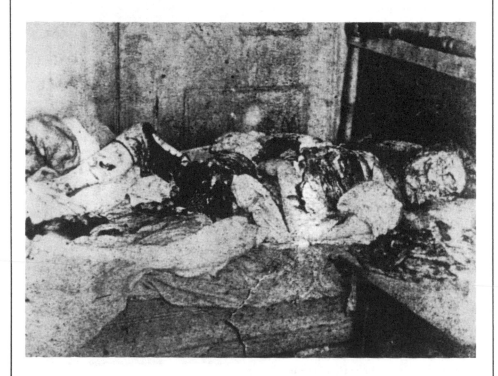

Mary Kelly as she was discovered in Miller's Court

Murder on a Railway Train
The Murder of Mr THOMAS BRIGGS
by FRANZ MÜLLER
on Saturday the 9th of July 1864
aboard a Railway Train of the North London Line,
between Bow and Hackney Wick

HORRID

MURDER

OF

A GENTLEMAN,

IN A

RAILWAY CARRIAGE.

Another base and dreadful murder,
　Now again, alas, has been,
One of the most atrocious murders
　It is, as ever yet was seen;
Poor Thomas Briggs, how sad to mention,
　Was in a first-class railway carriage slain,
Between Old Ford and Hackney Wick,
　Which caused excitement, care and pain.

Oh, listen to this railway murder
　Poor Briggs received the fatal wound,
Between Old Ford Bridge and Hackney Wick
　And very near great London town.

They found a hat in the railway carriage,
　Made in Crawford-street, St. Marylebone,
In which poor Thomas Briggs was riding,
　On his journey to his home;
Alas, poor man, he little thought
　That he would be deprived of life,
In the railway carriage, by a villain,
　At ten o'clock that fatal night.

Oh, little did he think they'd kill him,
　He had no thought he was to die,
Upon that fatal Saturday evening,
　On the 9th day of July;
The villains in the carriage slew him,
　For plunder Thomas Briggs was killed,
In a first-class carriage they did rob him,
　And all around his blood was spilled.

Thomas Briggs was a faithful servant,
　To Robarts, Lubbock and Company,
Three hundred pounds rewards is offered,
　Soon may the murderer taken be,

And brought to justice for the dreadful
　Deed he done, as we may hear,
And glad we are there is before us,
　A clue to the wicked murderer.

They have traced his watch-chain in the city,
　The very key, as we are told,
Stole from poor Briggs that fatal evening,
　Albert curb, with swivel seal in gold.
Robbed of nearly all that he possessed,
　He was, upon that fatal night,
Between Old Ford and Hackney Wick,
　In the Railway Carriage in daylight.

This sad affair has caused excitement,
　Far and near, for miles around,
And thousands to the spot are going
　From all around great London town.
And on the spot they look with horror,
　Where poor Thomas Briggs was killed,
They view with grief, with pain and sorrow,
　Where his crimson blood was spilled.

Oh, God above, look down from Heaven,
　Point the murdering villains out,
Let stern justice close pursue them,
　Never let them roam about;
On him, or them, we all are certain,
　Has on the brow the mark of Cain,
Thus ends the brutal horrid murder,
　Which has caused such grief and pain.

On that fatal Saturday evening,
　They left him in his crimson gore,
July the 9th, in a railway carriage,
　Eighteen hundred and sixty-four.

On July 9th, 1864 – a Saturday – Thomas Briggs, seventy years old, and expensively dressed, was unlucky enough to be travelling on that branch of the recently introduced railway that ran from Fenchurch Street in London to Hackney Wick.

It was unlucky because his sole travelling companion in that carriage was Franz Müller. Between them they were going to create a First. Franz Müller was to commit the first murder on a British train; Briggs was to be the first victim. Müller, a 25-year-old German national, was a tailor by trade; he had arrived in England having failed to make his fortune in the Fatherland; he had failed to make it in England as well and, at the time of his journey with Thomas Briggs, was planning to try again in America. And it seems likely that Müller viewed his travelling companion's heavy gold watch and chain as a move in this direction.

What is certain is that at Bow, travellers boarding the train at that carriage found the compartment empty. Uninhabited, that is; for it contained a black bag, an expensive walking stick, a large quantity of blood, and a hat. The unfortunate Briggs was later found where he had been thrown on to the track between Hackney Wick and Bow, alive, but only for a short time.

It was Scotland Yard's Chief-Inspector William Tanner who traced the stolen gold chain; to a jeweller in Cheapside by the name of John Death, who clearly remembered exchanging the chain for a newer one and a ring – for a customer with a foreign accent. A description of the hat left in the railway carriage – known not to belong to Mr Briggs, so assumed to be one left by mistake by his killer – also led to identification; its last owner had been a German tailor named Franz Müller. A search of Müller's lodgings revealed hasty flight, though another lucky break for Tanner came when an acquaintance of Müller's volunteered the information that the culprit was at that moment aboard the *Victoria* bound for New York. The rest was easy. The steamship *City of Manchester*, numbering Tanner and Detective-Sergeant George Clarke among its passengers, overtook the *Victoria* by a couple of weeks. After the formality of the quayside arrest, Müller's baggage was searched and found to contain Thomas Briggs's gold watch,

Franz Müller in 1864

and the poor man's now rather truncated hat, picked up by mistake at the scene of the murder.

Franz Müller's trial before Mr Baron Martin at the Old Bailey opened on 27 October 1864. For the prosecution, the Solicitor-General, Sir Robert Collier; Müller's defence was in the hands of the formidable Serjeant John Humffreys Parry (paid for by the German Legal Protection Society). The fame of the Briggs hat, which the defendant had shortened by some inches in order to disguise it, extended far beyond the confines of the court. Indeed, the 'Müller' style entered into the history of fashion, and was affected by many fashionable young gentlemen of the day. It was also the hat that hanged Franz Müller. For after a retirement of only fifteen minutes, the jury returned a 'Guilty' verdict, and the prisoner was sentenced to hang. Due punishment was carried out on November the 14th.

A postscript reflected the understandable worry of railway passengers subsequent to the Müller affair, and the attempts by several of the railway companies to reassure their customers by the cutting of peep-holes between the compartments. Christened by passengers 'Müller's Lights', these holes so restricted privacy – a valued commodity in the day – that the scheme was eventually abandoned.

"An evil, cynical, and depraved man"

The Abduction of KEIGHLEY BARTON

on Saturday the 10th of August 1985
from near her home in Sebert Road, E7

and her subsequent Murder by her Stepfather
RONALD WILLIAM BARTON

Most contemporary murders attract little more than a mention in the newspapers. It is only the exceptional case, exceptional in the personalities involved or the sequence of circumstances, which catches the headlines and enters the public imagination. There are also occasionally crimes which encapsulate a social dilemma, which seem somehow to be crimes of their time. The abduction and murder of 14-year-old Keighley Barton is not a pleasant story, but it did encapsulate a very particular and far-reaching social dilemma. It helped to bring into the public consciousness a very painful and emotive subject which people would prefer not to entertain the sexual abuse of children within the supposed 'safe haven' of the family.

Ronald Barton was forty-five years old when he was arrested in 1985, and had been a mini-cab driver, though he was unemployed at that time. For the origins of the crime, however, it is necessary to go back fourteen years to the time when Barton began to live with his 22-year-old girlfriend, Theresa, and the five-month-old baby girl, Keighley, that she had borne to another man. Two years later, in 1974, the couple were married and

subsequently had two other children, both boys. What Theresa Barton was not aware of when she married was that her husband already had a long police record of sexual offences. The full list gives some idea of the potential danger that young Keighley was placed under in the family home.

1959 –Unlawful sex with a girl, aged 14 – Absolute Discharge.
1961 –Indecent assault on a girl, aged 15 – Conditional Discharge.
1962 –Indecent assault on a girl, aged 16 – Six Months in Gaol.
1963 –Indecent assault on a girl, aged 16 – One Year in Gaol.
1965 –Grievous bodily harm to a girl – Nine Months in Gaol.
1966 –Assault with intent to rob – Eighteen Months in Gaol.
1968 –Indecent assault on a girl.
1970 –Indecent assault on a girl, aged 15 – Twenty-one Months in Gaol.

It cannot be known exactly when Ronald Barton began to interfere with Keighley, but the first time that the matter came to the attention of the authorities was in 1980,

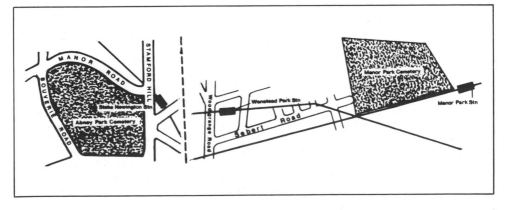

when, with both Keighley and her mother giving evidence against him, Ronald Barton was given a one-year suspended sentence for acts of gross indecency on Keighley. Keighley Barton was just eight years old.

Barton was later to claim that he took medical advice about his problem after this incident, but if he did it had little effect. It may be wondered why Mrs Barton, now aware of the full extent of her husband's 'tendencies', continued to live with Barton and subject herself and her daughter to the inevitable risks. Ronald Barton was a very violent, aggressive and domineering man. He thought nothing of keeping his family in a constant state of fear with threats of injury and worse; indeed, he seemed to positively enjoy it. Mrs Barton later stated that on a number of occasions both she and Keighley were forced to submit to sexual acts under the direct persuasion of a gun barrel. It must have taken a great deal of courage in the first place to inform the authorities of Barton's behaviour. It took even greater courage to accuse him again, as Mrs Barton did in 1982, though at the last minute Keighley refused to testify under the direct threat once more of a gun placed to her head. This did, however, alert the authorities sufficiently for them to place her in care in a council hostel.

Unfortunately, Keighley was unhappy at the hostel and soon ran away, back to her home, to her mother whom she loved and was very worried about; but also back to the brutalities of Ronald Barton. In 1984 Mrs Barton finally decided that something drastic needed to be done. A court order was obtained, banning Barton from going within a quarter of a mile of the family home at Sebert Road, Forest Gate. At the same time Mrs Barton and Keighley together held the threat over his head that they would testify to his indecent assaults on the young girl if he caused any more trouble. And this was a considerable threat to make to Barton, who had been in prison before and knew well the kind of 'treatment' he could expect inside as a molester of young girls. So he moved out and took a flat in Mildenhall Road, Clapton. Mrs Barton took a new 'friend', Eric Cross, into the family home and Keighley was sent back to the council hostel. When Barton visited her there she stood up to his bluster and told him that he must give up the idea of living with her mother or he would go to prison for a long time.

This seemed at first to be a workable solution to the tragedy, but it didn't take account of the bruising that Barton's massive ego had suffered. Apart from the frustration of his libidinous urges, Barton also felt a bitter resentment at his humiliating dismissal from the family home and the separation from his own two sons. As he immersed himself in this anger and hatred, a vicious plan of revenge began to form in his mind. If Keighley were removed from the scene the principal witness to his unnatural crimes would be silenced, and at the same time he would pay back his wife for defying him. Much later, in prison, he told the police, "She took my two boys away from me. I took her girl. Now she can suffer. I hate her. She has ruined my life."

Keighley had again run away from the council home and returned to live with her mother, her two brothers and her mother's new boyfriend. Barton began to spy out the land. On August 5th 1985 he again confronted his wife. He warned her that he had a gun and assured her that he would take somebody with him if he ever had to use it; he told her that he would put her ten feet under if she ever testified against him. On the evening of the 9th he was again spying on the family, watching Mrs Barton, her boyfriend, Keighley and his sons through the back window as they looked at television. At 11.30pm Keighley had a row with her mother about going to bed, which ended in her running upstairs and locking herself in her room. On the morning of Saturday, the 10th of August 1985 it was raining, but Keighley decided to take the family alsatian, Rex, out for a walk on a piece of wasteland near the house. Later in the morning the dog returned alone. Keighley Barton would never be seen alive again.

Ronald Barton was immediately suspected of being responsible for his stepdaughter's disappearance. His circumstances gave him the obvious motive; and then there was his inescapable record. When he was questioned he denied all knowledge of the matter, but in such a surly and uncooperative fashion that the suspicions of the police were merely heightened. On the 17th of August he was arrested, but then bailed. There was no real proof that Keighley was actually dead. Returning to his flat, Barton asked a neighbour if the post had arrived, as he was expecting an important letter. In the next few days two important letters did arrive, one for Barton, the other for Mrs Barton. They were both in Keighley's handwriting. In both she said that she had lied when she had made allegations against Barton. In her mother's letter she also called the new boyfriend a 'creep'.

For some time no new evidence emerged, despite extensive publicity about Keighley's disappearance. There were the inevitable crop of possible sightings, but none of them seemed to lead anywhere. The police became convinced that she was dead, and had been dead since soon after her disappearance. She would have remained alive only as long as it took Barton to coerce her into writing those very convenient letters.

On the 23rd of October Ronald Barton was officially charged with the abduction and murder of Keighley and remanded in Brixton Prison. He now made the great mistake of boasting of his cleverness to a fellow-prisoner. Barton was under the common misapprehension that a man cannot be convicted of murder without the evidence of a body. He bragged that he had paid £50 to have his old Peugeot car crushed, with Keighley's body inside it. He said that when the metal was melted the corpse "would come to the top as dross and there would be no other trace of her". He also tried to persuade another prisoner to give him a false alibi. Every word of this went straight back to the police.

Ronald Barton's trial was set for the 25th of February, 1986, but evidence was immediately brought by Mr Henry Grumwald for the defence that Keighley had been sighted by several witnesses over the past six months. The case was necessarily adjourned.

It finally came to court at the Old Bailey on the 7th of October 1986, with Mr Justice Turner presiding, Mr Michael Worsley QC for the prosecution and Mr Robin Gray QC defending. It began with the unusual step of the judge himself summoning two witnesses, Mrs Linda Jackson, a teacher in Keighley's school, and her young son, who thought they had seen Keighley alive and well in Walthamstow Market in July 1986. The main

case then went ahead. The prosecution's evidence was necessarily circumstantial, with no body as proof, and they were further hampered by being unable (under the rules of evidence) to present Barton's previous history as a sex offender. The defence response was twofold. Their strongest card was the slimness of the evidence that Keighley was actually dead. Then Barton put forward a most unlikely alibi to cover his movements on the 10th of August, the day of Keighley's disappearance. It seems that he had gone up to London to watch the Changing of the Guard and had then spent the rest of the day just walking around aimlessly because, he said, he was brooding and needed to be around people. Unfortunately, he was unaware, when cross-examined, that Central London was teeming with football fans on that particular morning, up for the Everton versus Manchester United Charity Shield game.

The jury were out for nearly two days, but returned on the 30th of October and, by a verdict of ten to two found Ronald Barton guilty on the two counts of the abduction and the murder of Keighley Barton. Mr Justice Turner, passing sentence, said, "I am satisfied that you for many years abused a girl who should have been entitled to regard you as her father. You started to gratify your unnatural desires when that girl was only eight years old. . . You not only debased Keighley, but you were prepared to commit the ultimate crime of murder against that poor girl, in an effort to avoid the punishment which awaited you. . . There is no question that you are an evil, cynical and depraved man, whom society – including your wife and family – are entitled to be and will be protected from for many years." The judge then sentenced Barton to life imprisonment, to last a minimum of twenty-five years. As Ronald Barton was taken down Mrs Barton screamed at him from the gallery, "I hope you rot, you bastard!"

The very day after he was sentenced, Barton requested to see the Assistant Governor of Wormwood Scrubs, where he was held. He admitted to the murder of Keighley Barton and then rebutted his earlier assertion that he had disposed of the body in a car crusher. He now said that the body had been buried in Abney Park Cemetery, Stoke Newington, near to his flat in Clapton. Whether this was a last-minute fit of remorse, an attempt to draw attention to his cleverness, or a piece of enlightened self-interest is impossible to know. As a convicted child abuser and killer he was certainly in need of the cooperation of the prison authorities to protect him from the rough justice that awaits such despised offenders behind prison walls.

A police team led by Detective Superintendent Charles Farquhar instituted a search of the old overgrown cemetery grounds. In the last sweep of the day a young girl police cadet discovered a skirt, a cardigan and a piece of shoe in the undergrowth. Beneath these sad relics was buried a decomposed body. On the finger was a cheap, fake Mexican ring that Keighley always wore. At the inquest, on the 18th of February 1987, the pathologist, Dr Peter Vanezis, was able to state that she had been stabbed five times in the chest. The six defence wounds on her left arm bore witness to the spirited attempt she had made to ward off the murderous attack.

On the 25th of February the body of Keighley Barton was finally laid to rest in Manor Park Cemetery, Forest Gate, just at the end of the road where she had lived out most of a short, frightened and brutalized existence of just fourteen years.

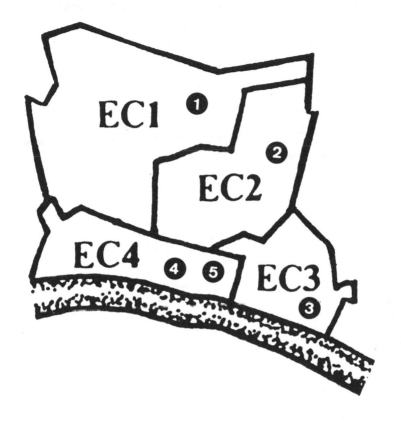

East-Central London

1. Michael BARRETT 152
2. John PRICE 154
3. Robert BLAKESLEY 156
4. William JOHNSON and Jane HOUSDEN 157
5. Elizabeth BROWNRIGG 159

The Patriot Game

The Incidental Killing of SARAH ANN HODGKINSON and Others by MICHAEL BARRET and other Fenians in an attempt to rescue their comrades from the Clerkenwell House of Detention, EC1 on Friday the 13th of December 1867 and their subsequent Trial for Murder

The Irish Problem has been a festering cause of violence, dissension and hatred for centuries. It may recede from public prominence for periods of time, but the underlying resentments are always waiting to be brought back to the surface and there are always men of strong conviction prepared to go to any lengths to speed up that process. The formation of the secret Fenian Brotherhood in the middle years of the nineteenth century was an attempt by Irish Nationalists to use violence to force the English politicians into a serious consideration of the Irish problem.

1867 was an important date in this process. Riots in Dublin were followed by a successful attempt to rescue two Fenian prisoners by Allen. Gould, and Larkin from a police wagon in Manchester, involving the fatal shooting of Police Sergeant Brett [see *Murder Club Guide No.3*]. This incident gave the Fenians the confidence to attempt an even greater coup, the rescue of Richard O'Sullivan Burke and Joseph Casey from Clerkenwell Prison in London.

On the 12th of December 1867 an attempt was made to dynamite the wall of Clerkenwell Prison, but the fuse failed to take. The next day, the 13th, at 3.45pm the plan was tried again. A wagon brought a large cask of dynamite up to the prison wall, a white ball was thrown over the wall to warn the two prisoners (who should have been exercising in the yard at that time) and the fuse was lit. Unfortunately for the would-be rescuers, the police had got wind of a plot and the two prisoners had been judiciously removed elsewhere. A huge explosion pierced the wall and also devastated the block of tena-

ments opposite. As an eye-witness later described, "Many adjacent tenaments were stripped clearly of their frontages and left open like Doll's Houses, with the kettles still singing on the hobs." Six persons were killed immediately, six more died later and one hundred and twenty were injured. All the victims were women and children, because of the time of day.

Five men and a woman were quickly arrested and brought for trial at the Old Bailey before Lord Chief Justice Cockburn and Baron Bramwell, charged with the murder of Sarah Ann Hodgkinson, one of the victims. The prosecution was led by the Attorney-General and the Solicitor-General, but the defendants, having no money, had only junior counsel to defend them. The main defendant, Michael Barrett, who was accused of having actually lit the fuse, made a particular contrast to the other ragged and wretched prisoners, standing erect and proud in a claret-coloured coat and grey trousers. Two of the other defendants soon turned Queen's evidence against Barrett,

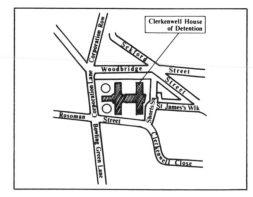

and even had the gall to demand part of the reward that had beeen offered at the time of the explosion. The woman prisoner, who had tried to hang herself in her cell, was soon acquitted for lack of evidence and kissed Barrett's hand as she left the court.

Although Barrett continued to maintain his innocence of the ghastly deed, and made one of the most effective and affecting appeals to the bench to grace the dock at the Old Bailey, his fate was in little doubt. Barrett was convicted, while the other defendants were acquitted. In a final impassioned reply to the bench Barrett spoke with sentiments that echo down the centuries of Irish nationalism, "If it is murder to love Ireland more deeply than life, then indeed I am a murderer . . . If it should please the God of Justice to turn to some account, for the benefit of my suffering country, the sacrifice of my poor worthless life, I could, by the grace of God, ascend the scaffold with firmness, strengthened by the consoling reflection that the stain of murder did not rest upon me, and mingling my prayers for the salvation of my immortal soul with those for the regeneration of my native land."

The public execution of Michael Barrett was set for the 26th of May, 1868, outside the Debtor's Door of Newgate Prison. Large crowds gathered to witness the spectacle. Barrett's proud and noble demeanour in the face of death earned hushed respect from the crowd. When the trap-door fell Barrett's body did not so much as shudder. Calcraft, the hangman, returning to cut down the body after the customary one hour was met with cries from the still assembled populace of "Come on, body snatcher! Take away the man you've killed."

The hanging of Michael Barrett was the last public execution to be held in Britain. Three days after Barrett suffered the ultimate sanction, the Capital Punishment Act was given royal assent [see Appendix to *Murder Club Guide No.2*]. Henceforth executions in Britain would be carried out within the privacy of prison walls.

The final testament to Michael Barrett must, however, be the words of William Ewart Gladstone, that the Clerkenwell Explosion and the other Irish Republican activities at that time had "first induced the British people to embrace, in a manner forcign to their habits in other times, the vast importance of the Irish controversy".

The explosion at Clerkenwell Prison, the force of which killed twelve people and destroyed the frontage of the houses opposite

The Hangman Hanged

The Murder of ELIZABETH WHITE
by Hangman JOHN PRICE

in the year 1718
on Bunhill Fields, EC2

In the year 1718, while George I ruled Great Britain and Ireland, John Price, ex-sailor and confirmed villain, reigned as Common Hangman. His occupancy of this throne was a short one, culminating in his ignominious death at the end of his successor's rope – hanged for the murder of a woman whose audacious crime was to resist Price's attempt at assault.

It is recorded of John Price that he "first drew his breath in the fog-end of the suburbs of London, and, like Mercury, became a thief as soon as ever he peeped out of the shell. So prone was he to vice, that as soon as he could speak he would curse and swear with as great a passion and vileness as is frequently heard round any gaming table. Moreover, to this unprofitable talent of profaneness he added that of lying."

Sentenced to death the first time by the Chelmsford magistrate, he was reprieved on the recommendation of his former master, whose position of High Sheriff of the County of Essex enabled him to bestow such gratuitous – and in this case undeserved – kindness.

On his way once more to London, Price was next apprehended as a pickpocket, and cast into the Bristol Newgate and flogged. He fared little better at sea, discovering that life on board a man-o'-war, far from leading him out of temptation, encouraged him to pilfer from his fellow-seamen, a habit which even such characteristically nautical punishments as whipping at a gun, pickling with brine, and keel-hauling failed to break by the time the ship re-entered Portsmouth harbour two years later.

Price's career in crime was marginally more successful on dry land – at least in so far as he tended to get caught less often, though the good times finally came to an end and, chastened by a spell in Newgate and another

flogging at the cart's tail, Price endeavoured to change his fortune by marriage.

His wife, Betty, was employed at Newgate Gaol – where probably they met – in the capacity of a run-around; that is, she ran errands for such of the prisoners as had money to pay for the service. It was through his wife's contacts that John raised himself to the position of hangman for the county of Middlesex.

Nevertheless the new hangman, shiftless by nature, could not long stay out of trouble and despite a salary approaching £40 per year, and the customary perquisite of the condemned man's clothing to sell, John Price soon found himself in the Marshalsea Prison and out of a job as executioner.

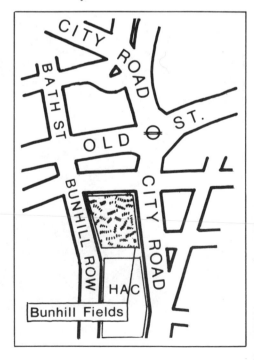

Bunhill Fields

When we next encounter the fortunes of John Price he has been released from the Marshalsea, and is about to slip into even deeper trouble:

> What brought him to this end was his going one night over Bunhill Fields in his drunken airs, when he met an old woman, named Elizabeth White, a watchman's wife, who sold pastry-ware about the streets. He violently assaulted her in a barbarous manner, almost knocking one of her eyes out of her head, giving her several bruises about her body, breaking one of her legs, and wounding her in the belly. Whilst he was acting this inhumanity two men came along at the same time, and hearing dreadful groans supposed somebody was in distress, and having the courage to pursue the sound as well as they could, at last came up to the distressed woman, which made Price damn them for their impudence. However, they secured him, and brought him to the watch-house in Old Street, from whence a couple of watchmen were sent to fetch the old woman out of Bunhill Fields, who within a day or two died, under the surgeon's hands.
>
> (*The Annals of Newgate*)

Newgate. Enter Price yet again.

At length the fatal day came wherein he was to bid adieu to the world, which was on a Saturday, the 31st of May, 1718. As he was riding in the cart he several times pulled a bottle of Geneva out of his pocket to drink before he came to the place of execution, which was in Bunhill Fields, where he committed the murder. Having arrived at the fatal tree, he was, upon Mr Ordinary's examination, found so ignorant on the ground of religion that he troubled himself not much about it; but valuing himself upon his former profession of being hangman, styled himself finisher of the law, and so was turned off the gibbet, aged upwards of forty years.

(*The Annals of Newgate*)

Bunhill Fields Burial Ground: it is said that Bunhill is a corruption of 'Bone Hill' through 'Bonhill', and derives from the transfer here, in 1549, of 100 cartloads of bones to ease the congestion in St Paul's Cathedral charnel-house. It later became the main burying-ground for the Non-Conformists, and served to accommodate many victims of the Plague

"My wife, or my life!"
The Murder of his Brother-in-Law JAMES BURDON by ROBERT BLAKESLEY
on Tuesday the 21st of September 1841
at the *King's Head* (now demolished), 44 Eastcheap, EC3

Robert Blakesley was born into a life of relative comfort and advantage; his early employment was in his father's clothing business in Leadenhall Street, London. A handsome, plausible and ambitious young man, he soon chaffed at family restrictions and left home to set up on his own as a butcher at Sevenoaks in Kent. Unfortunately, his business acumen was not quite equal to his ambition and he had to borrow large sums of money in order to build a slaughterhouse on to his establishment.

In 1841, at the age of twenty-seven, he decided to marry, and borrowed further sums to pay for the wedding and the purchase of a substantial residence at Seal, near Sevenoaks, for his bride, Sarah. Having exhausted all other sources of finance to keep his waning business afloat, Blakesley approached his new brother-in-law, James Burdon, the owner of the *King's Head* public house in Eastcheap, London, for a loan. Burdon, knowing nothing of his dubious reputation, readily agreed, with the suggestion that Sarah should stay with her sister and himself at the hostelry until Blakesley had straightened out his circumstances. This arrangement was agreed to, and Blakesley settled to spending much of his time at the inn.

By chance, however, Burdon happened to visit Sevenoaks on business and was quickly made aware of the full scale of Blakesley's debts and the general opprobrium with which he was regarded in Kent. In a stormy confrontation Burdon revoked his loan and refused Blakesley entrance to the inn to visit his wife. Blakesley, who had a foul temper, took this none too well, lurking menacingly around the neighbourhood and drinking heavily. He was heard to say, pointing to a knife in a butcher's window, "If I had that, I think I should have used

it" and talked further about going to visit his 'old woman' the next day.

The next day, the 21st of September 1841, Blakesley bought a knife in Aldgate High Street and asked for it to be sharpened. Nothing further was seen of him until late into the evening, when he suddenly burst into the bar of the *King's Head*, where his wife was helping to serve customers. With a cry of "My wife, or my life!" he plunged a knife into her left side. Turning round, he saw Burdon asleep in a chair. Leaping across the bar in a paroxysm of rage, he stuck the blade into Burdon's abdomen, ripping open his intestines with fatal effect. Turning towards Mrs Burdon, his sister-in-law, he struck out at her, but the knife was partially deflected by his staggering, wounded wife. Leaving the two bleeding women clutching one another, he walked towards the doorway, threw down the knife, paused to take in the bloody scene with a look of immense satisfaction and then ran out into the night.

Having thus made his escape, Blakesley wandered, penniless and confused, for some days. He was seen in woods near Potter's Bar and later, selling off his few meagre possessions (a razor strop, a corkscrew and a hairbrush) and begging for food near Hatfield. He continued in this demented state until he was eventually taken into custody for destitution. In the cell he kept repeating "I am a miserable man" and then asked a policeman if he had heard of 'the murder', saying "I am the man!". On being told that his wife was still alive, he replied "Thank God!", then continued, "Oh, that shriek! That shriek! I hear it now. I did not mean to hurt Burdon or his wife. I meant to kill my own wife and then myself."

Blakesley was tried at the Old Bailey before Lord Abinger, on Thursday 21st October. He sat throughout the trial with a handkerchief over his face, reacting wildly when the sentence of death had been passed. In prison, awaiting execution, he admitted that he had been feigning madness and went to his death eventually with some self-possession, though he was observed to struggle mightily on the rope. Just days later his wife passed away, not so much from her wounds as from sheer despair and misery.

Murder in the Old Bailey
The Murder of Mr SPURLING, a Turnkey
by WILLIAM JOHNSON and JANE HOUSDEN
in early September 1714
at the Old Bailey Session House, EC4

Johnson was a native of Northamptonshire, where he served his time as a butcher, and removing to London, he opened a shop in Newport Market; but business not succeeding to his expectation, he pursued a variety of speculations, until at length he sailed for Gibraltar, where he was appointed a mate to one of the surgeons of the garrison. Having saved some money at this place, he came back to his native country, where he soon spent it, and then had recourse to the highway for a supply. Being apprehended in consequence of one of his robberies, he was convicted, but received a pardon. Previously to this he had been acquainted with Jane Housden, his fellow in crime, who had been tried and convicted of coining, had obtained a pardon, but who was again in custody for a similar offence. On the day that she was to be tried, and just as she was brought down to the bar of the Old Bailey, Johnson called to see her; but Mr Spurling, the head Turnkey, telling him that he could not speak to her till her trial was ended, he instantly drew a pistol and shot Spurling dead on the spot, in the presence of the Court

and all the persons attending to hear the trials, Mrs Housden at the same time encouraging him in the perpetration of this singular murder. The event had no sooner happened than the judges, thinking it unnecessary to proceed on the trial of the woman for coining, ordered both the parties to be tried for murder;

and, there being many witnesses to the deed, they were convicted, and received sentence of death. From this time to that of their execution, which took place on the 19th of September, 1714, and even at the place of their death, they behaved as if they were wholly insensible of the enormity of the crime which they had committed; and notwithstanding the publicity of their offence, they had the confidence to deny it to the last moment of their lives. Nor did they show any signs of compunction for their former sins. After hanging the usual time, Johnson was hanged in chains near Holloway, between Islington and Highgate. [see *Murder Club Guide No.2* for a note on Hanging in Chains]

(*The Newgate Calendar*, London, 1776)

In order to understand the extraordinary circumstance of an officer of the High Court being shot dead inside the Court itself, it helps to recognize the very different architectural and administrative structure of the Old Bailey in the eighteenth century. A significant point was that the 'new' Sessions House, erected in 1673 to replace the building destroyed by the Great Fire of London was, although under cover, open on one side to the air. This expedient (seen in the illustration) at least helped protect Justices and jurors from the threat of gaol-fever* being transmitted by the prisoners brought before them, and helped to dilute the foul stench coming off their unwashed bodies. Offenders were brought straight from the gaol and herded into the enclosure known as the Bail Dock; when their cases were called the prisoners were transferred to the Court Dock. A high prison population ensured that the Bail Dock was filled to capacity, necessitating a large number of those awaiting trial being kept in the verminous Hold beneath the Court. Selling places in the open air became, therefore, one of the perks of the Court gaoler – half-a-crown was what it required to keep a prisoner from the infections of the Hold.

It happens that Spurling was notoriously exploitative of his position, and his brutality to the prisoners in his care was legend. Indeed, it is certain that if William Johnson had not despatched him it would not have been long before somebody else did.

---

* See *Murder Club Guide No.4* for a note on the outbreaks of gaol-fever in England's prisons.

James Brownrigg, whose occupation is variously recorded as plumber and house-painter, after living seven years in Greenwich, came to London and took a house in Flower-de-Luce [Fleur de Lys] Court, Fetter Lane, where he carried on the greater part of his business; he also had a small dwelling at Islington used as an occasional retreat.

His wife Elizabeth was the mother of sixteen children, and having practised midwifery, helped feed the many hungry mouths by virtue of this skill. The fact that she was held in some respect is indicated by her appointment by the overseers of the poor of St Dunstan's parish to the post of midwife to the poor women in the workhouse; which duty she appeared to perform to the entire satisfaction of her employers and, it is said, with great care and tenderness.

Mary Mitchell, a poor girl in the care of the precinct of Whitefriars, was put out as an apprentice to Mrs Brownrigg in the year 1765; and at about the same time, Mary Jones, one of the children of the Foundling Hospital, was likewise placed with her in the same capacity; and she had other apprentices. Lest it be thought that Brownrigg was charity personified, it must be remembered that anybody willing to take on an 'apprentice' from the workhouse was given £5 towards expenses (as any reader of Dickens's *Oliver Twist* will remember). As Mrs Brownrigg also received pregnant women to lie-in privately at her home, these girls were taken with a view of saving the expense of women-servants. At first the workhouse orphans were used with some degree of civility; but this soon gave way to the most savage barbarity. Once, having laid Mary Jones across two chairs in the kitchen, she whipped her with such wanton cruelty that she was occasionally obliged to rest through sheer fatigue; this treatment was frequently repeated. The punishment was sometimes concluded by Mrs Brownrigg throwing water on the child when she had done whipping her, and sometimes she would dip her head into a pail of water. The room appointed for the girl to sleep in adjoined a passage leading to the street door, and, smarting under the many wounds on her head, shoulders and various parts of her body, she determined not to bear such treatment any longer if she could effectively escape.

Observing that the key was left in the street door when the family went to bed, Mary Jones opened the door cautiously one early morning and escaped into the street. Thus freed from her wretched confinement, she repeatedly inquired her way to the Foundling Hospital till she found it, and was admitted after describing in what manner she had been treated, and showing the bruises she had received. The child was examined by a surgeon, who found her wounds to be of a most alarming nature. The Governors of the Hospital therefore instructed Mr Plumbtree, their solicitor, to write to James Brownrigg, threatening a prosecution if he did not give a proper reason for the severities exercised on the child.

Seeing no notice of this letter being taken, and the Governors of the Hospital thinking it imprudent to indict at common law, the girl was discharged, in consequence of an application to the Chamberlain of London. The other girl, Mary Mitchell, continued with her mistress for the space of a year, during which she was treated with equal cruelty, and she also resolved to quit her service. Having escaped out of the house, she was met in the street by the Brownriggs' younger son, who forced her to return home, where her sufferings were greatly aggravated on account of her vain bid for freedom. In the interim the overseers of the precinct of

Whitefriars bound Mary Clifford apprentice to Brownrigg, and it was not long before she too experienced cruelties similar to those inflicted on the other poor girls, and possibly even more severe. She was frequently tied up naked and beaten with a hearth-broom, a horsewhip or a cane till she completely lost the power of speech. This unfortunate girl having a natural infirmity, the mistress would not permit her to lie in a bed, but placed her on a mat in a coal-hole that was remarkably cold; however, after some time, Mrs Brownrigg must have had a change of heart, and a sack and a quantity of straw

her hands tied behind her, and the chain still about her neck.

The husband being obliged to provide his wife's apprentices with adequate clothing, they were nevertheless repeatedly stripped naked, and kept so for whole days, if their garments happened to be torn. Sometimes Mrs Brownrigg, when determined to some uncommon severity, used to tie the girls' hands with a cord and pull them up to a water-pipe which ran across the ceiling in the kitchen. So often was this device made use of, that it eventually gave way,

Mrs Brownrigg flogging her apprentice Mary Clifford

was given to form her bed, in place of the mat. During her confinement in this wretched situation she had nothing to subsist on but bread and water; and her covering, during the night, consisted only of her own clothes, so that she sometimes lay and almost perished with the cold.

In the course of this most inhuman treatment a collar and chain was fixed round her neck, the end of which was fastened to the yard door, and then it was pulled as tight as possible without strangling her. A day being suffered of this savage treatment, the girl was remanded to the coal-hole at night,

and she desired her husband to fix a hook in the beam, through which the cord could be drawn. Their arms being thus extended, Brownrigg used to horsewhip the terrified creatures till she was quite exhausted, and till the blood flowed at every stroke.

Nor was the barbarity restricted to Brownrigg senior, for the eldest son one day directed Mary Clifford to erect a bedstead, but the poor girl was too weak with hunger, fatigue and ill-usage to do it; upon which he beat her till she could no longer stand the blows. At another time, when the mother had been whipping Mary in the kitchen till she had made herself absolutely tired, the son continued the savage treatment. Mrs. Brownrigg would sometimes seize the poor girl by the cheeks and, forcing the skin down violently with her fingers, cause the blood to gush from her eyes.

Mary Clifford, unable to bear these repeated tortures, complained of her harsh treatment to a French lady who lodged in the house; and she having taken Mrs. Brownrigg to task for such behaviour, that inhuman monster flew at the girl and savaged her tongue in two places with a pair of scissors. Mary Mitchell, the other orphan apprentice was forced to be present during this chastisement. While Clifford was washing herself Mrs. Brownrigg repeatedly struck her on shoulders already sore with former bruises, with the butt-end of a whip; and she treated the child in this manner five more times that same day.

Through the intervention of young Mary Clifford's aunt – who had been refused permission by the Brownriggs to see her niece – and through reports given by neighbours of the screaming of the children, the parish authorities were at length persuaded to take action. This action resulted in swift retribution in the person of Mr Grundy, overseer of St Dunstan's, causing James Brownrigg to be conveyed to the Wood Street Compter. His wife and son had already beat a hasty retreat, taking with them a gold watch and some money. Mr Brownrigg was taken before Alderman Crossby, who committed him for trial, and ordered the girls to be taken to St. Bartholomew's Hospital, where Mary Clifford died within a few days. A coroner's inquest was summoned, who found a verdict of wilful murder against James and Elizabeth Brownrigg, and John Brownrigg, their son.

In the meantime Mrs Brownrigg and the boy shifted from place to place in London buying clothes in a rag shop to disguise themselves, going finally to Wandsworth, where they took lodgings in the house of Mr. Dunbar, keeper of a chandler's shop.

The chandler, by chance reading a newspaper on the 15th of August, saw an advertisement which so clearly described his lodgers that he had no doubt but that they were the murderers. A constable was called to the house, and the mother and son were quickly conveyed to London. On September 2nd, 1767, during the ensuing Sessions at the Old Bailey father, mother and son were indicted. Elizabeth Brownrigg, after a trial of eleven hours, was found guilty of murder, and ordered for execution, to the unrestrained delight of the large crowd that had gathered outside the court. The man and his son, being acquitted of the higher charge, were detained to take their trials for a misdemeanour, of which they both were convicted and imprisoned for 6 months.

After sentence of death was passed on Mrs Brownrigg she was attended by a clergyman, to whom she confessed the enormity of her crime, and acknowledged the justice of the

Elizabeth Brownrigg

sentence by which she had been condemned. The parting between her and her family, on the morning of her execution, was said to be very moving. The son fell on his knees, and she bent over him and embraced him, while the husband knelt on the other side.

After execution her body was put into a hackney-coach, and in accordance with the law conveyed to Surgeon's Hall for dissection and anatomizing. Her skeleton was hung up in the Surgeon's Hall*.

---

* For a note on Surgeon's Hall, see Appendix One to this volume.

THE HOUSE OF DETENTION AT CLERKENWELL, E.C.

Rules Relating to the Conduct and Treatment of Prisoners, 1839
(An Extract)

1.   All prisoners shall, on admission, be placed in a separate cell. They shall be strictly searched by the governor, or by an officer appointed by him for that purpose, or by the matron and a female officer, or by two female officers appointed as aforesaid if a female prisoner. All knives, sharp instruments, dangerous weapons, or articles calculated to facilitate escape, or otherwise desirable at the discretion of the governor to be removed, shall be taken from them; all money and other effects brought in with them, or subsequently sent in for their use and benefit, shall be taken care of for them. The governor shall take charge of such money and effects, and make an inventory of them, to be entered in the prisoner's property book.

2.   Every prisoner shall be examined by the surgeon before being passed into his or her proper cell; having been examined, they shall be cleansed in a warm or cold bath, as the surgeon may direct. The hair of female prisoners shall only be cut in cases when necessary for the removal of dirt or the extirpation of vermin, or when the medical officer deems it requisite on the grounds of health; male prisoners shall be shaved at least once a week, and their hair cut when necessary for the preservation of health and cleanliness. No prisoner shall be stripped or bathed in the presence of any other prisoner.

3.   The wearing apparel of every prisoner shall be fumigated and purified; and if the surgeon thinks it necessary, clothing may be burned. Prisoners before trial may wear their own clothes, if sufficient and proper; but if the wearing apparel of prisoners before trial be insufficient, improper, or necessary to be preserved for the purposes of justice, such prisoners may be furbished with a plain suit of coarse cloth.

4.   As convenient places for the prisoners to wash themselves are provided, with a sufficient allowance of water, soap, towels, and combs, every prisoner shall be required to wash thoroughly once a day, and his feet at least once in every week.

5.   Every prisoner shall be provided with a separate hammock, in a separate cell. Every prisoner shall be provided with sufficient bedding for warmth and health; and, when ordered by the surgeon, with two sheets and a pillow in addition. The whole shall be kept properly clean.

6.   No tobacco shall be admitted for the use of any prisoner, except by written order of the surgeon.

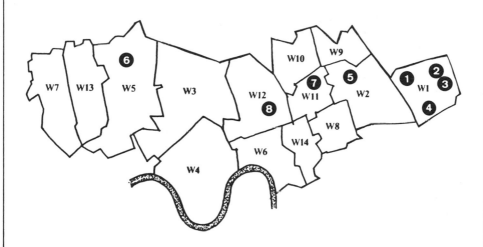

West London

1. Catherine HAYES 164
2. François Benjamin COURVOISIER 166
3. Louis VOISIN 170
4. Henry Julius JACOBY 172
5. Thomas Griffiths WAINEWRIGHT 174
6. Francis SMITH 177
7. John Reginald Halliday CHRISTIE 178
8. Harry ROBERTS, John WITNEY, and John DUDDY 184

Petit Treason*

The Murder of JOHN HAYES
by his wife CATHERINE, JOHN BILLINGS, and JOHN WOOD
in or around March 1726
at their home in Tyburn Road (now Oxford Street), W1

When Catherine Hall left Birmingham and entered the employ of Farmer Hayes at Worcestershire there was hope that she had left her dissolute past behind her. So agreeably did she present herself that young John Hayes, the son of the house, lost no time in leading her to the altar – very much to his father's consternation and, had he only

restlessness was only assuaged when she and Hayes migrated to the excitement of the country's teeming capital. There they took up residence in Tyburn Street (now Oxford Street), where Catherine started up a boarding house, among whose inhabitants were Thomas Billings and Thomas Wood. Billings it was who satisfied Mrs Hayes's

The turnpike at Tyburn Road

known it then, to his own greatest detriment.

For six years Catherine managed to maintain the appearance of domestic diligence, although what wild urgings smouldered inside her we can only now guess: her growing

---

* Petit Treason was aggravated murder and could happen, according to Statute of 25 Edward III (1351), in three ways:
  1. By a servant killing his master;
  2. By a wife killing her husband;
  3. By an ecclesiastic killing his superior.

carnal needs in her husband's absences from town on business. Soon Wood's gratitude to John Hayes – whose kindness had rescued him from destitution – was subordinated to Catherine's greed and debauchery, and he was enlisted in a terrible and treacherous plot by the illicit lovers to assassinate the unfortunate Hayes.

The following contemporary texts take up this story in which four lives are sacrificed to one woman's lust:

When Hayes was asleep, his wife apprised her associates that this was the opportune time to strike, and accordingly Billings entered the bed-chamber with a hatchet, with which he struck Hayes so violently that he fractured his skull. At the time, the unfortunate Hayes's legs were hanging over the edge of the bed, and so great was his anguish that his feet repeatedly stamped on the floor, which aroused Wood from his drunken reverie and he too joined in bludgeoning Hayes.

The murderers now consulted on the best manner of disposing of the body so as to most effectively prevent discovery. Mrs Hayes proposed cutting off the head, as if the body were found intact it would likely be identified. This plan agreed to, the assassins returned to the room with a candle and a pail. Sliding the body partly off the bed, Billings supported the head while Wood cut it off with his pocket knife; Catherine held the pail underneath to catch the head and to prevent the blood marking the floor. The deed being done, they emptied the blood out of the pail into a sink by the window. The woman now suggested boiling the head until the flesh should part from the bones, but it was thought that this would consume too much time, and it was decided to cast the grisly relic into the Thames where hopefully the tide would carry it off; the head was thus put into the pail, and Billings took it under his greatcoat, accompanied by Wood, to the river.

The head being thus disposed of, the murderers returned home. The next object of their endeavour was the disposal of the body, and Mrs Hayes proposed that it should be packed in a box and buried. The plan was decided upon, and a box purchased, but being found too small, the corpse had to be dismembered in order to

admit of being enclosed within it. However, the inconvenience of manhandling the heavy box soon became apparent, and the bits of mangled body were unpacked and wrapped in a blanket, this collection being deposited in a pond in the middle of a field in Marylebone.

In the meantime the head had been discovered, and the circumstances of a murder having been committed being obvious, every measure was taken to secure the discovery of its perpetrators. The magistrates, with this view, directed that the head should be washed clean, and the hair combed, and that it should be displayed on a pole in the churchyard of St Margaret's, Westminster, that an opportunity might be afforded to the public to identify it.

Thousands witnessed this extraordinary spectacle; and there were no few among that crowd that expressed the belief that the head belonged to Hayes. When the head had been exhibited for four days, it was thought expedient to preserve it, and Mr Westbrook, a chemist, consequently undertook to bottle it in spirits.

On the day of her death, Hayes received the Sacrament, and was dragged on a sledge to the place appointed for execution. When the wretched woman had finished her devotions, in pursuance of her sentence an iron chain was put around her waist, with which she was attached to the stake. When women were burned for petty treason, it was usual to strangle them by means of a rope passed around the neck and pulled by the executioner, so that they were mercifully insensible to the heat of the flames. But this woman was literally burned alive; for the executioner let go the rope too soon, in consequence of having his hand burnt by the flames. The flames burned fiercely around her, and the spectators beheld Catherine Hayes pushing away the faggots, while she rent the air with her cries and lamentations. Other faggots were instantly piled on her, but she survived amidst the flames for a considerable time, and her body was not perfectly reduced to ashes until three hours later.

The Treacherous Valet
The Murder of Lord WILLIAM RUSSELL
by FRANÇOIS BENJAMIN COURVOISIER
on Tuesday the 5th of May 1840
at 14 Norfolk Street (now Dunraven Street), W1

On the morning of Wednesday the 6th of May 1840 the 73-year-old Lord William Russell was found to have been murdered in his bed at his house in Norfolk Street, Park Lane, London.

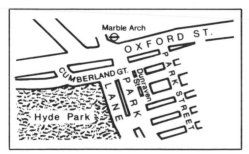

There was clear evidence of a forced entry through the back door to the house but although several pieces of jewellery had disappeared, there were sufficiently few of the house's treasures touched to make robbery an unlikely motive for the brutal attack.

The household below stairs consisted of two maids, a manservant, a coachman, and a groom. And François Benjamin Courvoisier, a young Swiss who for the past five weeks had occupied the position of Lord Russell's valet. It seems that his Lordship was in the habit of trusting his valet to act as the head of this small ménage and as was his custom had the previous morning given Courvoisier a number of instructions to transmit to the rest of the staff. One of these messages was that the coachman should be ready to collect Lord Russell from his club at five in the evening. As the valet omitted to pass that order on, it is understandable that when the master arrived home at length in a hired cab he should express some little dissatisfaction with his competence. It transpired that Courvoisier greatly resented this slight.

All this was noted by the investigating officers Inspector Nicolas Pearce and Sergeant Frederick Shaw. They felt that this misunderstanding in combination with clues like the missing jewellery being found in the valet's pantry, and bloodstained clothes in his room – not to forget his depositing some choice pieces of the Russell silver with Madame Piolaine, a Leicester Square hotelier – indicated a large measure of guilt on the part of Monsieur Courvoisier.

After sentence of death had been passed on him by Lord Chief Justice Tindal at the Central Criminal Court, Courvoisier obligingly confessed his crime:

François Benjamin Courvoisier

"His lordship was very cross with me and told me I must quit his service. As I was coming upstairs from the kitchen I thought it was all up with me; my character was gone, and I thought it was the only way I could cover my faults by murdering him. This was the first moment of any idea of the sort entering my head. I went into the dining room and took a knife from the sideboard. I do not remember whether it was a carving knife or not. I then went upstairs. I opened his bedroom door and heard him snoring in his sleep; there was a rushlight in his room burning at the time. I went near the bed by the side of the window, and then I murdered him. He just moved his arm a little; he never spoke a word."

The execution was carried out at Newgate on the 6th of July 1840.

EXECUTION
OF COURVOISIER,

GOING TO SEE A MAN HANGED
William Makepeace Thackeray

. . .I must confess then . . . that the sight has left on my mind an extraordinary feeling of terror and shame. It seems to me that I have been abetting an act of frightful wickedness and violence performed by a set of men against one of their fellows; and I pray God that it may soon be out of the power of any man in England to witness such a hideous and degrading sight. Forty-thousand persons (say the sheriffs), of all ranks amd degrees – mechanics, gentlemen, pickpockets, members of both the Houses of Parliament, streetwalkers, news-writers, gather together before Newgate at a very early hour; the most part of them give up their natural quiet night's rest, in order to partake of this hideous debauchery, which is more exciting than sleep, or than wine, or the last new ballet, or any other amusement that they can have. Pickpocket and peer, each is tickled by the sight alike, and has that hidden lust after blood that influences our race – government, a Christian government, gives us a feast every now and then: it agrees, that is to say, a majority in the two Houses agrees, that for certain crimes it is necessary that a man should be hanged by the neck. Government commits the criminal's soul to the mercy of God, stating that here on earth he is to look for no mercy; keeps him for a fortnight to prepare, provides him with a clergyman to settle his religious matters (if there be time enough, but government can't wait); and on a Monday morning, the bell tolling, the clergyman reading out the words of God, "I am the resurrection and the life," "The Lord giveth and the Lord taketh away," – on a Monday morning, at eight o'clock, this man is placed under a beam, with a rope connecting it and him; a plank disappears from under him, and those who have paid for good places may see the hands of the government agent, Jack Ketch, coming up from his black hole, and seizing the prisoner's legs, and pulling them, until he is quite dead – strangled. . .

. . .Look at the documents that came from the prison of this unhappy Courvoisier during the few days which passed between his trial and execution. Were ever letters more painful to read? At first, his statements are false, contradictory, lying. He has not repented then. His last declaration seems to be honest, as far as the relation of the crime goes. . . The horrid gallows is perpetually before him; he is wild with dread and remorse. Clergymen are with him ceaselessly; religious tracts are forced into his hands; night and day they ply him with the heinousness of his crime, and exhortations to repentance. Read through that last paper of his; by Heaven it is pitiful to read it...

...But murder is such a monstrous crime (this is the great argument) – when a man has killed another, it is natural that he should be killed. Away with your foolish sentimentalists who say no – it is *natural*. That is the word, and a fine philosophical opinion it is – philosophical and Christian. Kill a man, and you must be killed in turn. . . Blood demands blood!

. . .There is some talk, too, of the terror which the sight of this spectacle inspires, and of this we have endeavoured to give as good a notion as we can in the above pages. I fully confess, that I came away down Snow Hill that morning with a disgust for murder, but it was for *the murder I saw done*. As we made our way through the immense crowd, we came upon two little girls of eleven and twelve years: one of them was crying bitterly and begged, for Heaven's sake, that some one would lead her from that horrid place. This was done, and the children were carried to places of safety. We asked the elder girl – a very pretty one, what brought her into such a neighbourhood; the child grinned knowingly, and said, "We've koom to see the man hanged!" Tender law, that brings our babes upon such errands, and provides them with such gratifying moral spectacles. This is the 20th of July, and I may be permitted for my part to declare that, for the past fourteen days, so salutary has the impression of the butchery been upon me, I have had the man's face continually before my eyes; that I can see Mr Ketch at this moment, with an easy air, taking the rope from his pocket; that I feel myself ashamed and degraded at the brutal curiosity that took me to that brutal sight; and that I pray to Almighty God to cause this disgraceful sin to pass from among us, and cleanse our land of blood.

(*Fraser's Magazine for Town and Country*, Volume XXII No. CXXVIII. August 1840)

[*See* Murder Club Guide No.2 *for a fuller discussion of the Abolitionist movement.*]

NAKED MURDER

...but one circumstance (and a very curious one) is not known, as it only transpired to those immediately concerned. The murder was discovered very early in the morning, and when the police came in they were positive in the opinion that someone in the house was the murderer. No one had entered they were certain, though a window was opened to lead to that inference. Courvoisier was in his pantry, doing the usual morning's work; he was closely examined, and not the slightest trace of blood found on any of his clothes. The most stringent search failed to find any blood, except on a pair of gloves found in the housemaid's box. After Courvoisier's sentence, he was asked, I think by the under sheriff, how it was possible he could have cut the throat of his unfortunate master without a trace of blood on any of his clothes, and that nothing should have been discovered newly washed? His answer was that he had no clothes on, he committed the crime in a complete state of nudity, and had only to wash himself at the sink on coming down. He wore nothing but those gloves he placed afterwards in the housemaid's box, and which, being bloodstained, caused some suspicion for a time to attach to her. The immediate cause of the murder was Lord William having told him the night he committed it that he should leave his service the next morning. He had offended by taking a favourite watch-dog of his lordship's, which always slept at his bedroom door, and putting him into the stable; this he did three nights after his master had forbidden it. The consequence was Lord William telling him to collect his plate the first thing the next morning, and then leave his service. The dreadful catastrophe then took place..."

(*The Recollections of John Adolphus*, Emily Henderson; Published: T. Cautley Newby, London, 1871)

[Further reference is made to the wildly inaccurate *Recollections* of John Adolphus in the section on James Greenacre earlier in this volume.]

The Butcher in Charlotte Street
The Murder of Madame ÉMILIENNE GERARD
by LOUIS VOISIN
on Wednesday the 31st of October 1917
at 101 Charlotte Street, W1

The Voisin case opened, as do most murder cases, with the discovery of a body in suspicious circumstances; and there can have been few more suspicious circumstances than those which revealed themselves in Bloomsbury on November 2nd, 1917. A road-sweeper about his job in Regent Square found a large sacking-covered parcel in the central garden of the Square. When the package was opened it was found to contain the bloody trunk of a woman, dressed incongruously in delicate lace underwear; around the remains was another partial paper wrapper on which the misspelt message "Blodie Belgium" had been scribbled.

Medical examination was to place the time of death within the previous two days; more important, the dismemberment indicated some grasp of anatomy. A bloodstained sheet wrapped around the torso provided the most important clue – in one corner a laundry mark 'II H' had been embroidered; it was possible that the sheet had belonged to the victim.

And so it proved. A trawl of laundry shops led to No.50 Munster Square, in a run-down district of Regent's Park, where it was learned that Émilienne Gerard, a 32-year-old Frenchwoman, had been missing from her rooms since October 31st. A search of Mme Gerard's apartment produced a written IOU for the sum of £50, signed by a Louis Voisin, and a framed portrait of the same man, later identified as her lover.

Voisin was traced to a tenement at 101 Charlotte Street, Fitzroy Square, where he shared his life with Berthe Roche. Voisin's trade was butcher.

Though there was no more connection than *l'amour* provable between the butcher and Mme Gerard (if indeed she was the body in the parcel), Chief Inspector Wensley, in charge of the case, thought it wise to have

Voisin and Roche along to Bow Street for questioning. Wensley remembers Voisin as "a short, thick-set man, heavy-jawed and exceedingly powerful of frame". The man's story was that he had known the missing Émilienne Gerard for about 18 months, during which time an intimacy had developed between them. On October 31st they had met to say au revoir on the eve of her departure for France where she was to visit her husband, a cook with the French army. She had taken this opportunity to ask Voisin to pop in and feed her cat, and this he had dutifully done on two occasions.

After a night in detention, Voisin again faced Frederick Wensley "with a sort of aggressive determination"; on this occasion the detective asked him, through an interpreter, if he had any objection to writing out the words "Bloody Belgium" for him. Voisin had no objection, and with the painstakingly slow hand of the virtually illiterate, inscribed "Blodie Belgium" – five times. Wensley recalled "The final copy bore a very close resemblance in every particular to that of the original. I knew then that it was only a question of time before the other points of the case would be cleared up."

And cleared up they very speedily were. A return visit to Charlotte Street resulted in the first positive link between the dismembered trunk, Émilienne Gerard and Louis Voisin – in the cellar beneath No.101 Madame's head and hands were found in a barrel of sawdust. Furthermore, Voisin's kitchen was seen to be heavily stained with human blood. When he was charged with murder the Charlotte Street butcher simply shrugged and muttered, in broken English, "It is unfortunate."

A collaboration between the forensic brilliance of Bernard Spilsbury and the experience and imagination of Frederick Wensley was not long in piecing together a coherent reconstruction of the last hours of the unlucky Émilienne Gerard.

The night of 31st October had been marked by one of the worst Zeppelin raids yet suffered by the capital, and at around 11 o'clock, in response to the sirens, Émilienne Gerard fled first to the safety of the Underground, and from there to her lover's basement in Charlotte Street. The confrontation between the excitable Berthe and her rival – of whom she was until then unaware – must have been terrible to behold. Both women, their nerves already strained by the air raid outside, began a mutual tirade of accusations, recriminations and threats; the volatile Berthe pounced on the defenceless Madame Gerard, knife in hand, stabbing and slashing. This is the theory that supported Spilsbury's observation that a large number of the wounds suffered by the victim were by a far weaker hand than the powerful Voisin. It was at this point that Voisin, probably awakened by the fierce struggle, joined the fray to strike out the remaining life in the body of his hapless paramour. He then put in a little overtime with meat cleaver and saw.

Confronted with the findings at Charlotte Street and Munster Square (where closer examination had rewarded detectives with further bloodstains), Voisin modified his statement:

> I went to Madame Gerard's place last Thursday at 11am, and when I arrived the door was closed but not locked. The floor and carpet were soaked with blood. The head and hands were wrapped up in a flannel coat that is at my place now. They were on the kitchen table. The rest of the body was not there. I was so shocked by such a sight I did not know what to do…I remained there five minutes stupefied. I did not know what to do. I thought someone had laid a trap for me. I started to clean up the blood and my clothes became stained…Then I went back to my place and had lunch, and later returned to Madame Gerard's flat and took the packet [the head and hands] back home. I had no intention to harm Madame Gerard. Why should I kill her?

At the end of an unremarkable trial, Mr Justice Darling passed sentence of death – in French – on Louis Voisin. At his direction

A characteristically extravagent pictorial view of events in the Voisin Case

Berthe Roche was acquitted of murder, but charged as an accessory in a separate trial before Mr Justice Avory on March 1st. The jury found her guilty, and two years into a seven-year prison sentence Berthe Roche went mad and died in an institution. Voisin was executed on March 2nd, 1918. Ironically, the "Blodie Belgium" message, devised to mystify the police and send them on a false scent, had ended up hanging him.

The Naughty Pantry-Boy
The Murder of Lady ALICE WHITE
by HENRY JULIUS JACOBY
on Tuesday the 14th of March 1922
in the Spencer Hotel (now the Mostyn Hotel), Portman Street, W1

The murder committed by Henry Jacoby was foolish, prosaic and rather pathetic. It would probably have been forgotten were it not for the slight celebrity of his victim and the great publicity the case attracted at the time by being contrasted with the contemporary murder of a prostitute by the well-connected but insane Ronald True [see this volume].

Jacoby was an eighteen-year-old pantry boy at the Spencer Hotel, Portman Street, in central London; at the time of the murder, he had only been in the job for three weeks. In the early hours of the 14th of March 1922 Jacoby, who was sleeping in the basement, woke up thinking he had heard the sound of men whispering outside his room. He called Alfred Platt, the night porter, and together they searched the basement area but found nothing. Jacoby returned to bed but could not sleep. He began to reflect on his own mean circumstances and their comparison with the conspicuous wealth of the hotel guests, and gradually there grew in his mind an impulse to steal something from one of the rooms.

Taking the hammer from a workman's tool-bag which had been left in the basement, Jacoby took a circuitous route through the kitchens up to the guest rooms. After trying a number of doors, he found one which was unlocked. As though all his worst nightmares had been realized at once, the door creaked as he opened it; when he got inside he nervously shone a torch round the room. In one of two single beds was sleeping Lady White, the widow of a former chairman of the London County Council, Sir Edward

White. As the flashlight beam crept on to her Alice White woke up and began to scream. In terror now, Jacoby hit her on the head several times with the hammer and fled the room, stumbling down to the washroom to clean the bloody handle of the tool, returning it now to the toolbag...skulking back to bed.

When the body of Lady White was discovered the next morning the police quickly realized that they had a mystery on their hands. There was no evidence of robbery, or of a struggle, or even of forced entry to the room. This suggested an inside job,

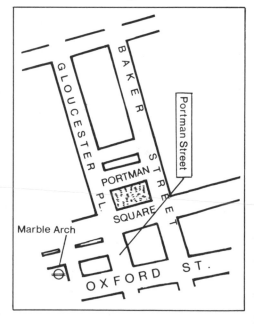

and questioning consequently began with the staff. Jacoby first drew attention to himself with the story of the whispering voices and the nocturnal search with the porter. Then it was discovered that he had given false details about his background and on instituting a search, police discovered amongst his clothing the two bloodstained handkerchiefs which had been used to wipe the handle of the hammer. But as if he had not already given his own worst testimony, Jacoby casually remarked to a police officer, "Isn't it funny how much strength a man's got?...we don't think of the punishment that comes after...but what's done can't be undone."

The trial of young Henry Jacoby began at the Old Bailey on the 28th of April 1922, with Percival Clarke prosecuting him, Mr Justice McCardie presiding and Mr Lucian for his defence. In the witness-box Jacoby again advanced the improbable story that he had heard the whisperers, had gone alone to search, taking with him the hammer, had thought Lady White was an intruder, and was so scared when he discovered his mistake that he tried to hide the evidence and keep the matter quiet. The judge reasoned that this would in any case make no difference to the verdict if the intention had been to inflict grievous bodily harm. Evidence in mitigation tried to suggest that Jacoby had been influenced by the violence in films – perhaps the first, but by no means the last, time that this defence has been used. Nevertheless, there was little doubt about the eventual verdict, though the jury offered a strong recommendation for clemency on account of Jacoby's youth.

There was much unease about the sentence of death. Newspapers made a comparison with the law's treatment of Ronald True, suggesting that there appeared to be one law for the rich and another for the poor. But in the end, this was an emotional argument, without a single legal point of similarity in the circumstances of the two cases. The authorities rejected all appeals on behalf of Jacoby, even one for him to be interred in consecrated ground.

He was hanged on the 5th of June 1922, and subsequently buried in the grounds of Pentonville Prison beneath the modest inscription 'H.J. 382'.

When he appeared before me, Jacoby looked both innocent and gentle. He was a good-looking lad with fair hair and a pale, pleasant face. He listened avidly to witness after witness, stared at the exhibits produced at the Inquest, and looked cheerfully round the packed court.

There is no doubt in my mind that he *enjoyed* the proceedings, extraordinary as such a statement may seem. His vanity was being glutted at last.

"What are the papers saying about me now?" he asked his warders again and again...

I am convinced from my own contact with this young ruffian that he would have developed into a dangerous criminal, with a tendency towards robbery and violence.

(*Memoirs of a London County Coroner*, H.R. Oswald)

"Pen, Pencil, and Poison"

The Suspected Murder of
Miss HELEN ABERCROMBY and Others
by THOMAS GRIFFITHS WAINEWRIGHT

during the years 1829-1837
at Linden House (now demolished), W2,
and Other Locations

Thomas Griffiths Wainewright was born to Thomas and Ann Wainewright in October 1794, in Chiswick. Sadly, Ann died in childbirth at the young age of twenty-one, and Thomas senior passed over not long afterwards, leaving young Thomas to the care of his maternal grandfather, Dr Ralph Griffiths, to whom he owed his second name, and who was at the time an editor on the influential *Monthly Review*. Griffiths had never entirely approved of his daughter's marriage, but seems to have taken to its offspring, officially adopting Thomas and taking him to live at Linden House, in what was then the village of Turnham Green.

Tragedy though the untimely death of his parents may have been for Thomas, he could hardly have had a more stimulating upbringing than that at Linden House. His grandfather's interests ensured that the boy came into contact with some of the most exciting artistic and literary minds of the age; luminaries like Fuseli and Flaxman. He attended the art academy held by Charles Burney, where he showed considerable talent as a draughtsman. By 1814 he had graduated to an apprenticeship in the studio of Thomas Phillips, though a certain shiftlessness was already beginning to make itself apparent, and to the young man-about-town a commission in the Guards promised greater attractions.

It was not long before Wainewright tired of this activity too. Leaving the service with no more than an uncommon appetite for whisky punch and a tendency to neurotic hypochondria, he was soon back in the dilettante circles that revolved around Linden House. He continued to paint, and to exhibit at the Royal Academy, but he was starting to discover talent in the direction of art-journalism and literature, at which he enjoyed a modest success, and under the pseudonyms Janus Weathercock and Egomet Bonmot he became a frequent contributor to John Scott's *London Magazine*. He became acquainted with Hazlitt, De Quincey, and Charles Lamb, for whom he was "kind light-hearted Wainewright". He met Wordsworth, and William Blake who spoke generously of his paintings.

Less indulgent contemporaries refer to his "white hands bespangled with regal rings, with an undress military air and the conversation of a smart, lively, heartless, voluptuous coxcomb"; and Procter records an effeminate manner and a voice rarely rising above a whisper.

His writing and sketching, plus a bit of shady art dealing, provided Wainewright with an income of something around two hundred pounds a year – a scant sum with which to indulge his accustomed lavish entertaining; and his marriage in 1821 to Frances Ward, a sweet girl, though penniless, merely contributed to the expenses.

By forging the signatures of the trustees controlling the small income he had from stock given by his grandfather, Thomas succeeded in laying his hands on a sum in excess of £2000 from the Bank of England. In fact, this represented half the capital sum of which he was only entitled to the interest. Unsurprisingly, former debts and current extravagance quickly swallowed this 'windfall', and in 1828 Thomas and Frances managed to inveigle themselves an invitation to live under the roof of their bachelor uncle George Edward Griffiths at Linden House.

Scarcely a year had passed of this new arrangement when poor Uncle George suddenly died; in great pain, from a mysterious illness. Coincidentally, Wainewright inherited, and once again the queue of creditors was shortened – though there were still too many hungry wolves baying at the door for comfort.

Thomas Wainewright's next move was to invite his wife's mother, Mrs Abercromby, and her two step-sisters, Helen and Made-

Self-description and portrait by Thomas Wainewright after his arrest

leine, to make their home at Linden House. In 1830, Helen's life was insured for £3000, and £2000, respectively with the Palladium and Eagle companies.

If only Mrs Abercromby could have seen into her future she might have allowed Thomas to go on and increase the value of the policies on Helen; as it was she obstructed the effort. Mrs Abercromby died suddenly in August 1930; in great pain, from a mysterious illness. It must have saddened the heart of Wainewright to have made no direct financial gain from his mother-

in-law's demise, but he consoled himself by increasing the insurance on Helen to £18,000. In December the family removed to No.12 Conduit Street, in London, where on the 21st of the month, in her twenty-first year, Helen Abercromby died – suddenly, in great pain, from a mysterious illness.

And mysterious was just the way the insurance companies chose to read it. In fact they refused outright to pay Wainwright a single penny on his policies. Wainewright instituted proceedings in court, borrowed £1000 on the security of his claim, and disappeared to Boulogne before the ravening jaws of the wolves locked on to his temporarily full pocket.

Little is definitely known of Wainewright's movements over the next five years, though he is recorded as having spent a time in prison in Paris. It is probably no coincidence that the man with whom Thomas was staying in France should have died suddenly; in great pain, from a mysterious illness! Or that his life was insured for £3000 in favour of Thomas Griffiths Wainewright.

In June 1837 Wainewright returned to England and was arrested at Covent Garden on a warrant issued by the Bank of England relating to the forgery of ten years previously. He also learned that the action against the insurance companies in the matter of Helen Abercromby's policies had been dismissed.

Although he was now openly known and referred to as "Wainewright the Poisoner", his appearance at the Old Bailey was on the charge of forgery only. Furthermore, by pleading guilty, he allowed the Bank the generosity of spirit to waive the capital charge (remember, this was 1835), and he was sentenced to transportation for life to Van Diemen's Land.

The story has been passed down that while in Newgate awaiting transportation Wainewright admitted to poisoning Helen Abercromby with strychnine – because, he said, he was offended by her very thick ankles. He is also claimed to have told a visitor in the commercial way of business, "Sir, you city men enter upon your speculations and take your chances of them. Some of your speculations succeed, and some fail. Mine happen to have failed."

Unlike so many of his fellows, Thomas Wainewright survived his voyage on the transports, and died in the convict hospital at Hobart Town in 1852. To the last he was boasting of his famous connections, of Wainewright the artist, Wainewright the author. It would no doubt have pleased him to know that in 1889 no less a celebrity than Oscar Wilde paid him tribute in his aesthetic study 'Pen, Pencil, and Poison'.

THE DEATH OF HELEN ABERCROMBY

[*After a trip to the theatre, in December 1830, Helen Abercromby fell mysteriously ill and languished in bed, between sickness and recovery for several days. On December 20th...*]

Helen had been upstairs just a week, and Mr and Mrs Wainewright held a little consultation together, and thought that Helen would be better off for a powder, of which the nauseous flavour could be disguised, as usual, by giving it in jelly; and Mr and Mrs Wainewright, having satisfied themselves that their patient had played them no trick, but had really taken what was good for her, went out for a stroll, leaving Helen under the control of an old and trusty servant, who had been at Linden House in the old Doctor's time, and who had known Mr Wainewright since he was a little boy. Mr and Mrs Wainewright promised to return as soon as possible, and nurse was to take every imaginable care of the invalid.

About two in the afternoon, not very long after the departure of her master and mistress, the woman was alarmed beyond measure by symptoms of violent convulsions, and by Miss Abercromby grasping her hand like a vice. Dr Locock was instantly summoned, and discovered, on examination, abnormal pressure on the brain; the poor young lady cried: "Oh doctor, I am dying! I feel I am, I am sure so!" He tried to reassure her, but she went on: "My mother died in the same way, yes, my poor mother! Oh my poor mother!" Locock wrote a new prescription which she took at once, and which appeared to relieve her; and when he left, pronounced the crisis averted; she was far easier and more composed, and in fact said to him: "Oh doctor, I was gone to heaven, but you have brought me back to earth!"

Before Dr Locock, however, could have reached his own house, the pains returned with aggravated violence. A local practitioner was called in and he did his utmost to alleviate the suffering; but Helen gradually sank, and breathed her last at four o'clock on the afternoon of that same day, without having the consolation of beholding once more the features of Mr and Mrs Wainewright.

Dr Locock called at four, and found that she had just expired. As he went out he met Mr Wainewright at the door, and told him what had happened. He appeared much shocked and astonished, as he had left her much better than she was on the night before. He inquired what was the cause of death. "Mischief in the brain", Dr Locock said."

(Introduction by William Hazlitt to his *Essays and Criticisms of Thomas Griffiths Wainewright*, Reeves and Turner, London, 1880)

HELEN FRANCES PHŒBE ABERCROMBY.

FROM AN ORIGINAL DRAWING
BY T.G.WAINEWRIGHT.

The Man who Shot a Ghost

The Murder of JOHN MILLWOOD
by FRANCIS SMITH

on Tuesday January the 3rd 1804
at the Churchyard in Black Lion Lane, W5

One of the capital's most celebrated hauntings was once associated with the churchyard at Hammersmith, in the year 1803 just one of the small villages skirting London. The restless spirit first displayed its malevolent nature to an unfortunate local who was quietly making her way home across the graveyard at ten o'clock at night. Half-way through the tombstones, she was accosted by something "very tall and very white", rising as though from the grave. Understandably terrified, the poor woman fled as fast as her legs could carry her; the ghost was quicker, overtaking his prey and enveloping her in its spectral arms. She remained in a faint until carried home by neighbours to her bed; a bed from which she never again rose.

Though this is the only record of a fatal encounter, enough people were sufficiently badly frightened for there to be formed an *ad-hoc* watch committee determined at least to discover whether the nuisance was caused, as some said, by the shade of a suicide who had cut his throat a year earlier or, as the cynics had it, by a misguided prankster.

Numbered among the courageous band of watchers was one fated to be the only man to appear before the bench at the Old Bailey charged with murdering a ghost.

At about half-past ten on the night of January the 3rd 1804, Mr John Locke met Mr Francis Smith. Smith, in agitation, confided to Locke that he had just killed the Hammersmith Ghost, and summoning a watchman, the trio made off up Limekiln Lane to Black Lion Lane, where lay a white figure, motionless on the ground. The figure proved to be human, and the reason for its immobility was a bullet from Smith's pistol lodged in its jaw.

It was then – as it is now – not etiquette to shoot a man – however much like a ghost he may look. And this, poor fellow, was the victim's only crime; for John Millwood was a bricklayer, and as a bricklayer wore the traditional clothing of his trade – white trousers, white apron, and a white linen jacket! Perhaps, though, his death could have been avoided if only he had listened to the advice of his mother-in-law; when she gave evidence at Smith's trial it transpired that "on the Saturday evening before his death, [Millwood] told her that two ladies and a gentleman had taken fright at him as he was coming down the terrace, thinking he was the ghost. He told them he was no more a ghost than any of them, and asked the gentleman if he wished for a punch in the head." Upon which the mother-in-law recommended that he wear a greatcoat to avoid future trouble.

As to Francis Smith, although he was able to call a number of character witnesses in his defence, each describing him as a mild and gentle man in the extreme, "The Lord Chief Baron, in his address to the jury, said that however disgusted they might feel in their own minds with any abominable person guilty of the misdemeanour of terrifying the neighbourhood, still the prisoner had no right to construe such misdemeanour into a

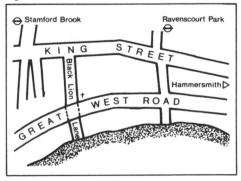

capital offence, or to conclude that a man dressed in white was a ghost. It was his own opinion, and was confirmed by those of his learned brethren on the bench, that if the facts stated in evidence were credible, the prisoner had committed murder."

The jury took a more lenient view, as juries often do, and returned with a verdict of "guilty of manslaughter".

On hearing this verdict the bench responded that "such a judgement can not be received in this case, for it ought to be either a verdict of murder or of acquittal. In this case there was a deliberate carrying of a loaded gun, which the prisoner concluded he was entitled to fire, but which he really was not; and he did fire it, with a rashness which the law did not excuse."

Chastened, the jury reconsidered their verdict. "Guilty of Murder."

And so it was that the man who shot a ghost was himself sentenced to die. Happily, history has provided a less austere ending, for Francis Smith earned an eleventh-hour reprieve, and was sentenced instead to one year's imprisonment.

The Problems of 'Reggie No-Dick'*
The Murder of Mrs ETHEL CHRISTIE and Others
by her Husband JOHN REGINALD HALLIDAY CHRISTIE
between 1943 and 1953
at 10 Rillington Place (now Ruston Mews), W11

Some thirty-five years ago, in the summer of 1953, the visitor to Notting Hill might have stumbled upon a cul-de-sac with the name Rillington Place. Almost certainly he would have felt inexplicably chilled by the look of its grim rows of terraced houses, one of which – No.10 – was being discussed in tones of horrified disbelief throughout Britain.

No.10 Rillington Place had little about it to justify a second glance; like its neighbours, the house told a tale of the gradual decline of a once respectable district from the time when such dwellings would have been home to a single Victorian family; they had long since been divided into smaller apartments. John Christie and his wife had occupied the ground-floor flat at No.10 for some years, and he was looked upon by the neighbours as a rather superior sort of fellow, with pretensions to education. To look at, Christie could be mistaken for any one of thousands of ordinary Englishmen. He dressed soberly, his thinning hair and studious-looking horn-rimmed spectacles did not attract any special attention, and his observable life-style was in perfect accord with his anonymous appearance.

The house, and Christie himself, had had one brief period of notoriety some years before. The Christies at that time shared the house with a Mr Kitchener, and a young couple named Evans who had had a baby daughter and occupied the top floor. On November 30th 1949 Timothy Evans walked into a police station in Wales and confessed to "disposing" of his wife. Subsequent investigation of the Evans home in Rillington Place revealed the body not only of Mrs Evans, but of baby Geraldine as well. Christie had been witness-in-chief for the prosecution, and it was in large part his evidence which subsequently hanged Evans.

But this moment of glory had faded into memory, and life at No.10 resumed its unremarkable tempo, so unremarkable that the lives of its residents once again became part of the city's grey background. Then two things happened to draw attention to the ground-floor occupant of No.10. Around December, Mr Christie's wife stopped being seen about her domestic activities. Ques-

---

* This unflattering jibe at Christie's physical shortcomings attached to him in youth where his unsatisfactory performances with his female peers resulted in several such unfortunate nicknames; 'can't-make-it-Christie' was another that stuck.

tioned by neighbours, Christie said that Ethel had "gone to the Midlands on medical grounds"; to have a special operation. This explanation was readily accepted because Christie was something of a self-promoted authority on health matters, always willing to advise when the need arose. The second occurrence was the disappearance from the locality of John Christie himself.

Such comings and goings, though, have a limited interest in a large city, and the Christies' rooms were eventually absorbed into the household of Mr Beresford Brown. Exploring his new territory on March 24th 1953, Brown was struck by a strange concoction of smells; at first it was the disinfectant that held the attention, but after a while another, less definable odour could be detected. These smells were at their strongest in the kitchen, and seemed to originate behind a section of wall that was hollow to the knock, and which on further investigation proved to be a papered-over door. Tearing off the paper from over a cut-out section of the door, Brown illuminated the inside with a torch. What he saw were the legs of a woman.

The local police took Mr Brown's discovery very seriously indeed, and they reported it straight on to the higher authority of Detective Chief Inspector Griffin of Scotland Yard, who in company with Dr Francis Camps the pathologist was soon at the premises.

The girl had been placed in a sitting position, with her back towards the room. The body was leaning, and would have fallen had it not been secured by a fastening attached to the back of the brassiere. The wrists had been tied with a handkerchief. Upon removal of the body, another girl was found hidden in the cavity, wrapped in a blanket with a pillow-case tied over her head. When this body was being removed, an incredible third was revealed, also covered with a blanket. A fourth victim was uncovered from rubble beneath the floorboards.

By the date of the inquest, March 30th, the following information had become available: Body Number One was identified by Robert MacLennan as his 26-year-old sister, Hectorina; the second body was Kathleen Maloney, aged twenty-six; and Number Three had been identified by Mrs May Langridge as her sister Rita Nelson, aged twenty-five. The body under the floorboards was that of Mrs Ethel Christie.

Meanwhile the police had begun to dig up the garden at the rear of the house, unearthing as they did so a large quantity of bones – many of them human – which were later to be built up by Dr Camps into two almost complete skeletons. Another significant find was a tobacco box in which had been arranged four lockets of pubic hair; one of these relics matched the hair on the body of Ethel Christie. The hunt was now under way for the absentee Christie himself.

By the end of the month of March the manhunt had been intensified, many people had been picked up for questioning, had proved to be other than John Christie, and had been released. The police were

John and Ethel Christie

trying to keep up with the hundreds of reported sightings of their quarry, from John O'Groats to Land's End.

What the police would have dearly loved to know was that Christie was still lurking about London, using his own name, and making little effort to lay low. In fact he had merely booked into a doss house. On the morning of Tuesday 31st March, Christie made his way from his lodging in Rowton House to Putney Bridge, where he stopped briefly to gaze into the Thames below.

Whatever his thoughts were that moment, they were interrupted by the words "You look like John Reginald Christie." Christie

suffering a great deal from persecution and assaults from the black people in the house No.10 Rillington Place* and had to undergo treatment at the doctor for her nerves. In December she was becoming very frightened from these blacks and was afraid to go about the house when they were about and she got very depressed. On December 14th I was awakened by my wife moving about in bed. I sat up and saw that she appeared to be convulsive, her face was blue and she was choking. I did what I could to try and restore breathing but it was hopeless. It appeared too late to call for assistance. That's when I couldn't bear to see her, so I got a stocking and tied it round her neck to put her to

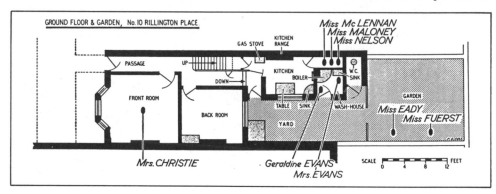

GROUND FLOOR & GARDEN, No. 10 RILLINGTON PLACE.

straightened up and faced PC Thomas Ledger; he was no longer the clean, well-groomed man who had left Rillington Place, hunger and lack of money, dossing down into an irregular and troubled sleep had taken their toll of him. "You are quite right, officer. I am Christie." The two men walked quietly towards Putney police station.

Later that day Christie was faced by Chief Inspector Albert Griffin and Inspector Kelly. Informed that the body of his wife had been uncovered from the front room floor of 10 Rillington Place, Christie began to weep, saying "She woke me up; she was choking; I couldn't stand it any longer. . ." The prisoner was then cautioned and made the first of several statements embodying his recollections of the murders:

I'll tell you as much as I can remember. I have not been well for a long while, about 18 months. I have been suffering from fibrositis and enteritis. I had a breakdown at the hospital. I got better by September 1952, but kept having attacks after. My wife had been

sleep. Then I got out of bed and saw a small bottle and a cup half full of water on a small table near the bed. I noticed that the bottle contained 2 phenobarbitone tablets and it originally contained 25. I then knew that she must have taken the remainder. I got them from the hospital because I couldn't sleep. I left her in bed for two or three days and didn't know what to do. Then I remembered some loose floorboards in the front room. . .I thought that was the best way to lay her to rest.

Christie then related his financial position, and described selling the furniture. The next significant recollection is of the meeting with Rita Nelson:

On the way back, in Ladbroke Grove, a drunken woman stood in front of me and

---

* This is quite untrue, though the Christies almost certainly entertained the same prejudices as the rest of a generation adjusting to the newly arrived immigrants from the West Indies.

demanded a pound for me to take her round the corner. I said, "I am not interested and haven't got money to throw away"...She then demanded thirty shillings and said she would scream and say I had interfered with her if I didn't give it to her. I walked away as I am so well known round there and she obviously would have created a scene. She came along. She wouldn't go, and she came right to the door still demanding thirty shillings. When I opened the door she forced her way in. I went into the kitchen, and she was still on about this thirty shillings. I tried to get her out and she picked up a frying pan to hit me. I closed with her and there was a struggle and she fell back on the chair. It was a deck chair. There was a piece of rope hanging from the chair. I don't remember what happened but I must have gone haywire. The next thing I remember she was lying still in the chair with the rope round her neck. I don't remember taking it off. It couldn't have been tied. I left her there and went into the front room. After that I believe I had a cup of tea and went to bed. I got up in the morning and went to the kitchen and washed and shaved. She was still in the chair. I believe I made some tea then. I pulled away a small cupboard in the corner and gained access to a small alcove. . . I must have put her in there. I don't remember doing it. . .

. . .Some time after this, I suppose it was February, I went into a cafe at Notting Hill Gate for a cup of tea and a sandwich. The cafe was pretty full, and there wasn't much space. Two girls sat at a table, and I sat opposite at the same table. They were talking about rooms, where they had been looking to get accommodation. Then one of them spoke to me. She asked me for a cigarette and then started a conversation. During the conversation I mentioned about leaving my flat and that it would be vacant very soon and they suggested coming down to see it together in the evening. Only one came down [she was Kathleen Maloney]. She looked over the flat. She said it would be suitable subject to the landlord's permission. It was then that she made suggestions that she would visit me for a few days. She said this so that I would use my influence with the landlord as a sort of payment in kind. I was rather annoyed and told her that it didn't interest me. I think she started saying I was making accusations against her when she saw there was nothing doing. She said that she would bring somebody down to me. I thought she meant she was going to bring some of the boys down to do me. I believe it was then that she mentioned something about Irish blood. She was in a violent temper. I remember she started fighting. I am very quiet and avoid fighting. I know there was something, it's in the back of my mind. She was on the floor. I must have put her in the alcove straight away. . .

Left to right: the systematic removal of the three female bodies from the kitchen cupboard at Rillington Place

. . .Not very long after this I met a man and a woman coming out of a cafe at Hammersmith [Alexander Pomeroy Baker and Hectorina MacLennan]...It was in the morning. The man went across the road to talk to a friend and while he was away she said they had to give up their diggings at the weekend. He was out of work. Then I told her that if they hadn't found anywhere I could put them up for a few days. They both came up together and stayed a few days. They said they had been thrown out of their digs. I told them they would have to go as he was being very unpleasant. He told me that police were looking for her for some offence. When they left the man said that if they couldn't find anywhere could they come back for that night. The girl came back alone. She asked if he had called and I said "No", but I was expecting him. She said she would wait, but I advised her not to. She insisted on staying in case he came. I told her she couldn't and that he may be looking for her, and that she must go, and that she couldn't stay there alone. She was very funny about it. I got hold of her arm to try and lead her out. I pushed her out of the kitchen. She started struggling like anything and some of her clothing got torn. She then sort of fell limp as I had hold of her. She sank to the ground and I think some of her clothes must have got caught round her neck in the struggle. She was just out of the kitchen in the passage-way. I tried to lift her up, but couldn't. I then pulled her into the kitchen on to a chair. I felt her pulse, but it wasn't beating. I pulled the cupboard away again and I must have put her in there. . .

This was the way in which Christie remembered the last hours of the three victims boarded up in the kitchen. Or rather, it is Christie claiming *not* to remember what happened. He 'forgets', for example, that in each case he had sexual intercourse with the victim during or immediately after killing them.

John Reginald Christie's next statement is dated 5th of June, and relates to the murders, some ten years previously, of Ruth Fuerst and Muriel Eady:

When I was in the Police War Reserve I met an Austrian girl in the snack bar at the junction of Lancaster Road and Ladbroke Grove. . .It was the summer of 1943. I was living in the ground-floor flat at No.10 Rillington Place, and my wife was away in Sheffield. . .The Austrian girl told me she used to go out with American soldiers and one of them was responsible for a baby she had previously. I got friendly with her and she went to Rillington Place with me two or three times. . .

. . .I have seen a photograph in a newspaper recently of a girl named Ruth Fuerst. I do not recognise the photograph now shown to me. . .One day when this Austrian girl was with me in the flat at Rillington Place, she undressed and wanted me to have intercourse with her. I got a telegram while she was there, saying that my wife was on her way home. The girl wanted us to team up together and go right away somewhere together. I would not do that. I got onto the bed and had intercourse with her. While I was having intercourse with her, I strangled her with a piece of rope. I remember urine and excreta coming away from her. She was completely naked. I tried to put some of her clothes back on her. She had a leopard skin coat and I wrapped this round her. I took her from the bedroom into the front room and put her under the floorboards. I had to do that because of my wife coming back. I put the remainder of her clothing under the floorboards too...during the [next] afternoon my wife went out. While she was out I pulled the body up from under the floorboards and took it into the outhouse. Later in the day I dug a hole in the garden and in the evening, when it was dark, about ten o'clock I should say, I put the body down in the hole and covered it up quickly with earth. It was the right-hand side of the garden, about half-way along towards the rockery. My wife never knew. I told her I was going to the lavatory. The only lavatory is in the yard. I buried all the clothing in the garden. The next day I straightened the garden up and raked it over. . .

. . .I was released from the War Reserve in December, 1943, and started work at Ultra Radio, Park Royal. I got friendly with a woman named Eady, who was about thirty. She used to live at Putney. I took this woman and her man friend to Rillington Place and introduced them to my wife. They came several times together and had tea, and on another occasion we all went to the pictures together. . .

. . .On one occasion she came alone. I believe she complained of catarrh, and I said I thought I could help her. She came by appointment when my wife was out. I believe my wife was on holiday. I think I mixed some stuff up, some inhalants, Friar's Balsam was one. She was in the kitchen, and at the time she was inhaling with a square scarf over her head. I remember now, it was in the bedroom. The inhalant was in a square glass jar with a metal screw-top lid. I had made two holes in the lid and through one of the holes I put a rubber tube from the gas into the liquid. Through the other hole I put another rubber tube, about two feet long. This tube didn't touch the liquid. The idea was to stop what was coming from smelling of gas. She inhaled the stuff from the tube. I did it to make her dopey. She became sort of unconscious and I have a vague recollection of getting a stocking and tying it round her neck. I am not too clear about this. I have got them confused. It may have been the Austrian girl that I used the gas on. I don't think it was both. I believe I had intercourse with her at the time I strangled her. I think I put her in the wash-house [outhouse]. That night I buried her in the garden on the right-hand side nearest the yard. She was still wearing her clothing."

In a further statement made on the 8th of June Christie confessed at length to the murder of Mrs Beryl Evans – the crime for which her unfortunate husband had been executed – though is uncertain what happened to the Evans baby. In this same statement he acknowledges that the collection of pubic hair was his and that the samples "came from the three women in the alcove and from my wife".

Christie's trial was a formality, and despite his confession to multiple murder he was charged only with the killing of his wife. On the judge's seat was Mr Justice Finnemore; prosecuting Christie was Sir Lionel Heald QC, the Attorney-General, defending him Mr Derek Curtis-Bennett QC. The court took four days to examine the prisoner's defence of Not Guilty by reason of insanity, and his catalogue of self-confessed crimes did much to confirm the plea – that, and Curtis-Bennett's frequent references to his client as "mad as a March hare", and "hopelessly and utterly mad". In his summing up the judge acquainted the jury with the finer points of the McNaghten Rules [see *Murder Club Guide No.3*] and invited them to measure Christie's behaviour against them. The jury took one hour and twenty minutes to decide that the prisoner was guilty, and Christie was sentenced to death. There was no appeal, and the statutory inquiry into his mental condition concurred with the jury's verdict.

John Christie was hanged at Pentonville on the 15th of July 1953. Too late to save poor Timothy Evans, who even then had to wait until 1966 to be granted a long-overdue free and posthumous pardon.

Portrait of John Reginald Christie by Philip Youngman Carter

Francis Camps, pathologist and the Christie Case, was an old friend of Colonel Youngman Carter, and records the artist's own impression of his subject*: "In the case of Christie", he wrote, "I would say that the man was the nearest thing I have ever encountered to unadulterated evil. . .Two days' association with [the picture] made me almost physically sick, and the woman cleaning my studio, who had no idea about the subject of the portrait, asked me to put it away whilst she was working because it was frightening. . .

---

* *The Investigation of Murder*, Francis Camps with Richard Barber. Michael Joseph, London, 1966.

Manhunt
The Murder of PC GEOFFREY FOX, DS CHRISTOPHER HEAD, and DC DAVID WOMBWELL
by HARRY ROBERTS, JOHN WITNEY, and JOHN DUDDY
on Friday the 12th of August 1966 in Braybrook Street, W12

On Friday August the 12th 1966 Police Constable Geoffrey Fox, Detective Sergeant Christopher Head and Detective Constable David Wombwell were on the 9am to 5pm shift in 'Q' Car Foxtrot Eleven, an unmarked police car. They had just been stood down from the gruesome 'Jack the Stripper' inquiry and the main job of the morning had been to ferry Detective Inspector Coote to Marylebone Magistrates Court. After lunch at the *Beaumont Arms*, Uxbridge Road, there was little to do before a call came through at about three o'clock to pick up DI Coote again. They set off up Wood Lane, turning left into Western Avenue and eventually reached Braybrook Street, East Acton, a road that runs along the perimeter of Wormwood Scrubs Prison. At this point they sighted a battered blue Standard Vanguard Estate Car. For some reason, maybe a combination of its disreputable appearance and its proximity to the prison, they decided to stop it and check on the driver.

Inside the blue car were three small-time criminals, John Witney, Harry Roberts and John Duddy. Witney, the owner and driver of the car, was a 36-year-old unemployed lorry driver with a number of previous convictions for petty theft. About a year before, Witney had teamed up with Harry Roberts and together they had done a number of jobs, stealing lead and other metals. Roberts, aged thirty, had a similarly long criminal record, but was a much harder man, having done his National Service in Malaya, which had taught him guerrilla warfare and jungle survival techniques. He had recently served a four-year stretch and had resolved that he'd do almost anything to avoid getting caught again. John Duddy was a heavy drinker and had a history of petty theft, but

had always avoided violence. He had joined the other two more recently and they had begun to carry out a series of small robberies on betting shops and rent collectors. For this purpose they had decided to get 'tooled up' with firearms to use as a 'frightener'. Between the two front seats of the estate car was a canvas holdall containing three guns.

It was about a quarter-past three. The police car overtook the Vanguard Estate and flagged it down. Sergeant Head and DC Wombwell got out of their car and walked back to the driver's window of the Estate. Head asked to see the Road Fund Licence and Witney replied that he was awaiting his MOT Certificate. This was followed by a request for Witney's driving licence and insurance, the details of which Wombwell wrote down in his notebook. Head then moved round to inspect the rear of the car, and Witney said "Can't you give me a break. I've just been pinched for this a fortnight ago." As Wombwell inclined his head towards the driver's window to reply, Roberts drew a gun and shot him in the left

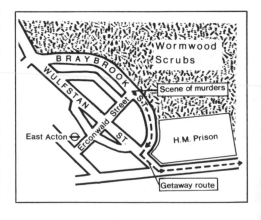

eye. DC Wombwell fell to the ground and Roberts and Duddy clambered out of the car in pursuit of Sergeant Head. Head ran back towards the Q Car and Roberts fired a shot, which missed. The Sergeant was trying to crouch behind the bonnet of the Q Car as Roberts shot him in the back. Meanwhile Duddy had run up to the Q Car and fired three shots through the driver's window at PC Fox, one of them hitting him in the left temple and killing him instantly. This released the brake pedal of the police car which, horrifyingly, ran over the body of the dying Sergeant Head, trapping him against the rear wheels. The two criminals then turned and ran to their car, which reversed back down the road in a panic and, turning, sped away past a surprised young couple driving in the opposite direction. Thinking that this might be a prison escape, they took the number of the van, PGT 726, and drove on to be faced by the scene of bloody devastation.

By nine o'clock that evening, the number of the car had been traced to Witney and the police had organized a raid on his house, where they found him and immediately took him into custody. His first story was that he had sold the car that lunchtime to a man in a pub for £15. That evening a description of the car was put out over the TV and radio, which was heard by a man who had seen it parked outside a lock-up garage in Tinworth Road, Vauxhall. Again the police pounced and discovered the car in the garage, complete with three .38 cartridges and Duddy's .38 gun on the back seat. On the Sunday Witney was formally charged with the three murders. Deciding that he had nothing to gain and an awful lot to lose by holding out any longer, Witney confessed to his part in the murder and named Roberts and Duddy as the main perpetrators of the crime.

Meanwhile, Roberts and Duddy had met up on the Saturday morning and, after burying the remaining guns on Hampstead Heath, decided they should separately make a run for it.

Duddy made for Glasgow, his home town, and was arrested several days later in a Carlton tenament. On his way back to London by plane, he confessed his part in the murders.

Roberts thought that his best chance of survival was to lay low for a while until the heat died down. He decided the safest way of achieving this was by living rough, a technique in which the Army had so thoughtfully trained him during his National Service. Accompanied by his common-law wife, Mrs Margaret Perry, he bought the camping gear he required in Tottenham Court Road and caught a bus from Camden Town to the *Wake Arms* in Epping. There, Mrs Perry left him, to return to her flat and the waiting attentions of the police. Roberts set out into Epping Forest.

So shocking did the senseless murder of three ordinary policemen seem that public outrage was instantly galvanized; one of many spontaneous gestures of sympathy was the production of this book, the proceeds from which were given to help the officers' dependants

On August the 16th a picture of Roberts was issued to the media and the biggest and most sustained manhunt in criminal history was about to begin. A reward of £1000 was offered for information leading to his capture and 16,000 posters bearing his picture were distributed. For three months his was the most famous face in Britain. Over six thousand reported sightings had to be followed up and the police were nearly swamped by the sheer volume of mainly useless information they had to check.

On the 31st of August the three unfortunate policemen were buried, and on September the 6th a memorial service was held for them in Westminster Abbey, attended by the Prime Minister, Mr Wilson, and many other dignitaries. Fifty thousand people sent money to a fund set up for the dependants of the three victims and petitions were circulated for the reintroduction of capital punishment, which had been abolished only a year previously. This seemed to be all the proof that the retentionists needed of the anarchy which would prevail without the ultimate sanction.

Still nothing substantial had been heard of Roberts. The authorities decided that they must go ahead with proceedings against Witney and Duddy, and the trial was set for November the 14th at the Old Bailey.

On November the 14th 1966 a gypsy farm labourer, John Cunningham, came across a man living in a tent in Thorley Woods, Bishop's Stortford. Being no friend of the police, he crept away and kept silent about it. A couple of days later he was being questioned on another matter by a local policeman and mentioned it in passing. The sighting was followed up and the camp site found. It was empty, but fingerprints found there matched those of Harry Roberts. The area was surrounded by 100 policemen and at dawn the next day a systematic search was begun. Just before noon Roberts was discovered hiding in a disused hangar on the edge of near-by Nathan's Wood. He gave himself up without a struggle.

It was decided to suspend the trial of Witney and Duddy so that Harry Roberts could join them in the dock. The new trial began at the Old Bailey on December the 6th, with Mr Justice Glyn-Jones presiding, the Solicitor-General, Sir Dingle Foot, representing the Crown and Mr W.M. Hudson, Mr James Comyn QC and Mr James Burge QC representing Witney, Duddy and Roberts respectively. Witney and Duddy pleaded not guilty to all the charges and Roberts pleaded guilty to the murder of DC Wombwell and DS Head, but not guilty to the killing of PC Fox. All three were found guilty on all counts. Witney and Roberts appealed, but their appeals were dismissed. The sentence was life imprisonment, with a recommendation from the Judge that they should each serve a minimum of thirty years. John Duddy died in Parkhurst Prison in February, 1981. Witney and Roberts are still serving their sentences.

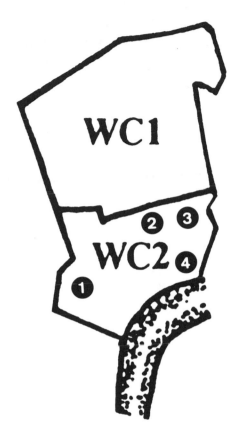

West-Central London

1. Major George STRANGEWAYS.. 188
2. Theodore GARDELLE 191
3. Marie-Marguerite FAHMY 195
4. Edwin BUSH 198

A Matter of Honour

The Murder of Mr FUSSEL
by Major GEORGE STRANGEWAYS

in the month of February 1658
at the sign of the George and Half Moon, Temple Bar
(site in present-day Fleet Street), WC2

Mr George Strangeways was the second son of Mr James Strangeways, a gentleman of an ancient and unblemished family whose seat was in the county of Dorset. George was generous of spirit and was framed, it is said, "to the most masculine proportion of man". As his youthful inclinations were suited more to the path of Mars than that of the Muses, he pursued and attained the rank of Major in the service of King Charles I (when loyalty to that monarch was neither very popular nor very safe), which military office he held with a great deal of bravery and gallantry during the whole course of the Civil War. Only in love did he appear unfulfilled, for he never married.

At the death of his father, the Major was left in possession of the family farm, and his elder sister, Mabellah, was created executrix by the will.

> This sister, being then an ancient maid, rented her brother's farm, and stocked it at her own cost; engaging herself to him in a bond of £350, which she borrowed towards the procuring of the said stock. The Major entrusted her not only with the bond, but also with that part of the stock, and such utensils of the house as by his father's will, properly belonged to him.*

In simpler terms, everything passed into Mabellah's legal possession, including the title-deeds and bonds. George's reason in doing this was to avoid the unthinkable consequence of his lack of loyalty to Cromwell – the sequestration of his goods by the Commonwealth.

> But all of a sudden the scene altered,

---

* Quotations are taken from an early edition of *The Malefactor's Register*.

and she, whom he thought sufficiently proof against all inclinations to matrimony, began to express some affection for Mr Fussel, a gentleman well esteemed at Blandford, the place of his residence, and of much repute for his eminent abilities in matters of law. Miss Strangeways made it now the least part of her care to disguise her sentiments concerning him; so it was not long before her brother came to a perfect knowledge of their mutual resolutions.

No sooner had he heard of the proposal of marriage – and the consequent transfer of his inheritance to the suitor – than George Strangeways spoke absolutely against it, and lost no opportunity in telling his sister of his disapproval. Just as often, and just as stubbornly, Miss Mabellah affirmed the steadfastness of her purpose. So did the family quarrels result in a separation between the brother and sister; the Major crying loudly against his sister, accusing her of nothing less than a design to defraud him of his estate. These were the differences which first fomented a rage that was not to be quenched but by blood.

Soon afterwards, the wedding took place; succeeded by a challenge to combat by Strangeways; followed by a lawsuit commenced by Fussel, for which purpose both men were present in the city of London.

> Mr Fussel lodged up one pair of stairs at the sign of the George and Half Moon, three doors from the *Palsgrave's Head* tavern without Temple Bar, opposite a pewterer's shop. He came in one evening between nine and ten, and retired to his study, which fronted the street, sitting behind a desk, with his face towards the window, the curtains being so near drawn

that there was but just room enough left to discern him. In this manner he had not sat above a quarter of an hour before two bullets shot from a carbine struck him, the one through the forehead and the other in about his mouth; a third bullet, or slug, stuck in the lower part of the window. . .

. . .He dropped down upon his desk without so much as a groan, so that his clerk, who was in the room at the same time, did not apprehend anything of what was done; till at last, perceiving him to lean

this time of night in the public parts of the city.

By the time the watchmen had carried out a fruitless search, Fussel's son (by a previous marriage) had recalled to mind the bitter quarrel that had for some time existed between his father and Uncle George Strangeways, and suggested that the officers might like to apprehend him; which action they in general approved of.

Thus George Strangeways found himself, at two-thirty in the morning, dragged from his lodging in Bull Inn Court and before Mr

Temple Bar at the time of Mr Fussell's assassination

his head, and knowing him not apt to fall asleep as he wrote, he imagined something more than ordinary was the matter. Upon this he drew near, to be satisfied, when he was suddenly struck with such horror and amazement at the unexpected sight of blood that, for the present, he was incapable of any action. As soon as he had recollected himself, he called up some of the family . . . Instantly they all ran into the street, but could see nothing, everything appearing more silent and still than is usual at

Justice Blake; the latter listening dispassionately to his denials before committing him to Newgate. . .

where remaining till next morning, he was then conveyed to the place where Mr Fussel's body was. When he came there, he was commanded to take his dead brother-in-law by the hand, and touch his wounds before the coroner's inquest.*

---

* It was formerly customary to oblige persons suspected of murder to touch the murdered body

As this piece of hocus-pocus failed to produce any positive result, the problem was remanded back to the jury for further inquiry. One of the ways suggested was to inquire of all the gunsmiths in London and around what guns they had either sold or lent on the fatal day. Now it happened that a fellow member of that jury was himself a gunsmith, Mr Holloway of the Strand, and it was his opinion that it would be impossible to make such an inquiry without error owing to the number of that profession in London alone; indeed, he added, he had himself lent out a carbine on the very day in question, to Mr Thompson in Long Acre. Seeing the opportunity for positive action, the foreman of the jury ordered the apprehension of Thompson, but since this latter was away on business, and there being nobody else to arrest, his unfortunate wife was taken into custody. . .

but on the first news of his wife's confinement, Thompson returned hastily to London, where being examined before a justice of the peace, he confessed that he had borrowed a carbine from Mr Holloway – for the use of a Major Strangeways!

Strangeways had claimed that he was going on a deer hunt, and so the gun was loaded

---

to discover their guilt or innocence. This way of finding out murderers was first practised in Denmark by King Christian II, and permitted all over his kingdom; the occasion was this: certain gentlemen were drinking together one evening in a 'stove', or tavern, and falling out among themselves began to brawl and, the candles being knocked out, one man was fatally stabbed with a poignard. The murderer being unknown – because of the darkness and the number of persons involved – the king, one of whose pursuivants had been accused, caused them all to come together at the stove in a circle round the corpse. He commanded that they should each in turn lay their right hand on the corpse's naked breast, swearing that they had not killed him. The gentlemen did so, and no sign appeared against them; only the pursuivant remained, who went first of all to kiss the dead man's feet; but as soon as he had laid his hand upon his breast the blood gushed forth in abundance, out of both his wound and his nostrils; urged by this evident accusation, he confessed to the murder, and was immediately beheaded. Such was the origin of a practise which became common throughout Europe for the exposure of unknown murderers.

and passed to his keeping on the evening of the murder between the hours of seven and eight. Confronted by this weighty testimony, Strangeways could do nothing but agree, and to concur with Major Thompson in the fact that the gun was returned to his house between ten and eleven o'clock of the same evening.

What happened between these hours will never be known for certain. Strangeways admitted to having set up an alibi for himself, leaving a friend innocently in his apartment, whose movements were mistaken for his own; a friend who slipped quietly away on his return. George Strangeways acknowledged culpability for the fact of Fussel's death, but not for firing the shot.

On the 24th of February, 1685, Major George Strangeways was brought to his trial at the sessions house in the Old Bailey; where, his indictment being read, and he being commanded to plead, he absolutely refused to comply with the method of the Court unless, he said, he might be permitted, when he was condemned, to die in the same manner as his brother-in-law [that is, by shooting, which in his eyes meant the firing squad as a military 'honour']. If they refused this, he told them, he would continue in his contempt of the Court, that he might preserve his estate, which would be forfeited on his conviction, in order to bestow it on such friends as he had most affection for, as well as to free himself from the ignominious death of a public gibbet.

Many arguments were urged by Cromwell's Lord Chief Justice, Mr Serjeant Glyn, and the rest of the bench, to induce him to plead; particularly the terror of the death which his obstinate silence would oblige them to inflict upon him. But still he remained immovable, refusing either to plead or to discover who it was that fired the gun; only affirming that, whoever did it, it was done by his direction.

When it was clear that no argument would alter his resolution the Lord Chief Justice passed on Major Strangeways the terrible sentence of 'Peine Forte et Dure' to be his punishment until death.

On the last day of February – a Monday – at eleven o'clock in the morning, the Sheriffs of London and Middlesex, accompanied by several of their officers, met at the Press-Yard in Newgate. . .

After a short stay, Major Strangeways was guarded down, clothed all in white – waistcoat, stockings, drawers and cap, over which was cast a long mourning cloak. From whence he was conducted to the dungeon, the dismal place of execution. . .

He took his solemn last leave of all his lamenting friends, and prepared himself for the dreadful assault of Death, with whom he was speedily to encounter. He desired his friends, when he gave the signal, to lay on the weights, and they placed themselves at the corners of the press for that purpose.

His arms and legs were extended, according to the sentence, in which action he cried out, "Thus were the sacred limbs of my ever blessed Saviour stretched forth on the cross, when He suffered to free the sin-polluted world from an eternal curse." Then crying with a sprightly voice, "Lord Jesus receive my soul," which were the words he had told them, his mournful attendants performed their dreadful task. They soon perceived that the weight they laid on was not sufficient to put him suddenly out of pain, so several of them added their own weight, that they might the sooner release his soul. While he was dying, it was horrible to all who stood by, as well as dreadful to himself, to see the agonies he was put into, and hear his loud and doleful groans. But this dismal scene was over in about eight or ten minutes, when all his spirit departed, and left her tortured mansion, till the great day that shall unite them again. . .His body having laid some time in the press, was brought forth and exposed to the public view, so that a great many people beheld the bruises made by the press, one angle of which being purposely placed over his heart, he was the sooner deprived of life, though he was denied what is usual in these cases, to have a sharp piece of timber under his back to hasten execution. The body appeared void of scars, and not deformed with blood, save where the extremities of the press came on the breasts and the upper part of the belly. The face was bloody, not from any external injury, but the violent forcing of the blood from the larger vessels into the veins of the face and eyes. After the dead corpse had been thus examined it was put into a coffin, and in a cart that attended at the prison door conveyed to Christ Church, where it was interred.

[*See Appendix Five to this volume for an additional note on the punishment of Peine Forte et Dure.*]

The Fine Art of Murder
The Murder of Mrs KING, his Landlady
by THEODORE GARDELLE
on the 19th of February 1761
at her house in Leicester Fields (now Leicester Square), WC2

Theodore Gardelle* was a foreigner, and a man of education and talents in his profession, the fine art of painting. He was born at Geneva, a city which is famed for giving birth to great men, in both the

---
* The text has been adapted from *The Life of Theodore Gardelle*, published in London in 1761.

---

arts and sciences. He chose the miniature style of painting, and, having acquired its first rudiments, went to Paris, where he gained great proficiency in the art. He then returned to his native place and practiced his profession for some years, with credit and emolument; but, it appears, unhappy in his domestic concerns, he repaired to London, and took lodgings at Mrs King's, in Leicester Fields, in the year 1760.

Some time afterwards, for the benefit of purer air, he removed to Knightsbridge, but finding that place too far from his business he returned to his former residence, where he pursued his business until the fatal cause arose which brought him to an ignominious death.

On Thursday, the 19th of February 1761, in the morning, the maid got up about seven o'clock and opened the fore parlour windows. There was a fore parlour and a back parlour; both had a door in the passage from the street door, and there was also a door out of one into the other: the back parlour was Mrs King's bedchamber, and the door which entered it from the passage was secured on the inside by a drop-bolt, and could not be opened on the outside when locked, though the drop-bolt was not down, because on the outside there was no keyhole. The door on the fore parlour was also secured on the inside by Mrs King when she went to bed, and the door of the fore parlour into the passage was left open. When the maid had entered the fore parlour by this door and opened the windows she went to the passage door of the back parlour, where Mrs King was in bed, and knocked, in order to get the key of the street door, which Mrs King took at night into her room. Mrs King drew up the bolt and the maid went in. She took the key of the street door, which she saw lying upon the table by a looking-glass, and her mistress then shut the passage door and dropped the bolt, and ordered the maid to open the door that communicated with the fore parlour, which she did and went out. She then kindled the fire in the fore parlour, that it might be ready when her mistress arose, and about eight o'clock went up into Gardelle's room, where she found him in a red-and-green nightgown, at work. He gave her two letters, a snuff box, and a guinea, and desired her to deliver the letters, one of which was directed to one Mozier, in the Haymarket, and the other to the person who kept the snuff-shop next door, and to bring from thence a pennyworth of snuff.

The girl took the messages, and went again to her mistress, telling her what Gardelle had desired her to do; to which her mistress replied: "Nannie, you can't go, for there is nobody to answer the street door." The girl being willing to oblige Gardelle, or being for some reason desirous to go out, answered that Mr Gardelle would come down and sit in the parlour till she came back. Then she went again to Gardelle and told him what objection her mistress had made, and what she had said to remove it. Gardelle then said he would come down, as she had proposed, and he did come down accordingly.

The girl immediately went on his errand, and left him in the parlour, shutting the street door after her, and taking the key to let herself in when she came back.

Immediately the girl had gone out, Mrs King, hearing the tread of somebody in the parlour, called out, "Who is there?" and at the same time opened her chamber door. Gardelle was at a table, very near the door, having just taken up a book that lay upon it, which happened to be a French grammar. He had some time before drawn Mrs King's picture, which she wanted to have made very handsome, and had teased him so much about it that the effect was just contrary.

It happened, unfortunately, that the first thing she said to him, when she saw it was he who she had heard walking about in the room, was something reproachful about this picture. Gardelle was provoked at the insult, and, as he spoke English very imperfectly, he, for want of a less improper expression, told her, with some warmth, that she was an impertinent woman. This threw her into a transport of rage, and she gave him a violent blow with her fist on the breast – so violent, that he said he would not have thought such a blow could have been given by a woman. As soon as the blow was struck she drew back a little, and at the same instant he laid his hand on her shoulder and pushed her from him, rather in contempt than anger, or with a design to hurt her; but her foot happening to catch the floor-cloth she fell backwards, and her head came with great force against the corner of the bedstead. The blood immediately gushed from her mouth, not in a continued stream, but as if by different strokes of a pump. He instantly ran to her and stooped to raise her, expressing his concern at the accident; but she pushed him away, and threatened, though in a feeble voice, to punish him.

He was exceeding terrified at the thought of being condemned for a criminal act upon her accusation, and again attempted to assist her, by raising her up, as the blood still gushed from her mouth in great quantities; but she still exerted all her strength to keep him off, and still cried out, mixing threats with her screams. He then seized an ivory comb with a sharp taper point continued from the back for adjusting the curls of the maid, by saying that her mistress had discharged her. She left the house, and the murder was not discovered until the next Saturday week, when a constable and some others went to the house, where they found Gardelle, and charged him with the murder. He denied it, but soon after dropped into a swoon. When he recovered, they demanded the key of Mrs King's chamber; but he said she had taken it with her to the country. The

Leicester Square in about 1750

her hair, which lay upon her toilet, and threatened her in his turn to prevent her crying out; but she still continuing to cry out, though with a voice still fainter and fainter, he struck her with this instrument, probably in the throat, upon which the blood flowed from her mouth in yet greater quantities, and her voice was quite stopped. He then drew the bedclothes over her to prevent her blood spreading on the floor, and to hide her from his sight. He stood some time motionless beside her, and then fell down by her side in a swoon. When he came to himself he perceived the maid had come in. He therefore went out of the room without examining the body to see if the unhappy wretch was quite dead, and his confusion was then so great that he staggered against the wainscot and hit his head, so that a bump was raised over his eye.

By means of a ruse, Gardelle got rid of constable therefore got in at the window and opened the door that communicated with the parlour, and they all went in. They found that there had been a fire in the garret, and some fragments of bones, half consumed, were found in the chimney. To this force of evidence Gardelle at length gave way, and confessed the fact. He was sent to New Prison, where he attempted to destroy himself by swallowing some opium, which he had kept several years by him as a remedy for the toothache. When he found the opium did not produce the effect he desired, he swallowed twelve halfpence.

On the 2nd of March he was brought to Newgate, and diligently watched, to prevent any further attempts on his life. On Thursday, the 2nd of April, he was tried at the Old Bailey; and, in his defence, he insisted only that he had no malice to the deceased, and that her death was the consequence of the fall. He was convicted, and sentenced to be executed on Saturday the 4th.

He was executed, amidst the shouts and hisses of an indignant populace, in the Haymarket, near Panton Street, to which he was led past Mrs King's house, where the cart made a stop, and at which he just gave a look. His body was hung in chains upon Hounslow Heath.

[*See* Murder Club Guide No.2 *for a note on Hanging in Chains*].

The Oriental Underneath

The Murder of Prince ALI KAMEL FAHMY BEY
by his Wife MARIE-MARGUERITE FAHMY
on Monday the 9th of July 1923
in their suite at the Savoy Hotel, Strand, WC2

Within the personalities and the lifestyles of its two leading characters lay all the ingredients that together make either a great Romance, or a great Crime of Passion. It was to be the meeting of two quite alien cultures that set this runaway train of emotions hurtling towards the latter course.

He was Prince Ali Kamel Fahmy Bey, a volatile young Egyptian playboy, holding a nominal diplomatic post with his Government's embassy in Paris, and heir to his father's immense fortune. She was a beautiful, sophisticated Parisienne ten years his senior.

When they met in Paris in 1922 Fahmy fell instantly in love with the beautiful Marie-Marguerite Laurent, a recent divorcée, and pursued her relentlessly and passionately. He followed her to Deauville, where they became lovers, and in December Marguerite was converted to the Muslim faith and the couple married, embarking on a life that revolved around the fashionable high-spots of Egypt and Paris. Subsequent events were to illuminate the dark recesses that lay behind this outwardly bright and carefree extravagance.

The beginning of July found the Fahmys ensconced in a luxury suite at London's famous Savoy Hotel.

On the evening of the 9th the couple fell into bitter disagreement over an operation that Marguerite wished to have performed in Paris, but her husband insisted be carried out in London – or he would not provide the money to pay for it. The quarrel accompanied them to supper in the hotel restaurant, where Madame Fahmy was overheard threatening to crack a bottle over Prince Ali's head.

Later on, as part of his customary courtesy, the leader of the restaurant's small orchestra approached the Fahmys' table to ask Madame if there was any particular tune that she would like them to play. "I don't want any music", she replied, "my husband has threatened to kill me tonight." With a polite bow the conductor made a tactical withdrawal with the words "I hope you will still be here tomorrow, Madame."

Twice during that tense evening Fahmy asked his wife to dance with him; twice she refused; twice she accepted the same invitation from his personal secretary, Said Ernani. They returned to their fourth floor suite at about 1.30am, the squabbling clearly continuing to escalate. John Beattie, a luggage porter, passing on his business past the Fahmy rooms was startled to see the door fly open, and the Prince launch himself into the corridor complaining, "Look at my face; look what she has done." The porter recollected seeing nothing more alarming than a small red blemish on the Egyptian's face, and before he could gather himself for a response Madame Fahmy came out of the room talking loudly, excitedly, and in French. With what must be considered great tact, Beattie persuaded the warring couple to return to their room and stop making a

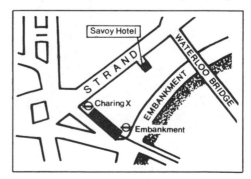

public nuisance of themselves. Turning his head as he resumed his way along the corridor, the porter caught a glimpse of Fahmy, still outside his room, crouched down whistling and snapping his fingers at a small dog. Before he had reached the end of the passage, three sharp, loud noises obliged him hastily to retread his steps. The sound was from a gun; Madame Fahmy's gun; and when he arrived back at the entrance to their suite it was Marguerite Fahmy herself holding it. Her husband lay on the floor, bleeding from the head.

Ali Fahmy was to die shortly after admission to hospital; at about the same time Madame Fahmy was being charged with his murder.

By the opening of the trial at the Central Criminal Court on September 10th 1923, sufficient information was already publicly available to ensure that the case was a sensation even before the first witness took the stand.

That first witness (for the prosecution), under the expert cross-examination of popular defender Sir Edward Marshall Hall, began to reveal the grim story of repression, mental cruelty, and physical abuse which had led poor Marguerite to her most desperate method of escape. The witness was Fahmy's secretary, Said Ernani, and he agreed that the couple were always in dispute because of his master's strong views on the position of women; that having wooed her with

Madame Marie-Marguerite Fahmy

sugar-coated promises and elegant flattery, Fahmy forced her to become a Muslim before their wedding as it was a condition on which a large legacy from his mother depended. Despite Fahmy's promise that a clause would be entered into the marriage contract allowing Marguerite the right to initiate a divorce if things became intolerable, he had this agreement struck out of the document, so that only he could annul the marriage. As to the physical side of things, Said Ernani denied that Fahmy had sworn on the Koran to kill his wife, but reluctantly admitted a series of lesser bodily attacks – once occasioning Marguerite a dislocated jaw.

Warming to his defence, Marshall Hall read out to the court a letter written by Fahmy to Marguerite's younger sister: "Just now I am engaged in training her. Yesterday, to begin with I did not come in to lunch nor to dinner and also I left her at the theatre. This will teach her, I hope, to respect my wishes. With women one must act with energy and be severe – no bad habits. We still lead the same life of which you are aware – the opera, theatre, disputes, high words, perverseness."

Madame Fahmy's gun passed into Marshall Hall's collection of memorabilia and came under the auctioneer's hammer in January 1987

Sir Edward then touched on the bizarre (certainly in the eyes of the 1920s) sexual appetites of the Prince, and in particular the homosexual relationships which he enjoyed with (among others) the witness himself – a liaison which had become popular gossip in Egypt. Referring to Fahmy's sexual use of his wife, the defender elicited such information as to suggest that the very complaint for which she wished to attend a Paris clinic, and which had initiated the quarrel on the night of the murder, almost certainly arose from complications associated with persistent anal intercourse.

Marshall Hall's closing speech – as indeed his whole handling of the defence – has gone down as one of his most outstanding, relying as it did on emphasising the fatal consequences of intermarriage between the sons and daughters of East and West:

"She made one great mistake," [he told the jury] "possibly the greatest mistake a woman of the West can make. She married an Oriental. I dare say the Egyptian civilization is, and may be, one of the oldest and most wonderful civilizations in the world. But if you strip off the external civilization of the Oriental, you get the real Oriental underneath. It is common knowledge that the Oriental's treatment of women does not fit in with the way the Western woman considers she should be treated by her husband. . .The curse

Prince Ali Kamel Fahmy Bey

of this case is the atmosphere which we cannot understand – the Eastern feeling of possession of the woman, the Turk in his harem, this man who was entitled to have four wives if he liked for chattels. which to us Western people with our ideas of women is almost unintelligible, something we cannot deal with."

He then came to the night of the murder, and in one of those moments of dramatic brilliance which illuminated his career, Marshall Hall took up the pistol which had shot Fahmy dead. He crouched in imitation of Ali Fahmy, stealthily advancing towards his wife, about to spring like a wild animal upon her, "she turned the pistol and put it to his face, and to her horror the thing went off": the jury found themselves momentarily looking down the barrel of that same gun. Then, as his words died in the silence, he dropped the weapon with a deafening clatter on to the courtroom floor.

"I do not ask you for a verdict," he told the jury, "I demand a verdict at your hands."

Mr Justice Swift, at the time the youngest judge sitting on a High Court Bench, followed with his summing-up. It concluded: "A person who honestly believes that his life is in danger is entitled to kill his assailant if that is the only way he honestly and reasonably believes he can protect himself. But he must be in real danger, and it must be the only way out of it."

Quite clearly the jury found this the perfect description of Madame Fahmy's predicament; at any rate it took them little over an hour to return a verdict of "Not guilty".

Those two words were all but drowned by the outburst of cheers from the court, and taken up by the huge crowd outside, all awaiting just such a result.

For Marshall Hall the undying gratitude of a beautiful woman, and the unstinting respect of his peers. Only the Egyptian Government was less than impressed, and cabled the Attorney-General complaining bitterly about the derogatory remarks made about the Orientals.

For Marie-Marguerite Fahmy the love and admiration of a nation; and now, the freedom to "be forgotten by everybody except my own friends."

The Face of Crime
The Murder of Mrs ELSIE MAY BATTEN
by EDWIN ALBERT BUSH
on the 3rd of March 1961
at 23 Cecil Court (formerly Louis Meier's antique shop), WC2

The Identikit system of identification was the culmination of research and development carried out by the Los Angeles Police Department, notably by Hugh McDonald. At its inception the 'kit' comprised a set of interchangeable transparencies of drawings. These depicted variations on facial features – eyes, noses, ears, etc. – which in a collaboration between the police operator and a witness could be assembled to give a composite picture of the wanted person. In theory it was possible to combine the components into thousands of millions of likenesses; in practice the system proved rudimentary and inaccurate, even, as in the case of the 'A6 Murder', a possible hindrance to the course of justice.

In 1959 the concept of Identikit was introduced to the investigating officers of Scotland Yard, but it was not until 1961 that the system was put to practical use...

Britain's first Identikit Face was that of 21-year-old Edwin Albert Bush, author of a senseless and lacklustre crime in the heart of London's theatreland. Bush, obligingly enough for the launch of Identikit, was a fairly distinctive half-caste Indian who had walked into Louis Meier's antiquities shop in Cecil Court on March 2nd 1961, the day before the murder, and made inquiries as to the cost of a dress sword. He had been told £15, and went from here across the pedestrian court, to the shop of a gunsmith named Roberts who replied to his question that, yes, he did occasionally buy swords, but would need to see it before agreeing a price.

On the following morning Bush returned to Louis Meier's shop, where he stabbed to death Meier's assistant, Mrs Elsie Batten, wife of the President of the Royal Society of Sculptors Mark Batten, and helped himself to a dress sword. At 10am he re-opened his transaction with the gunsmith, leaving the ill-gotten blade in the care of his son Paul Roberts, suggesting a price of say £10. He never returned to hear the gunsmith's verdict, but Bush (as prime suspect in the murder) could now be reliably identified by three people. This enabled a fairly accurate Identikit portrait to be made; accurate enough, anyway, for Police Constable John Cole to identify and arrest the subject while on patrol in Old Compton Street, Soho, on the 8th of March.

At Bow Street police station where he was interviewed by Detective Chief Superintendent John Bliss, Bush expressed the opinion that the Identikit looked like him, but denied any connection with the killing of Elsie Batten. However, it was not long before Edwin Bush was making his statement: "I went to the back of the shop and started looking through the daggers, telling her I might want to buy one, but I picked one up and hit her in the back...I then lost my nerve and picked up a stone vase and hit her with it. I grabbed a knife and hit her once in the stomach and once in the neck."

But aside from his confession, Edwin Bush's catalogue of carelessness had not ended at

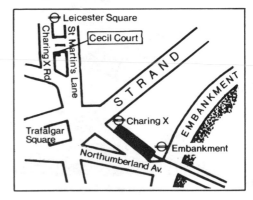

198

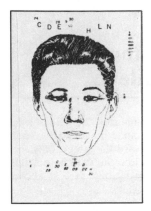  

Edwin Bush, flanked by his Identikit likenesses, the first time the system was used in Britain

regularly showing his face in the area where he had committed murder; he had also left behind in the shop an identifiable footprint. There was blood on his clothing, and two fingers and a palm print on the sheet of paper he had used to wrap the sword.

Edwin Bush stood trial at the Old Bailey on May 12th and 13th. In his evidence he admitted going into Mr Meier's shop with the intention of stealing a cermonial sword; he was then, he said, going to sell the sword to Mr Roberts in order to buy an engagement ring for his girl-friend. Bush then began to haggle over the price and: "She let off about my colour and said, 'You niggers are all the same. You come in and never buy anything', I lost my head..." he then repeated his previous account of the killing.

Bush had the benefit of Mr Christmas Humphreys QC as his defender, but at the end of the trial he was convicted, sentenced to death by Mr Justice Stevenson, and hanged. Of PC Cole's part in the apprehension of Mrs Batten's killer, the judge commented: "You deserve the congratulations and gratitude of the community for the great efficiency you displayed in recognizing Bush. You have been the direct instrument of his being brought to justice. Your vigilance deserves the highest praise, and I hope it will be clearly recognised by the highest authority."

Some Brief Notes on the History of Newgate and the Old Bailey

. . .That most celebrated place,
Where angry Justice shows her awful face;
Where little villains must submit to fate,
That great ones may enjoy the world in state.
(Sir Samual Garth, *The Dispensary*)

HISTORY AND DESCRIPTION

There is some dispute as to the origin of the name 'Old Bailey', for while some think it implies the Ballium, or outer space beyond the wall, Maitland* refers it to Bail Hill, an eminence where the bail, or bailiff, lived and held his court. Stow** thinks the street was called from some old court held there, as, in the year 1356, the tenement and ground upon Houndsditch, between Ludgate on the south and Newgate on the north, was appointed to John Cambridge, fishmonger and Chamberlain of London, "whereby," he says, "it seems that the Chamberlains of London have kept their courts as now they do by the Guildhall; and to this day the mayor and justices of this City kept their sessions in a part thereof now called the Sessions Hall, both for the City of London and Shire of Middlesex."

Strype describes the Old Sessions House as a fair and stately building, very commodious, and with large galleries on both sides for spectators,

> The court-room, being advanced by stone steps from the ground, with rails and banisters, enclosed from the yard before it; and the bail-dock, which fronts the court where the prisoners are kept until brought to their trials, is also enclosed. Over the court-room is a stately dining-room, sustained by ten stone pillars, and over it a platform, headed with rails and banisters. There be five lodging-rooms,

* Frederick William Maitland (1850-1906); Barrister and legal historian, author of *History of the English Law.*
** John Stow (1525-1605); English antiquarian best known for his formidable *Survey of London.*

and other conveniences, on either side of the court. It standeth backwards, so it hath no front toward the street; only the gateway leadeth into the yard before the house, which is spacious. It cost above £6000 the building.

A Court-house was erected here in 1773; it was destroyed in the 'No Popery' riots of 1780, but was rebuilt and enlarged in 1809 by the addition of the site of the old Surgeon's Hall (see below).

The old constitution of this court for malefactors is given in Strype:

> It is called the King's Commission on the Peace of Oyer and Terminer, and the Gaol Delivery of Newgate, for the City of London and County of Middlesex, which court is held at Justice Hall, in the Old Bailey, commonly called the Sessions House, and generally eight times, or oftener, every year. The judges are the Lord Mayor, Recorder, and others of His Majesty's Justices of the Peace of the City of London, the two Sheriffs of London being always present; and oftentimes the judges (being always in these commissions) come, and sit to give their assistance. The jurors, for all matters committed in London, are citizens of London . . . and the jurors for crimes and misdemeanours committed in Middlesex, are freeholders of the said county.

Under the general title, 'The Central Criminal Court', are joined both what are called the Old Court and the New. The former deals with the more weighty cases – those of deepest dye – and has echoed, without doubt, to more tales of the romance of crime than any other building in the kingdom. Here are tried crimes of every kind, from treason to the pettiest larceny, and even offences committed on the high seas.

As to the number of persons who are here brought into the public notice, Mr Sheriff

Laurie, writing to *The Times* of November 28th 1845, says, "I find upon investigation that upwards of two thousand persons annually are placed at the bar of the Old Bailey for trial. About one-third are acquitted, one-third are first offences, and the remaining portion have been convicted of a felony before." Trials go on at the Old Bailey almost all the year round.

The interior of the Old Court has been described by a writer in Knight's *Cyclopaedia of London* (1851)*:

Passing through a door in the wall which encloses the area between Newgate and the courts, we find a flight of steps on our right, leading up into the Old Court. This is used chiefly for prosecutors and witnesses. Farther on in the area, another flight of steps leads to a long passage into a corridor at the back of the court, with two doors opening into the latter, by one of which the judges and sheriffs reach the bench, and by the other, the barristers

* Charles Knight (1791-1873); Popular author and publisher of *Popular History of England* and the *Penny Cyclopaedia*.

their place in the centre at the bottom. Both doors also lead to the seats reserved for visitors. We enter, pause, and look round. The first sentiment is one of disappointment. The great and moral power and pre-eminence of the court makes one, however idly and unconsciously, anticipate a grander physical exhibition. What does meet our gaze is no more than a square hall of sufficient length, and breadth, and height, lighted up by three large square windows on the opposite wall, showing the top of the gloomy walls of Newgate, having on the left a gallery close to the ceiling, with projecting boxes, and on the right, the bench, extending the whole length of the wall, with desks at intervals for the use of judges, whilst in the body of the court are, first, a dock for the prisoners below the gallery, with stairs descending to the covered passage by which the prisoners are conveyed to and from the prison; then, just in advance of the left-hand corner of the dock, the circular witness-box, and in a similarly relative position to the witness box, the jury box, below the windows of the

The Sessions House built in about 1673 to replace its predecessor which was consumed in the Great Fire of 1666

The interior layout of the Central Criminal Court in the middle of the nineteenth century

court, an arrangement that enables the jury to see clearly and without turning, the faces of the witnesses and of the prisoners; that enables the witness to identify the prisoner; and lastly, that enables the judges on the bench, and counsel in the centre of the court below, to keep jury, witnesses, and prisoners all at once within the same, or nearly the same, line of view. We need only add to these features of the place the formidable row of law-books which occupies the centre of the green-baized table, around which are the counsel; the double line of reporters occupying the two seats below us; the sherriff in attendance for the day, looking so spruce in his court suit, stepping noiselessly in and out. Where, then, is the judge? one naturally asks; when, looking more attentively, we perceive for the first time, some one writing, taking frequent but brief glances at the prisoners or the witnesses, but never turning his head in any other direction, speaking to no one on the bench, and unspoken to. That is a judge of the land, quietly doing the whole business of the court."

PUBLIC EXECUTIONS

The Old Bailey – that part of the street opposite to Newgate – became the scene of public executions in 1783, on the 9th of December, in which year the first culprit suffered here the extreme penalty of the law. Before that time the public executions took place at Tyburn [near present-day Marble Arch]. The gallows of the Old Bailey was built with three cross-beams for as many rows of victims, and between February and December, 1785, ninety-six persons suffered by the 'new drop', an ingenious invention which took the place of the cart.

The front of Newgate continued to be the place of execution in London from 1783 to 1868, when an Act was passed directing executions to take place within the walls of prisons. This Act was the result of a commission on capital punishments, appointed in 1864, which in their report of 1865 recommended, among other things, that executions should not be public, [see *Murder Club Guide No.2* for a note on the early Abolitionist movement]. The number of executions throughout the country gradually decreased over many years, as laws became less severe. What a contrast to the old times when the law of the gallows and the scaffold kept our forefathers in order! In the thirty-eight-year reign of Henry VIII it is said that no fewer than 72,000 criminals were executed in England!

About 1786 was witnessed in the Old Bailey the end of an old practice: the body of the criminal just executed was burned for the last time. A woman was the sufferer in this case. She was hung on a low gibbet, and on life being extinct fagots were heaped around her and over her head, fire was set to the pile, and the corpse was burned to ashes.

Public chastisement at the pillory in Sessions House Yard

The Debtors' Door from Newgate Prison. Criminals who had been condemned to death were led through this door to the public scaffold in front of the gaol. The door can now be seen in the Museum of London

THE PILLORY

Offenders frequently stood in the pillory in the Old Bailey, and there they were often, as was customary, stoned by the mob, and pelted with rotten eggs, and other equally offensive missiles. The pillory generally consisted of a wooden frame, erected on a scaffolding, with holes and folding boards for the admission of the head and hands of him whom it was desired to render less publicly infamous.

SURGEON'S HALL

The Surgeon's Hall used to stand in the Old Bailey, on the site of the New Sessions House, until 1809. Tennant, in his *London*, makes the observation, in connection with the old Court of Justice, that the erection of the Surgeon's Hall in its neighbourhood was an exceedingly convenient circumstance:

By a feat of second sight, Surgeon's Hall was built near this court of conviction near Newgate, the concluding stage of the lives forfeited to the justice of their country, several years before the fatal tree was removed from Tyburn to its present site. It is a handsome building, ornamented with Ionic pilasters, and with

203

Surgeon's Hall

a double flight of steps to the first floor. Beneath is a door for the admission of the bodies of murderers and other felons, who, noxious in their lives, make a sort of reparation to their fellow-creatures by becoming useful after death.

The bodies of murderers, after execution, were dissected in the Surgeon's Theatre, according to an Act passed in 1752, and which was only repealed in the reign of William IV.

Anatomizing in the Surgeon's Theatre

THE ROAD TO TYBURN

As clever Tom Clinch, while the rabble
    was bawling,
Rode stately through Holborn to die in
    his calling,
He stopt at the *George* for a bottle of
    sack.
And promised to pay for it when he
    came back.
His waistcoat and stockings and breeches
    were white,
His cap had a new cherry ribbon to tie 't.
The maids to the doors and the balconies
    ran,
And said 'Lack-a-day! he's a proper
    young man!'
But as from the windows the ladies he
    spied,
Like a beau in the box he bowed low
    on each side!
And when his last speech the loud
    hawkers did cry,
He swore from his cart, 'It was all a
    d-----d lie!'
The hangman for pardon fell down on
    his knee,
And clever Tom gave him a kick – for
    his fee!

(Daniel Defoe, 1660-1731)

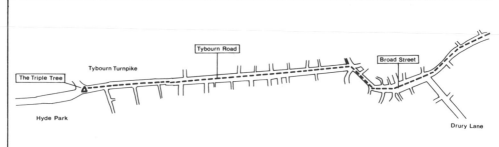

The route to Tyburn

When criminals were conveyed from Newgate to Tyburn the cart passed up Giltspur Street, and through Smithfield, to Cow Lane. Skinner Street had not then been built, and the Crooked Lane which turned down by St Sepulchre's, as well as Ozier Lane, did not afford sufficient width to admit of the cavalcade passing by either of them with convenience, to Holborn Hill – or "the Heavy Hill", as it used to be called. The procession seems at no time to have had much of the solemn element about it. "The heroes of the day were often", wrote a popular author, "on good terms with the mob, and jokes exchanged between the men who were going to be hanged and the men who deserved to be."

ST SEPULCHRE'S

Many interesting associations – principally, however, connected with the annals of crime and execution of the laws of England – belong to the Church of St Sepulchre, or St 'Pulchre.

As this was the nearest church to Newgate prison, that connection naturally was intimate. Its clock served to give the time to the hangman when there was an execution in the Old Bailey, and many a poor wretch's last moments must it have regulated.

A curious custom observed at St Sepulchre's was the presentation of a nosegay to every criminal on his way to execution at Tyburn. No doubt the practice had its origin in some kindly feeling for the poor unfortunates who were so soon to bid farewell to all the beauties of earth. One of the last to receive a nosegay from the steps of St Sepulchre's was 'Sixteen-string Jack', alias John Rann, who was hanged in 1774. Sixteen-string Jack wore the flowers in his button-hole as he rode dolefully to the gallows.

THE BELLMAN OF ST SEPULCHRE

It was an old practice on the night preceding the execution of condemned prisoners for the sexton, or bellman, of the parish of St Sepulchre, to pronounce two solemn exhortations to the criminals; the first

"You prisoners that are within,
Who, for wickedness and sin,
after many mercies shown, you are now appointed to die tomorrow, in the forenoon; give ear and understand that tomorrow morning, the great bell of St Sepulchre's shall toll for you, in the manner of the passing bell as used to be tolled for those that are at the point of death. To the end that all goodly people hearing that bell, and knowing it is for you going to your deaths, may be stirred up heartily to pray to God to bestow his grace and mercy upon you whilst you live."

Succeeded by the ringing of his handbell and the recitation of the following piece of friendly advice:

All you that in the condemn'd hold do lie,
Prepare you, for tomorrow you shall die.
Watch all and pray the hour is drawing near
That you before the Almighty must appear.
Examine well yourselves, in time repent,
That you may not t'eternal flames be sent
The Lord above have mercy on your souls!"
Past Twelve o'Clock.

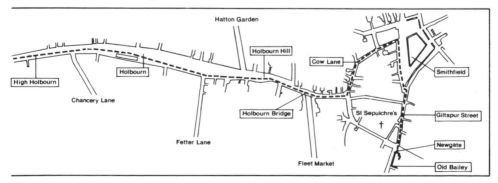

John Stow, the English chronicler and antiquarian, sketches in the origin of the custom in an edition dated 1618 of his *Survey of London*.

> Robert Doue (or Dow), a Citizen and Merchant Taylor, of London, that deceased 1612, gave to the parish church of St Sepulchres, the somme of 50*l*. That after the several sessions of London, when the prisoners remain in the gaol, as condemned men to death, expecting execution on the morning following; the clarke [that is, the parson] of the church should come in the night time, and likewise early in the morning, to the window of the prison where they lie, and there ringing certain toles with a handbell, appointed for the purpose, he doth afterwards (in a most Christian manner) put them in mind of their present condition, and ensuing execution, desiring them be prepared therefor as they ought to be. When they are in the cart, and brought before the wall of the church, there he standeth ready with the same bell, and after certaine toles rehearseth an appointed praier, desiring all the people there present to pray for them. The beadle also of Merchant Taylors Hall hath an honest stipend allowed to see that this is duely done.

APPENDIX TWO
The Coward's Weapon: 1

ACONITE

This drug is obtained from the common garden plant known as 'monkshood' (*Aconitum anglicum*), though in some parts of the country it is called 'wolfsbane', and in Ireland 'blue rocket'.

The active principle of aconite is an alkaloid called aconitine, which varies greatly in the roots according to the conditions under which the plant is grown. In medicine it was formerly administered in the form of tincture of aconite or as a linament – usually for the relief of sciatica and rheumatism, where its heat-producing and mildly anaesthetic properties gave comfort. Though it can still be found listed in the pharmacopoeias, aconitine fell into disfavour when it was found that even rubbing preparations on the skin produced the symptoms of poisoning by ingestion.

It is commonly from the root that the alkaloid aconitine is prepared. Until well into this century it was the most virulent poison known, one-fiftieth of a grain having proved fatal, while it is certain that one-tenth of a grain would always cause death. It is a white powder without any definite crystalline structure; hardly soluble in water, but dissolved by alcohol or weak acids. One-thousandth of a grain can be distinguished through the tingling sensation set up.

The symptoms of poisoning by this drug are as follows: In from a few minutes to an hour from the time the poison has been taken, the patient experiences a tingling sensation in the mouth and throat, which are much parched. If a large quantity has been administered, this tingling becomes a very severe burning. The tingling rapidly extends to the hands and feet, and soon the whole surface of the body is affected. The skin of the extremities is cool and clammy to the touch, but at the same time the patient complains that he feels as if his limbs have been flayed. There is a loss of power in the legs, and sometimes sight and hearing are much dulled, though usually the victim remains in full possession of his faculties till death ensues. Occasionally convulsions take place. The pulse becomes weak and variable; the pupils of the eyes dilated; and the least exertion may bring on a fatal syncope. Death, however, usually results from failure of the respiratory organs. Aconite may be said to paralyse all the organs in turn, and so destroy life. The fatal period can be from eight minutes to three or four hours.

The poison has rarely been used for criminal purposes, the most notable in England being the case of Dr Lamson, who killed his brother-in-law Percy John at Wimbledon in 1881 [see this volume]. In Scotland Dr Edward William Pritchard's use of aconite helped earn him a place on the scaffold [see *Murder Club Guide No.8*]. It may be pointed out that though there are few reliable antidotes for this deadly drug, there are most excellent tests for its detection in the body, so that a murderer who selected aconite, or aconitine would probably slay the victim, but would not long escape the consequences.

ARSENIC

No metallic poison has been so much used by criminals as arsenic. In the earliest days it was administered in the form of yellow sulphide, the bright colour of which convinced the ancient alchemists that it must be a source of gold.

The more common white oxide of arsenic was traditionally prepared by roasting the ore slowly and putting the resulting product into a vessel and applying greater heat; the vapours produced condense as a heavy white powder, or a crystalline mass. The vapour, which smells strongly of garlic, is very poisonous, and the greatest care has to be taken to avoid inhaling it.

The symptoms of arsenic poisoning vary a great deal, according to the form and dose which is administered. In a typical case of poisoning by white oxide the patient experiences a feeling of sinking and depression, followed by sickness, and an intense burning pain in the stomach, which is increased by pressure. These symptoms are followed by vomiting and diarrhoea, which is more or less violent, and often accompanied by cramp in the calves of the legs. Collapse rapidly comes on, and the patient dies from exhaustion. One of the most marked external characteristics is cyanosis – blueness of the skin caused by lack of oxygen in the bloodstream. Post-mortem examination reveals the lining membrane of the stomach to be very much inflamed, and in many cases badly ulcerated. Arsenic is therefore a distinct irritant poison.

There are several curious points about arsenic. It can be found in every part of the body of a person poisoned by it, and even after the body has been buried for years it may be found in the bones and hair. Again, arsenic can be administered in almost any form, but its post-mortem effects are the same. The poison can pass through the skin, and yet the stomach will be inflamed. It can be inhaled as a vapour, and the same symptoms will be found. It is one of the strongest of the irritant poisons.

Of its use to poisoners, one must note that even in comparatively large doses arsenic is virtually tasteless, and even the slightly metallic sweetness can be easily masked by administering it in food. Arsenic can also have a cumulative effect, so that the toxin can be built up in the body (particularly the kidneys and the liver) over a period of time until a quite small dose is lethal.

HYOSCINE

. . .Upon my secure hour thy uncle stole
With juice of cursed hebenon in a vial,
And in the porches of mine ears did pour
The leprous distilment. . .
(Hamlet, Act I Sc. 5)

Hyoscine is a vegetable drug occurring naturally in several plants: in deadly nightshade where it is mixed with atropine (belladonna), in thorn apple (called Jimson Weed), and in henbane. It is commonly called 'scopolamine' to distinguish it from another drug, hyoscyamine.

All of the effects of hyoscine are related to depression of the central nervous system, and characteristics depend on the size of dose administered. Very tiny amounts can be effective in the treatment of anxiety-related problems, and it is sometimes prescribed against travel-sickness. Larger doses begin to break down the patient's ability to discriminate and make reasoned judgements, which has led to its use as a so-called 'truth drug'. Still larger amounts cause hallucinations, and in particular the sensation of floating – it was this effect which so endeared henbane to witches and sorcerers of former times for use in 'flying ointment'; this ability to be as toxic when administered externally as internally renders it a doubly useful substance for both physician and poisoner. Unfortunately, hyoscine is unpredictable in its effect on different people, making it hazardous to administer even the smallest of doses. Death occurs when the nerves of the heart become affected and that organ ceases to function.

Hyoscine as a murder weapon was introduced to the world in 1910 by Dr Crippen [see this volume], who used it to dispose of his wife.

CHLOROFORM

Chloroform is the result of adding chlorinated lime to alcohol, and then distilling the mixture. To look at it is a heavy colourless liquid, with a sweet spirituous taste and a pleasant smell. To correct several popular misapprehensions regarding this useful drug, it must be stated that it is almost impossible to chloroform a sleeping patient without awakening them in the process. Furthermore, the time taken for its effects to become apparent is longer than implied by writers of detective fiction; two or three minutes is rarely sufficient, and there have been many cases where the patient was fully conscious of the drug taking fifteen minutes to produce results. As the drug begins to take effect the patient in many instances exhibits strong convulsions, and has to be held down by assistants. One has often read of a criminal laying a handkerchief saturated with chloroform over a sleeping householder's face to ensure his unconsciousness of the burglary about to take place; in reality the effect would be either to wake the sleeper or to severely blister his face – this latter being a characteristic consequence of chloroform applied to the skin.

In only one murder trial has chloroform featured as an alleged poison, and that was the so-called Pimlico Mystery of 1886 [see this volume] where, strange to say, the drug was taken internally, and not by inhalation. The trial lasted for three days, at the end of which Adelaide Bartlett was acquitted of the killing of her husband. How it was possible to administer such an extremely irritant poison without severe damage to the digestive system is one of crime's enduring mysteries.

APPENDIX THREE
The Prison Hulks at Woolwich

The following texts have been adapted from the researches of Henry Mayhew, the eminent nineteenth century social historian, who wrote in 1862, in collaboration with John Binney, *The Criminal Prisons of London.*

THE HISTORY OF THE HULKS

The idea of converting old ships to prisons arose when, on the breaking out of the American War of Independence, the transportation of convicts to our transatlantic possessions became an impossibility. An Act of George III (19th Geo.III., cap.74), had already laid down:

> . . . for the more severe and effectual punishment of atrocious and daring offenders, be it further enacted that, from and after the First Day of July, one thousand seven hundred and seventy-nine, where any male person...shall be lawfully convicted of Grand Larceny, or any other crime, except Petty Larceny, for which he be shall be liable by law to be transported to any Parts beyond the seas, it shall and may be lawful for the Court . . . to order and adjudge that such Person . . . shall be punished by being kept on Board Ships or Vessels properly accommodated for the Security, Employment, and Health of the Persons to be confined therein, and by being employed in Hard Labour in the raising of Sand, Soil, and Gravel from, and cleansing, the River Thames, or any other River navigable for Ships of Burthen. . .

The *Justitia*, an old Indiaman, and the *Censor*, a frigate, were the first floating prisons in England, and by January 1841 there were 3,552 convicts on board the various hulks. Some idea of the sanitary condition of these establishments may be gathered from the report of Mr Peter Bossy, surgeon of the *Warrior* hulk, which shows that in the year 1841, among 638 convicts on board, there were no less than 400 cases of admission to hospital, and 38 deaths. At this period there were no less than 11 ships used by the British Government for the purposes of penal discipline (including those stationed at Bermuda). . ."we were assured by one of the warders who had served under the old hulk regime, that he well remembers seeing the shirts of the prisoners, when hung out upon the rigging, so black with vermin that the linen positively appeared to have been sprinkled over with pepper; and that when the cholera broke out on board the convict vessels for the first time the Chaplain refused to bury the dead until there were several corpses aboard, so that the coffins were taken to the marshes by half-dozen at a time, and there interred at a given signal from the clergyman; his reverence remaining behind on the poop of the vessel, afraid to accompany the bodies, reading the burial service at the distance of a mile from the grave, and letting fall a handkerchief when he came to 'ashes to ashes and dust to dust', as the sign that they were to lower the bodies."

It was impossible that a state of affairs so scandalous could last; and the successive reports of the directors of convict prisons are evidence of the anxiety with which they urged upon the government the reform – if not the abandonment – of the hulk system altogether; for, to the disadvantage inseparable from the conduct of prison discipline on board ship, the governors of hulks were forced to add the rottenness of the vessels entrusted to them . . . "The *Warrior*", they said, "is patched up as well as her unsoundness will permit, but there is no knowing how soon she may become quite unfit for further use, and it will be advisable to take the earliest opportunity that offers of transferring the prisoners to some more suitable place of confinement, as any serious repairs would be quite thrown away on so decayed a hulk. She is rotten and unsound from stem to stern." But still the *Warrior* remained, with canvas drawn over her leakages, to keep the damp from the wards, moored off the Woolwich dockyard, with 436 convicts between her crumbling ribs.

The hulk system, condemned, as we have already observed, even from the date of its origin, was the despair of all penal reformers. Originally adopted as a makeshift under pressing circumstances, these old men-of-war remained during nearly half a century the receptacles of the worst class of prisoners from all the gaols of the United Kingdom – a striking instance of the inertness of government, as well as of its utter callousness as to the fate or reformation of the criminal.

CONVICT LABOUR AT WOOLWICH

. . .This labour was of the description called "hard"; that is to say, the exercise of irksome brute force, rather than the application of

The convicts returning to the Hulks from their labour in the arsenal

self-gratifying skill . . . The directors stated that the kind of work performed by the convicts was chiefly labourers work, such as loading and unloading vessels, moving timber and other materials, and stores, cleaning out ships, etc., whilst at the Royal Arsenal the prisoners were employed at jobs of a similar description, with the addition of cleaning guns and shot, and excavating the ground for the engineer department.

THE CONVICTS' BURIAL GROUND

We approached a low piece of ground – in no way marked off from the rest of the marsh – in no way distinguishable from any section of the dreary expanse, save that the long rank grass had been turned in one place lately, and that there was an upset barrow lying not far off. Heavy, leaden clouds were rolling overhead, and some heavy drops of rain pattered upon our face as we stood there.

A DAY ON BOARD THE *DEFENCE* HULK

THE DAILY DISTRIBUTION OF TIME ON BOARD THE "DEFENCE" HULK.

Occupation.	In Summer (longest day).			In Winter (shortest day).		
	(In intermediate seasons, the hours vary according to light).					
	A.M.	A.M.	Hrs. Min.	A.M.	A.M.	Hrs. Min.
Prisoners rise, wash, and roll up hammocks	5 30	6 0	= 0 30	5 30	6 0	= 0 30
Breakfast (officers and servants)	6 0	6 30	= 0 30	6 0	6 30	= 0 30
Cleaning classes	6 30	7 15	= 0 45	6 30	7 15	= 0 45
In readiness to turn out to work (preparing the boats, &c.)	7 15	7 30	= 0 15	7 15	7 30	= 0 15
Labour, including landing and marching to and from working ground	7 30	12 noon	= 4 30	7 30	12 noon	= 4 30
Dinner for officers and prisoners	12 noon	1 P.M.	= 1 0	12 noon	1 P.M.	= 1 0
Labour, including mustering and marching to and from working ground	1 P.M.	5 30	= 4 30	1 P.M.	4 0	= 3 0
Prisoners are mustered, wash, and prepare for supper	5 30	6 0	= 0 30	4 0	4 45	= 0 45
Supper, washing-up, &c.	6 0	6 45	= 0 45	4 45	5 30	= 0 45
Evening prayers, school, and those not at school repairing clothing, &c., mustered intermediately	6 45	8 30	= 1 45	5 30	7 30	= 2 0
Sling hammocks	8 30	9 0	= 0 30	7 30	8 0	= 0 30
All in bed	9 0			8 0		
	Total from 5.30 A.M. to 8.0 P.M.		15 30	Total from 5.30 A.M. to 8.0 P.M.		14 30

ABSTRACT OF THE ABOVE.

	Summer		Winter	
Meals	2	15	2	15
Labour, including mustering, and moving to and from	9	0	7	30
In-door occupation, evening instruction, &c., &c.	4	15	4	45
	In Summer...... 15	30	In Winter.... 14	30

We thought it was one of the dreariest spots we had ever seen. "This", said the Governor, "is the Convicts' Burial Ground".

We could just trace the rough outline of disturbed ground at our feet. Beyond this was a shed, where cattle found shelter in bad weather; and on the right the land shelved up between the marsh and the river. There was not even a number over the graves; the last, and it was only a month old, was disappearing. In a few months the rank grass will have closed over it, as over the story of its inmate. And it is, perhaps, well to leave the names of the unfortunate men, whose bones lie in the clay of this dreary marsh, unregistered and unknown. But the feeling with which we look upon its desolation is irrepressible.

Then there is a legend an old, old, legend, that has passed down to the present time – about a little pale-blue flower, with purple leaves – the *Rubrum lamium* – which, it is said, grows only over the convict's grave – a flower, tender and unobtrusive as the kindness for which legend gives it credit.

APPENDIX FOUR
Benefit of Clergy

This remarkable loophole in the English law originated in the separation, in the Middle Ages, of the ecclesiastical and secular courts, which enabled the clergy to exempt themselves from secular jurisdiction. Thus, persons in Holy Orders accused of a crime were sent before the Bishop's Court, a notable feature of which was its powerlessness to pass sentence of death.

[It was to reverse such encroachments by the church courts upon secular law that Henry II appointed Thomas Becket Archbishop of Canterbury in 1162. Becket proved less compliant than his former friend had supposed, and the archbishop – as much a victim of his own arrogance as of Henry's displeasure – was assassinated in Canterbury Cathedral in 1170.]

This Benefit of Clergy was subsequently extended to all persons who were *eligible* for ordination into the Church – effectively anybody who could read. So corrupt, however, were the courts that in order to 'Plead' it was necessary only to learn by heart the first verse of the 51st Psalm, which became known as the 'neck-verse':

Have mercy upon me, O God, according to thy loving kindness; according unto the

A felon 'Burned in the Hand'

multitude of thy tender mercies blot out my transgressions.

The judge would ask: "*Legit aut non legit?*" ("Can he read or not?"). The Chaplain replied: "*Legit ut clericus*" ("He reads like a clerk"). Sentence would then be reduced to some other form of physical punishment, like flogging, or imprisonment or fining. Nor was it entirely necessary to learn the saving verse by heart; a few coins in the chaplain's hand would ensure a few promptings in the felon's ear.

By a statute of 1490 it became possible for secular prisoners only to plead benefit of clergy once. To ensure this laymen were marked by branding on the ball of the thumb (colourfully described as 'glymming in the paw', or 'burning in the hand'). There always having been 'one law for the rich and another for the poor', it comes as no surprise that many judges were prepared, either for money or favour, to allow the use of a cold iron.

Benefit of Clergy was abolished in England in 1827, but is said to have been successfully invoked in the state of Carolina, USA, in 1855.

APPENDIX FIVE
The Punishment of 'Peine Forte et Dure'

The punishment of 'Peine forte et dure', or 'Pressing to Death', was first adopted in England around the year 1406, and though it fell into gradual disuse was not abolished until 1772. Indeed, the prevalence of this torture led to the Newgate exercise yard being given the name 'Press-Yard', as well as the so-called 'Press-Room' where the Pressing was carried out.

The procedure was as simple as it was cruel, and the form was embodied in the words of the judge's sentence: "That the prisoner shall be remanded to the place from whence he came, and be put in some low, dark room, and there laid on his back, without any covering except a cloth round his middle; and that as many weights shall be laid upon him as he can bear, and more; and that he shall have no more sustenance but the worst of bread and water, and that he shall not eat on the same day on which he drinks, nor drink on the same day on which he eats; and he shall so continue till he die."

This was later somewhat refined: "That the prisoner shall be remanded to the place from whence he came, and put in some low, dark room, that he shall lie without any litter or anything under him, and that one arm shall be drawn to one quarter of the room with a cord, and the other to another, and that his feet shall be used in the same manner, and that as many weights shall be laid on him as he can bear, and more. That he shall have three morsels of barley bread a day, and that he shall have the water next the prison, so that it be not current, and that he shall not eat. . . etc."

The punishment was originally developed to 'encourage' prisoners to plead. To understand this we must recognize that until the time of its introduction a person could not be tried by a court until he had pleaded "guilty" or "not guilty" to the charge brought against him. This fact, combined with another – that the property of a convicted felon was forfeit to the State – made it not uncommon for a criminal to affect muteness in the hope of preserving the estate for his heirs. Though a majority of sufferers will clearly have been persuaded by Pressing to talk, there are ample records of those who bore the punishment until death, thus depriving the Crown of its 'booty'. There also exist tragic reports of the genuinely mute perishing under 'Peine forte et dure'.

"At the Kilkenny Assizes, in 1740, one Matthew Ryan was tried for highway robbery. When he was apprehended, he pretended to be a lunatic, stripped himself in the jail, threw away his clothes, and could not be prevailed on to put them on again, but went as he was to the court to take his trial. He then affected to be dumb, and would not plead; on which the judges ordered a jury to be empannelled, to inquire and give their opinion, whether he was mute and lunatic by the will of God, or wilfully so. The jury returned in a short time, and brought in a verdict of 'wilful and affected dumbness and lunacy'. The judges on this desired the prisoner to plead; but he still pretended to be insensible to all that was said to him. The law now called for the peine forte et dure; but the judges compassionately deferred awarding it until a future day, in the hope that he might in the mean time acquire a juster sense of his situation. When again brought up, however, the criminal persisted in his refusal to plead; and the court at last pronounced the dreadful sentence, that he should be pressed to death. This sentence was accordingly executed upon him two days after, in the public market place of Kilkenny. As the weights were heaping on the wretched man, he earnestly supplicated to be hanged; but it being beyond the power of the sheriff to deviate from the mode of punishment prescribed in the sentence, even this was an indulgence which could no longer be granted to him."

(*The Terrific Register*, Edinburgh, 1825)

MUTE OF MALICE

The nineteenth century saw a more enlightened approach to overcoming the difficulty of a prisoner refusing to plead. The original motivation for silence, it is true, had disappeared, but by reason of contempt, or a misinformed feeling that no plea means no trial, (and by some, it must be credited, "mute by the visitation of God") an accused would periodically stand silent.

The law now required that a jury should first decide upon the question of ability to plead. The following example shows that formula in operation:

Friday, November 8, 1912

TITUS, Stephen (27, tailor) was indicted and charged on coroner's inquisition with the wilful murder of Esther May Towers. . .

Mr Bodkin and Mr Perceval Clarke prosecuted.

Prisoner, called upon to plead, stood mute. A jury was sworn to try whether prisoner stood mute of malice.

Sidney Reginald DYER, principal medical officer Brixton Prison: "Prisoner has been under my observation since September 28. I have had various conversations with him, and he has answered the questions I have put to him and understood the English language. He had no difficulty whatever in hearing and answered as a person would who heard and understood. I had a conversation with him last night. Now and again he has been in a morose condition. I saw him before he came to the Court this morning and he was in that condition then. He is in the same condition now, but he quite understands, and I think he is fit to plead and follow the course of the trial and give the necessary instructions for his defence."

The jury found that the prisoner stood mute of malice.

Mr Justice Phillimore then directed a plea of Not Guilty to be entered upon each indictment and requested Mr Waldo Briggs to represent the prisoner.

(*Sessions Papers of Central Criminal Court*, G. Walpole and Co.)

Select Bibliography

The following Bibliography makes no claim to completeness, and when one single volume is considered to provide a balanced, reliable account of a crime, this title alone is listed; for example, one in the remarkable Notable British Trials series. Published by William Hodge, the 83 volumes provide an unparalleled panorama of British crime, notably the crime of Murder. It is a matter of regret that the series is now long out of print and only occasional single volumes appear on the second-hand book shelves.

Tribute must also be paid to the publishers of this present series of *Guides* for their consistent, imaginative programme of publishing of true crime titles; the Harrap list is particularly strong in the field of the forensic sciences. Happily, many of these are either in print or periodically reprinted.

For many of the historical cases (for example, that of James Greenacre) there are few reliable modern sources. In this event contemporary references (most of them used by the authors in compiling this *Guide*) have been cited, though they are not freely available outside the national archives and book depositories.

As a postscript, this may be an appropriate occasion on which once again to thank the staff of the British Library Reading Room for their unfailing courtesy and expertise. Much of this series was compiled at desk T9, and it is no exaggeration to say that it would have been far poorer in content were it not for the BL resources.

BARRETT, Michael
Lesson of the Scaffold, David D. Cooper. Allen Lane, London, 1974.

BARTLETT, Adelaide
Notable British Trials, ed. Sir John Hall, 1927.
Poison and Adelaide Bartlett, Yseult Bridges. Hutchinson, London, 1962.
The Trial of Adelaide Bartlett for Murder, Edward Beal. Stevens and Hayes, London, 1886.

BELLINGHAM, John
Assassination of the Prime Minister, Mollie Gillen. Sidgwick and Jackson, London, 1972.

BRAIN, George
Cherrill of the Yard, Fred Cherrill. Harrap, London, 1954.

BROWNRIGG, Elizabeth
More Famous Trials, Earl of Birkenhead. Hutchinson, London, 1928.

CHARING CROSS TRUNK MURDER (John ROBINSON)
Trunk Crimes: Past and Present, Leonard Lewis. Hutchinson, London, 1934
Detective Days, Frederick Porter Wensley. Cassell, London, 1931.

CHRISTIE, John Reginald Halliday
Notable British Trials, ed. F. Tennyson Jesse, 1957.
The Investigation of Murder, Francis Camps with Richard Barber. Michael Joseph, London, 1966.
Medical and Scientific Investigations in the Christie Case, Francis Camps. Medical Publications, London, 1953.

Ten Rillington Place, Ludovic Kennedy. Gollancz, London, 1961.
Murder with a Difference, Molly Lefebure. Heinemann, London, 1958.

CHRISTOFI, Styllou
Famous Criminal Cases No.2, Rupert Furneaux. Allan Wingate, London, 1955.
Murderess, Patrick Wilson. Michael Joseph, London, 1971.

COURVOISIER, François Benjamin
Two Studies in Crime, Yseult Bridges. Hutchinson, London, 1959.

CREAM, Dr Thomas Neill
Notable British Trials, ed. W. Teignmouth Shore, 1923.
The Gentleman from Chicago, John Cashman. Hamilton, London, 1974.

CRIPPEN, Dr Hawley Harvey
Notable British Trials, ed. Filson Young, 1950.
Crippen: The Mild Murderer, Tom Cullen. Bodley Head, London, 1977.
I Caught Crippen, Walter Dew. Blackie, London, 1938.
Ethel le Neve: Her Story, Ethel le Neve. Daisy Bank Printing Co., Manchester, 1910.

DOBKIN, Harry
Old Bailey Trials: Harry Dobkin, ed. C.E. Bechhofer Roberts. Jarrolds, London, 1944.
Forty Years of Murder, Professor Keith Simpson. Harrap, London, 1978.

DUDDY, John (see ROBERTS, Harry)

ELLIS, Ruth
Celebrated Trials Series: Ruth Ellis, Patrick

Pringle and Jonathan Goodman (general ed.). David and Charles, Newton Abbot, 1974.
Ruth Ellis, Robert Hancock. Weidenfeld, London, 198[5].
Ruth Ellis: A Case of Diminished Responsibility?, Laurence Marks and Tony Van der Bergh. Macdonald and Jane's, London, 1977.

FAHMY, Marie-Marguerite
They Died by a Gun, Rupert Furneaux. Herbert Jenkins, London, 1962.
Life of Sir Edward Marshall Hall, Edward Majoribanks. Gollancz, London, 1929.

GARDELLE, Theodore
The Life of Theodore Gardelle, London, 1761.
Classics in Murder, Robert Meadley. Xanadu, London, 1984.

GREEN, Robert, BERRY, Henry, and HILL, Lawrence
The Killing of Justice Godfrey, Stephen Knight. Granada, London, 1984.

GREENACRE, James
The Life of James Greenacre, Robert Huish. William Wright, London, 1837.
The Paddington Tragedy, O. Hodgson, London, 1837.

GREENWOOD, David
Reminiscences of an Ex-Detective, Francis Carlin. Hutchinson, London, 1927.
A Book of Trials, Sir Travers Humphries. Heinemann, London, 1953.

HALLIWELL, Kenneth
Joe Orton's Diaries, ed. John Lahr. Methuen, London, 1986.
Prick Up Your Ears, John Lahr. Allen Lane, London, 1978.

HAYES, Catherine
More Famous Trials, Earl of Birkenhead. Hutchinson, London, 1928.

JACK THE RIPPER
The Harlot Killer, Allan Barnard. Dodd Mead, [London], 1953.
Autumn of Terror, Tom Cullen. Bodley Head, London, 1965.
Jack the Ripper, Daniel Farson. Michael Joseph, London, 1972.
Clarence, Michael Harrison. W.H. Allen, London, 1972.
Jack the Ripper: A Bibliography. . ., Alexander Kelly, Assoc. of Asst. Librarians, 1973.
Jack the Ripper: The Final Solution, Stephen Knight. Harrap, London, 1976.
The Identity of Jack the Ripper, Donald McCormick. Jarrolds, London, 1959.
Jack the Ripper in Fact and Fiction, Robin Odell. Harrap, London, 1965.
The Complete Jack the Ripper, Donald Rumbelow. W.H. Allen, London, 1975.
A Casebook on Jack the Ripper, Richard

Whittington-Egan. Wildy, London, 1976.

JACOBY, Henry Julius
Forty Years of Man-Hunting, Arthur Fowler Neil. Jarrolds, London, 1932.
Memoirs of a London County Coroner, H.R. Oswald. Stanley Paul, London, 1936.

LAMSON, Dr George Henry
Notable British Trials, ed. Hargrave Lee Adam, 1912.
Doctors of Murder, Simon Dewes. John Long, London, 1962.

MANNING, Frederick and Maria
Classics in Murder, Robert Meadley, Xanadu, London, 1984.
The Bermondsey Murder, G. Vickers, London, 1849.

MORRISON, Stinie
Notable British Trials, ed. H. Fletcher Moulton, 1922.
The Corpse on Clapham Common, Eric Linklater. Macmillan, London, 1971.
Stinie: Murder on the Common, Andrew Rose. Bodley Head, London, 1985.

MULLER, Franz
Notable British Trials, ed. H.B. Irving, 1911.
The Railway Policeman, J.R. Whitbread. Harrap, London, 1961.

NILSEN, Dennis
Killing for Company, Brian Masters. Jonathan Cape, London, 1985.

PATEMAN, George Baron
The Detective-Physician, Philip Willcox. Heinemann Medical, London, 1970.

PEARCEY, Mary Eleanor
Lady Killers, J.H.H. Gaute and Robin Odell. Granada, London, 1980.
Murderess, Patrick Wilson. Michael Joseph. London, 1971.

ROBERTS, Harry, WITNEY, John, and DUDDY, John
No Answer From Foxtrot Eleven, Tom Tullett. Michael Joseph, London, 1967.

ROBINSON, John (see CHARING CROSS TRUNK MURDER)

SEDDON, Frederick Henry
Notable British Trials, ed. Filson Young, 1952.
Trial of the Seddons, Edgar Wallace. George Newnes, London, 1966.

STAUNTON, Patrick and Louis
Notable British Trials, ed. J.B. Aklay, 1952.
Penge Mystery: The Story of the Stauntons, Hargrave Lee Adam. Mellifont (Celebrated Crimes Series), London, [1936].

TRUE, Ronald
Notable British Trials, ed. Donald Carswell, 1925.

VOISIN, Louis
Mr Justice Avory, Stanley Jackson. Gollancz, London, 1935.
Detective Days, Frederick Porter Wensley. Cassell, London, 1931.

WAINEWRIGHT, Thomas Griffiths
Janus Weathercock, Jonathan Curling. Nelson, London, 1938.
Suburban Gentleman, John Lindsey. Rich and Cowan, London, 1942.
The Genteel Murderer, Charles Norman. Macmillan, New York, 1956.

WAINWRIGHT, Henry and John
Notable British Trials, ed. H.B. Irving, 1920.

WILLIAMS, John (RATCLIFFE HIGHWAY MURDERS)
The Maul and the Pear Tree, P.D. James and T.A. Critchley. Sphere Books, London, 1971.

WITNEY, John (see ROBERTS, Harry)

WOOD, Robert
Notable British Trials, ed. Basil Hogarth, 1936.
The Camden Town Murder, Sir David Napley. Weidenfeld & Nicholson, London, 1987.
Murder Mistaken, John Rowland. John Long, London, 1963.

APPENDICES

NEWGATE AND THE OLD BAILEY
The Triple Tree, Donald Rumbelow. Harrap, London, 1982.
The Chronicles of Newgate, Arthur Griffiths, London, 1883.

PRISON HULKS
The English Prison Hulks, W. Branch Johnson. Phillimore, London, 1970.
The Criminal Prisons of London, Henry Mayhew and John Binney. Charles Griffin, London, 1862.

GENERAL REFERENCE BOOKS

The Guilty and the Innocent, William Bixley. Souvenir Press, London, 1957.
Sir Bernard Spilsbury: His Life and Cases, Douglas G. Browne and Tom Tullett. Harrap, London, 1951.
The Murderers' Who's Who, J.H.H. Gaute and Robin Odell. Harrap, London, 1979.
Murder Whatdunit, J.H.H. Gaute and Robin Odell. Harrap, London, 1982.
Murder Whereabouts, J.H.H. Gaute and Robin Odell. Harrap, London, 1986.
The Railway Murders, Jonathan Goodman, Allison and Busby, [London], 1985
The Seaside Murders, Jonathan Goodman. Allison and Busby, [London], 1984.
Murders of the Black Museum, Gordon Honeycombe. Hutchinson, London, 1982.
Francis Camps, Robert Jackson. Hart-Davis MacGibbon, London, 1975.
Poisoner in the Dock, John Rowland. Arco, London, 1960.
Forty Years of Murder, Professor Keith Simpson. Harrap, London, 1978.
Cause of Death, Frank Smyth. Orbis, London, 1980.
Companion to Murder, E. Spencer Shew. Cassell, London, 1960.
Clues to Murder, Tom Tullett. Grafton Books, London, 1986.
Strictly Murder, Tom Tullett. Bodley Head, London, 1975.
A Casebook of Murder, Colin Wilson. Leslie Frewin, London, 1969.
Encyclopaedia of Murder, Colin Wilson and Patricia Pitman. Arthur Barker, London, 1961.

PICTURE CREDITS

Index

NOTE

Bold type indicates the Name of a Murderer.
Italic type indicates the Location of a Murder.
CAPITALS indicate Murder Method or other
  Key Subject

Abercromby, Helen, 174 *et seq.*
Abinger, Mr Edward, 117
Abney Park Cemetery, 150
ABOLITION OF CAPITAL PUNISHMENT,
  57–58, 65, 167–168
abortion, 67 *et seq.*
ACQUITTALS, Bartlett, Adelaide; Dyson,
  George; Fahmy, Marie-Marguerite; le Neve,
  Ethel; Rhodes, Alice; Seddon, Margaret Ann;
  Wood, Robert.
Adolphus, Mr John, 75, 124, 169
Agar Grove (see *St Paul's Road*), 38 *et seq.*
Allen, Graham, 34
Allen, Gould, and Larkin, 152
Armstrong, Major Herbert Rowse 10
Atkins, 'Irish' Rose, 126 *et seq.*
Atkins, Mr Justice, 89
Avory, Mr Justice, 172

bail dock, 157–158
Barlow, Malcolm, 33
Barrett, Michael, 152 *et seq.*
Barrow, Miss Eliza, 19 *et seq.*
Bartlett, Adelaide, 107 *et seq.*
Bartlett, Edwin, 107 *et seq.*
Barton, Keighley, 147 *et seq.*
Barton, Ronald William, 147 *et seq.*
Batten, Elsie May, 198 *et seq.*
Becket, Thomas (Archbishop of Canterbury), 211
Bedloe, Captain William, 49, 51
Bellingham, John, 104 *et seq.*
Bellman of St Sepulchre, 205–206
Belsize House, 46 *et seq.*
Belsize Lane, 46 *et seq.*
BENEFIT OF CLERGY, 103, 211–212
Berner Street (see *Henriques Street*), 143
Beron, Leon, 113 *et seq.*
Beron, Solomon, 115, 116
Berry, James (hangman), 38
Berry, Henry, 48 *et seq.*
Biggs, James, 132 *et seq.*
Billings, John, 164
Black Lion Lane, 177 *et seq.*
Blake, Mr Justice, 189
Blakeley, David, 56 *et seq.*
Blakesley, Robert, 156 *et seq.*
Blenheim House School, 124 *et seq.*
BLUDGEONING, Brain; Hayes; Hocker;
  Jacoby; Manning; Morrison; Müller; Price; San
  Dwe; True; Williams
Bonati, Minnie Alice, 111 *et seq.*
Bowen, David (Professor of Forensic Medicine),
  30
Brain, George, 126 *et seq.*
Braybrook Street, 184 *et seq.*
Briggs, Thomas, 145 *et seq.*
BRIXTON PRISON, 116, 120
BROADMOOR CRIMINAL LUNATIC
  ASYLUM, 121
Brown, Beresford, 179
Brown, Hannah, 72 *et seq.*
Brownrigg, Elizabeth, 159 *et seq*
Bucknill, Mr Justice, 21
Buck's Row (now *Durward Street*), 141 *et seq.*
Bunhill Fields, 154 *et seq.*
Burdon, James, 156 *et seq.*
Burge, Mr James QC, 186
BURNING (disposal of body), Christofi, Dobkin,
  Good; Nilsen
BURNING AT THE STAKE, 166
BURNING IN THE HAND, 211–212
Bush, Edwin, 198 *et seq.*
Butler, Ivan, 9
Button and Badge Murder, 85 *et seq.*
Byrne, Mr L.A., 93

Calcraft, William (hangman), 47, 121, 153
Cameron, Dr James (pathologist), 76 *et seq.*
Camps, Professor Francis, 179, 183
Carlin, Det. Chief Insp. Francis, 87 *et seq.*
Carpenters Buildings, No.6, 72 *et seq.*
Carter, Philip Youngman, 183
'Cassandra' (Sir William Connor), 57–58
Cecil Court, No.23, 198 *et seq.*
Chambers, Det. Chief Supt. Peter, 31 *et seq.*
Channell, Mr Justice, 84
Chapman, Annie, 140 *et seq.*
Chapman, Mr Justice, 79
Charing Cross Trunk Murder, 111 *et seq.*
Charlotte Street, No. 101, 170 *et seq.*
child abuse, 147 *et seq.*
Christie, Ethel, 178 *et seq.*
Christie, John Reginald Halliday, 178 *et seq.*
Christofi, Hella, 52 *et seq.*
Christofi, Stavros, 53 *et seq.*
Christofi, Styllou Pantopiou, 52 *et seq.*
Churchill, Winston, (Home Secretary), 117
Cinnamon Street, 135
Clapham Common 113 *et seq.*
Clarke, Sir Edward, 110
Claverton Street, No. 85, 107 *et seq.*
CLERKENWELL HOUSE OF DETENTION,
  152 *et seq*, 162

Clifford, Mary, 159 *et seq.*
Clover, Matilda, 66 *et seq.*
Coal Harbour Lane (now *Coldharbour Lane*), 74
Cockburn, Lord Chief Justice, 152
COLDBATH FIELDS PRISON, 135
Coleman, Mr Justice, 47
Coleridge, Mr Justice, 47
Collier, Sir Robert (Solicitor-General), 146
Collins, Det. Insp. Charles, 84
Colman, William, 93 *et seq.*
Colney Hatch Lunatic Asylum, 117
Coltman, Mr Justice, 124
Comyn, Mr James QC, 186
Confait Case, The, 76 *et seq.*
Confait, Maxwell, 76 *et seq.*
Cony, Nathaniel, 102 *et seq.*
Courvoisier, François Benjamin, 166 *et seq.*
Cranley Gardens, No. 23, 29 *et seq.*
Cream, Dr Thomas Neill, 66 *et seq.*
Cresswell, Mr Justice, 63
Crippen, Cora (see Elmore, Belle)
Crippen, Dr Hawley Harvey, 10, 24 *et seq.*
Curtis-Bennett, Mr Derek, QC, 183
Curtis-Bennett, Sir Henry, 45, 121

'Dark Blue For Courage', 185
Darling, Mr Justice, 89, 116, 171
DARTMOOR PRISON, 117
De La Rue, James, 46 *et seq.*
De La Rue, Thomas, 46 *et seq.*
Denman, Mr Justice, 37, 124
Deptford High Street, No.34, 82 *et seq.*
De Quincey, Thomas, 130 *et seq.*
Dew, Chief Insp. Walter, 26 *et seq.*
Dickens, Charles, 64, 65
Dimmock, Phyllis, 38 *et seq.*
DISMEMBERMENT, Crippen; Dobkin;
   Greenacre; Hayes; Nilsen; Robinson; Voisin;
   Wainwright
Dobkin, Harry, 90 *et seq.*
Dobkin, Rachel, 90 *et seq.*
DOCTORS, Cream; Crippen; Lamson
Dogget Road, No.27, 76 *et seq.*
Donworth, Ellen, 68 *et seq.*
Du Cann, Richard, 79
Duddy, John, 184 *et seq.*
Duffey, Martyn, 33
Dunkley, Susan, 28, 60
Dunraven Street (see *Norfolk Street*)
Durward Street (see *Buck's Row*)
Dyson, Rev. George, 107 *et seq.*

Eady, Muriel, 182 *et seq.*
'Eagle' public house, 39 *et seq.*
Eastcheap, No.44, 156 *et seq.*
Eddowes, Catherine, 140 *et seq.*
Edgware Road, 73
Egomet Bonmot, 174
Ellis, Ruth, 55, 56 *et seq.*
Elmore, Belle, 24 *et seq.*
Eltham Common, 85 *et seq.*
Evans, Beryl, 178, 183

Evans, Timothy John, 178 *et seq.*
EXECUTIONS, Barrett; Bellingham; Brain;
   Christie; Christofi; Colman; Courvoisier;
   Cream; Crippen; Dobkin; Ellis; Evans; Good;
   Green, Berry and Hill; Greenacre; Hayes;
   Hocker; Lamson; Manning; Pateman;
   Robinson; Seddon; Strattons; Voisin;
   Wainwright

Fahmy, Marie-Marguerite, 195 *et seq.*
Fahmy Bey, Prince Ali Kamel, 195 *et seq.*
Farquhar, Det. Supt. Charles, 150
Farrow, Ann, 82 *et seq.*
Farrow, Thomas, 82 *et seq.*
Fenians, 152 *et seq.*
Finborough Road, No.13a, 118 *et seq.*
FINGERPRINTS, Strattons
Finnemore, Mr Justice, 183
Fisher, Sir Henry Arthur, 81
Fleur de Lys Court, 159 *et seq.*
Foot, Sir Dingle (Solicitor-General), 186
Foot, Paul, 10
Forbes Road, No.34 (now *Mosslea Road*), 95 *et seq.*
Fox, Det. Chief Insp., 82 *et seq.*
Fox, PC Geoffrey, 184 *et seq.*
'Foxtrot Eleven' (Q Car), 184 *et seq.*
'Fraser's Magazine for Town and Country', 168
Fuerst, Ruth, 182 *et seq.*
Fulton, Mr Forrest, 37
Furniss, Harold, 8
Fussel, Mr, 188 *et seq.*

Gale, Sarah, 72 *et seq.*
Gallichan, David, 32
GAOL-FEVER, 158
Gardelle, Theodore, 191 *et seq.*
Garnet Street (previously *Gravel Lane*), 134–135
Gerard, Émilienne, 170 *et seq.*
GHOSTS, 28, 177 *et seq.*
Gladstone, William Ewart, 153
Glyn, Mr Serjeant, (Lord Chief Justice), 190
Glyn-Jones, Mr Justice, 186
Godfrey, Sir Edmund Berry, 48 *et seq.*
Good, Daniel, 121 *et seq.*
Goode, Winston, 77 *et seq.*
Granard Lodge, 121 *et seq.*
Grantham, Mr Justice, 42
Gravel Lane (now *Garnet Street*), 134–135
Gray, Mr Robin, QC, 149
Green, Mr Allan, 34
Green, Robert, 48 *et seq.*
Greenacre, James, 72 *et seq.*
Greenberry Hill, 52
Grumwald, Mr Henry, 149
Greenwood, David, 85 *et seq.*
Griffin, Det. Chief Insp. Albert, 179 *et seq.*
Gurney, Mr Russell, 124

Hall, Sir Edward Marshall, 21, 41, 196 *et seq.*
Halliwell, Kenneth, 16 *et seq.*
Hambrook, Det. Insp. Walter, 44

Hammersmith Ghost, 177 *et seq.*
Hanbury Street, No.29, 141
Hatton, Det. Chief Insp., 90, 93
Hawkins, Mr. Justice, 70, 96–97
Hayes, Catherine, 164 *et seq.*
Hayes, John, 164 *et seq.*
Haymarket, 102 *et seq.*
Hazlitt, William, 176
Head, DC Christopher, 184 *et seq.*
Heald, Sir Lionel (Attorney-General), 183
Henriques Street (see *Berner Street*)
**Herbert, Philip, Earl of Pembroke and
     Montgomery**, 102 *et seq.*
The Highway (see *Ratcliffe Highway*)
Hill, Lawrence, 48 *et seq.*
Hilldrop Crescent, No.39, 24 *et seq.*
Ho, Andrew, 32
Hocker, Thomas Henry, 46 *et seq.*
Hodgkinson, Sarah Ann, 152 *et seq.*
Hogg, Frank, 36 *et seq.*
Hogg, Phoebe, 36 *et seq.*
HOMOSEXUAL MURDERS, Confait Case;
     Nilsen
Honeycombe, Gordon, 9
HORSEMONGER LANE GOAL, 64
Houndsditch Murders, 114
Housden, Jane, 157 *et seq.*
House of Commons, 104 *et seq.*
House of Lords, 102–104
Howlett, John, 33
Hudson, Mr W.M., 186
Humphreys, Mr Travers KC, 89
hunger strike, 118
Hutton, Mr Arthur, 37

identikit, 198 *et seq.*
Inglazer, Israel (real name Leon Beron), 114
Isaacs, Sir Rufus, 21
Ivor Street (see *Priory Street*)

Jack the Ripper, 10, 140 *et seq.*
Jacoby, Henry Julius, 121, 172 *et seq.*
Janus Weathercock, 174
Jardine, David, 8
Jay, Det. Chief Insp. Peter, 30 *et seq.*
Jenkins, Roy (Home Secretary), 80–81
John, Percy, 124 *et seq.*
'John the Guardsman' (see Howlett, John)
Johnson, Mr Justice Croom, 34
Johnson, William, 157 *et seq.*
Jones, Chief Supt. Alan, 78
Jones, Jane, 121 *et seq.*
Jones, Thomas, 93 *et seq.*
Jones, Sir William (Attorney-General), 52

Keeling, Det. Insp., 90
Kelly, Mary Jane, 140 *et seq.*
Kendall, Captain Henry, 27
Kennedy, Ludovic, 10
'Kentish Mercury' newspaper, 86 *et seq.*
King, Mrs, 191 *et seq.*

Lambeth Road, No.27, 66 *et seq.*
Lamson, Dr George Henry, 124 *et seq.*
Lane, Harriet, 136 *et seq.*
Langridge, May, 179 *et seq.*
Lattimore, Colin, 76 *et seq.*
Lawrence, Ivan, QC, MP, 34
Lawton, Mr F.H., 93
le Neve, Ethel, 25 *et seq.*
Leicester Fields (see *Leicester Square*)
Leicester Square (formerly *Leicester Fields*), 191 *et
     seq.*
Leighton, Ronald, 76 *et seq.*
'Lewisham Borough News' newspaper, 87
'Life and Recollections of Calcraft the Hangman',
     121
Limekiln Lane, 177
Linden House, 174 *et seq.*
Linfold, Alice, 59 *et seq.*
Lockwood, Mr Frank, 110
Lustgarten, Edgar, 9

MacLennan, Hectorina, 179 *et seq.*
McNaghten Rules, 107, 118, 183
'Madame Tussaud's Waxworks', 38
'Magdala Tavern' public house, 56
MAIDSTONE PRISON, 100
Maloney, Kathleen, 179 *et seq.*
Manning, Frederick George, 62 *et seq.*
Manning, Maria, 62 *et seq.*
Manor Park Cemetery, 150
Mansfield, Lord Chief Justice, 107
Marr Family, 130 *et seq.*
Marriage, John, QC, 79
MARSHALSEA PRISON, 154
Martin, Mr Baron, 146
Marwood, William (hangman), 126
'Mather's Chemical Fly Papers', 23
Maybrick, Florence, 10
Mayhew, Henry, 64
M'Cardie, Mr Justice, 121, 173
Melrose Avenue, No.195, 29 *et seq.*
Miller's Court, No.13, 144
Millwood, John, 177 *et seq.*
Minver (or Minerva) Place, No.3, 62 *et seq.*
Mitchell, Mary, 159 *et seq.*
Mitre Square, 143–144
'Monthly Review', 174
Morland, Nigel, 9
morphia (addiction to), 119 *et seq.*
Morrison, Stinie, 113 *et seq.*
Muir, Sir Richard, 84, 117, 121
Müller, Franz, 145 *et seq.*
'Müller's lights', 146
MULTIPLE MURDER, Jack the Ripper; Nilsen;
     Williams
Munro, Irene, 9
Mute of Malice, 213

Neil, Inspector Arthur, 41 *et seq.*
NEWGATE PRISON, 38, 52, 70, 124, 138, 153,
     154, 155, 167, 191, 200 *et seq.*
'News of the World', 40

newspapers (assisting investigations), 85
Nichols, Mary Ann, 140 *et seq.*
Nilsen, Dennis Andrew, 29 *et seq.*
Nobbs, Paul, 33
Noel Road, No.25, 16
Norfolk Street, No.14 (now *Dunraven Street*), 166
  et seq.
North London Railway, 145 *et seq.*

Oates, Titus, 48 *et seq.*
Ockenden, Ken, 33
O'Connor, Patrick, 62 *et seq.*
OLD BAILEY, 21, 28, 34, 37, 41, 45, 52, 55, 70,
  79, 84, 89, 93, 107, 110, 113, 116, 121, 137, 146,
  149, 153, 157–158, 161, 167, 173, 175, 186, 196,
  199, 200 *et seq.*
'Oliver Twist', 159
Ormond, Lord Justice, 81
Orton, Joe, 16 *et seq.*
Oswald, H.R., (coroner), 173

Paddington Tragedy, The, 72 *et seq.*
Paget, Sir James, 111
PARKHURST PRISON, 186
Parry, Serjeant John Humffreys, 146
Pateman, George Baron, 59 *et seq.*
'Pa Wa' The Sacred White Elephant, 45
Pearcey, Mary Eleanor, 36 *et seq.*
Pearson, Edmund, 9
Peers, Trial by, 102 *et seq.*
PEINE FORTE ET DURE, 190–191, 212–213
**Pembroke and Montgomery, Philip Herbert, Earl
of**, 102 *et seq.*
'Pen, Pencil, and Poison', 176
Penge Murder, The, 95 *et seq.*
PENTONVILLE PRISON, 22, 28, 113, 173, 183
Perceval, Rt. Hon. Spencer (Prime Minister), 104
  et seq.
Petit Treason, 164 *et seq.*
petitions, 100, 117
phenobarbitone, 180
pillory, 203
Pitman, Patricia, 9
playing cards, 50–51
POISON, Aconite,
  Lamson, 206–207
POISON, Arsenic,
  Seddon, 207
POISON, Chloroform,
  108 *et seq*, 208
POISON, Hyoscine,
  Crippen, 207–208
POISON, Strychnine
  Cream, 175
Police (as victims of murder), 184 *et seq.*
Popish Plot, The, 48 *et seq.*
Portman Street, 172 *et seq.*
Prance, Miles, 49, 51
Pressing to Death (see Peine Forte et Dure)
Price, John, 154 *et seq.*
Primrose Hill, 49 *et seq.*
Prince of Wales Road, No.141, 36 *et seq.*

Priory Street, No.2. (now *Ivor Street*), 36 *et seq.*
PRISON HULKS, 93 *et seq*, 208 *et seq.*
Public Executions (see also EXECUTIONS),
  202–203
Putney Park Lane, 121

RAPE COMBINED WITH MURDER,
  Greenwood
Ratcliffe Highway (now *The Highway*), 130 *et seq.*
Rattenbury, Francis Mawson, 9
RAILWAY MURDERS, Muller
Rentoul, Mr Gervais, 21
REPRIEVE, Greenwood; Morrison; San Dwe;
  Smith, Francis; Staunton; True
Rhodes, Alice, 95 *et seq.*
Richardson, Harriet, (see Staunton, Harriet)
Rillington Place, No.10, (now *Ruston Mews*), 178
  et seq.
'Rising Sun' public house, 39 *et seq.*
Roberts, Harry, 184 *et seq.*
Robinson, John, 111 *et seq.*
Roche, Berthe, 170 *et seq.*
Rochester Row, No.86, 111 *et seq.*
Russell, Sir Charles, (Attorney-General), 110
Russell, Lord William, 166 *et seq.*
Ruxton, Buck, 92 *et seq.*
Ryhope House, 59 *et seq.*

Said Ali, 42 *et seq.*
St George's Road, Nos.1–2, 124 *et seq.*
St George's Turnpike, 135
St Paul's Road, No.29 (now *Agar Street*), 38 *et
seq.*
St Sepulchre's Church, 205–206
Salih, Ahmet, 76 *et seq.*
Salmon, Cyril, QC, 79
San Dwe, 42 *et seq.*
Sandy Wee (see **San Dwe**)
Savage, Mr Richard, 102–103
Savoy Hotel, 195 *et seq.*
Scarman, Lord Justice, 81
Scraggs, Lord Chief Justice, 52
Sebert Road, 147 *et seq.*
Seddon, Frederick Henry, 19 *et seq.*
Seddon, Margaret Ann, 19 *et seq.*
serology, 59 *et seq.*
Shew, Edward Spencer, 9
SHOOTING, Bellingham; Ellis; Fahmy; Johnson
  and Housden; Roberts, Witney and Duddy;
  Smith, Francis; Strangeways; Wainwright
Siege of Sydney Street, 114
Simpson, Professor Keith (pathologist), 81 *et seq*,
  90 *et seq.*
Sinclair, Stephen, 34
Smith, Francis, 177 *et seq.*
Smith, George Joseph, 9
Snelwar's Warsaw Restaurant, 114 *et seq.*
South Hill Park, No.11, 52 *et seq.*
Spencer Hotel (now *Mostyn Hotel*), 172 *et seq.*
Spilsbury, Sir Bernard (pathologist), 21, 89, 111 *et
seq.*
Spurling, Mr (turnkey), 157 *et seq.*

STABBING, Barton; Blakesley; Brain; Colman; Courvoisier; Voisin
Stake, (driven through heart of a suicide), 135
STARVATION, Stauntons
Staunton, Harriet, 95 *et seq.*
Staunton, Louis, 95 *et seq.*
Staunton, Mrs Patrick, 95 *et seq.*
Staunton, Patrick, 95 *et seq.*
Stein, Morris (see **Morrison, Stinie**)
Stewart, Douglas, 33
Stockwell, Det. Insp. Graham, 78 *et seq.*
Stott, Daniel, 67
Stotter, Carl (called Khara Le Fox), 33
Strand, 195 *et seq.*
Strangeways, Major George, 188 *et seq.*
STRANGULATION, Christie; Confait Case; Greenwood
Stratton, Albert, 82 *et seq.*
Stratton, Alfred, 82 *et seq.*
Stride, Elizabeth, 140 *et seq.*
suicide, 134–135
Surgeon's Hall, 161, 203–204
Sutherland, Billy, 33
Swanwick, Lord Justice, 81
Swift, Mr Justice, 45, 113, 197

Tanner, Det. Chief Insp. William, 146
Teare, Professor Donald, (pathologist), 79 *et seq.*
Temple Bar, 188 *et seq.*
'Terrific Register, The', 213
Thackeray, William Makepeace, 167–168
Thompson, Edith, 10, 55
THROAT CUTTING, Pateman; Pearcey; Williams; Wood
Tindal, Lord Chief Justice, 167
Titus, Stephen, 213
Tollington Park, No.63, 19
Touching the Corpse, 189–190
transportation, 175–176
Trew, Nellie Grace, 85 *et seq.*
True, Ronald, 118 *et seq.*
TRUNK MURDERS, Robinson
Turner, John 134–135
Turner, Mr Justice, 149
TYBURN, 52, 204–205
Tyburn Road (now *Oxford Street*), 164 *et seq.*

UNSOLVED MURDERS, Confait case; Jack the Ripper

Van der Elst, Mrs Violet, 59
Vanezis, Dr Peter (pathologist), 150
Vauxhall Road Baptist Church, 90 *et seq.*
Vine Court, 136 *et seq.*
Viney, Mr Lawrence, 113
Voisin, Louis, 170 *et seq.*
von Goetz, Baroness Hilda, 118

Wainewright, Thomas Griffiths, 174 *et seq.*
Wainwright, Henry, 136 *et seq.*
Wainwright, Thomas, 136 *et seq.*
WANDSWORTH PRISON, 90, 93, 117, 126, 128
Ward, Div. Det. Insp. Alfred, 114
Watling, Brian, 79
Well Hall Road, 85 *et seq.*
Wensley, Det. Insp. Frederick Porter, 114 *et seq.*
'West Kent Argus' newspaper, 86 *et seq.*
Wheeler, Mary Eleanor (see **Pearcey, Mary Eleanor**)
Wheeler, Thomas, 38
White, Lady Alice, 172 *et seq.*
White, Elizabeth, 154 *et seq.*
Whitechapel Road, No.215, 136 *et seq.*
Widgery, Lord Chief Justice, 81
Wilde, Oscar, 176
Willcox, Sir William, 21
Williams, John, 130 *et seq.*
Williamson Family, 134–135
Wills, Mr Justice, 110
Wilmot, Tony, 10
Wilson, Colin, 10
Wilson, Harold, (Prime Minister), 186
Witney, John, 184 *et seq.*
Wombwell, DC David, 184 *et seq.*
Wood, John, 164
Wood, Robert, 38 *et seq.*
WORMWOOD SCRUBS PRISON, 149
Worsley, Mr Michael, QC, 149
Wrottesley, Mr Justice, 93
Wyndham, Horace, 8

Yates, Gertrude, 118 *et seq.*
'Yorkshire Grey' public house, 46
Young, Olive (see Yates, Gertrude)
Young, Ruby, 40 *et seq.*

Zoo (London Zoological Gardens, Regent's Park), 42 *et seq.*

THE MURDER CLUB

The publication of this series of *Guides* has been timed to coincide with the Club's Public Membership launch.

Criminology will no longer be the exclusive domain of scientists, lawyers and writers, The Murder Club enables every one of its Members to become an arm-chair detective.

You, the readers, are invited to join in the Club's fascinating research programmes, to contribute your ideas to its publications and entertainments, its 'Notorious Locations' tours and presentations.

Or simply sit back and enjoy the regular packages of intriguing true-life crime material prepared by The Murder Club *exclusively* for its Members, stimulating the imagination with a little fireside detective work.

Membership benefits for 1988–1989 include, among other features:

★ The Murder Club's own unique badge, membership card, and personal Certificate of Membership. (Dispatched with Introductory Membership Pack.)

★ *The Murder Club Bulletin,* a two-monthly magazine devoted to all aspects of real-life crime – new cases, old cases, cases to marvel at, cases to solve. A fully illustrated miscellany of information and entertainment; plus full news of Murder Club activities in Great Britain and abroad. (Dispatched to Members bi-monthly.)

continued overleaf

THE MURDER CLUB

APPLICATION FOR MEMBERSHIP

I enclose the sum of £25*, being the annual Membership Fee of The Murder Club. I understand that this entitles me to all the benefits listed above and outlined in the introductory Membership Pack.

Name _____

Address _____

_____

_____

Signature _____

Please send completed form and remittance to:
The Murder Club
35 North Audley Street, London W1Y 1WG

*Due to high overseas postal rates, a small supplement of £5 will be charged to Members outside the British Isles.

★ *Murder World Wide,* a series of illustrated booklets covering Classics of Murder from around the world. Each issue is complete in itself and a printed slip-case will be presented to contain each series as an annual 'volume'. (Dispatched to Members monthly.)

★ *Cabinet of Crime,* a companion series of monthly publications dealing with immortal cases from the annals of British murder. Specifications as *Murder World Wide.*

★ *The Black Museum,* title of The Murder Club's own mail-order catalogue with a difference. A unique illustrated document covering a wide range of publications, facsimiles, posters, prints, photographs and objects, exclusively produced by the Club to enable its Members to build up their own 'home Black Museum' of thought-provoking conversation pieces. (Published annually with bi-monthly supplements.)

★ The Murder-Book Club. A service offered to Members through our contact with the specialist publishers of popular true-crime books. A two-monthly list of available titles will be issued – many of which are available through the Club at lower than publishers' catalogue prices. (Updated bi-monthly.)

★ Concessionary prices and privileges on a wide range of Murder Club and related products, entertainments, and activities.

For Annual Membership including Introductory Membership Pack and monthly supplements, please complete the form overleaf enclosing the sum of £25.

Or send £2.50 (deductible from Membership) for further information.